MODERATE VOICES IN THE EUROPEAN REFORMATION

Moderate Voices in the European Reformation

Edited by

LUC RACAUT and ALEC RYRIE

ASHGATE

Published by
Ashgate Publishing Limited
Gower House
Croft Road
Aldershot
Hants GU11 3HR
England

Ashgate Publishing Company
Suite 420
101 Cherry Street
Burlington, VT 05401-4405
USA

Ashgate website: http://www.ashgate.com

British Library Cataloguing in Publication Data

Moderate voices in the European Reformation – (St Andrews studies in
    Reformation history)
    1. Reformation 2. Moderation – Religious aspects –
    Christianity – History – 16th century
    I. Racaut, Luc II. Ryrie, Alec
    274'.06

Library of Congress Cataloging-in-Publication Data

Moderate voices in the European Reformation / edited by Luc Racaut and
    Alec Ryrie
        p. cm. – (St. Andrews studies in Reformation history)
    ISBN 0-7546-5021-9 (alk. paper)
    1. Reformation. 2. Moderation – Religious aspects – Christianity – History –
16th century. I. Racaut, Luc. II. Ryrie, Alec. III. Title. IV. Series.

    BR307.M59 2005
    274'.06–dc22

2004016095

ISBN 0 7546 5021 9

Printed on acid-free paper

Typeset in Sabon by Get Set Go, Bordon, Hampshire.

Printed and bound in Great Britain by MPG Books Bodmin, Cornwall

Contents

Notes on Contributors

Kenneth Austin is Lecturer in Early Modern History at St Anne's College, Oxford. His forthcoming publications include 'Immanuel Tremellius (1510–1580), the Jews and Christian Hebraica' in Achim Detmers (ed.), *Reformierter Protestantismus und Judentum im Europa des 16. und 17. Jahrhunderts* (Wuppertal: Foedus-Verlag, 2005); 'Immanuel Tremellius' Latin Bible (1575–79) as a Pillar of the Calvinist Faith', in David Adams and Adrian Armstrong (eds), *Elites, Printed Media and Social Control* (Aldershot, 2005); and a monograph, *From Judaism to Calvinism: The Life and Writings of Immanuel Tremellius 1510–1580* (Aldershot, 2005/6), based on his doctoral thesis (St Andrews, 2003).

Louise Campbell is a Teaching Fellow in the Department of Modern History at the University of Birmingham. Her doctoral research, funded by the Arts and Humanities Research Board, focuses on the career of Matthew Parker and the English Reformation from 1520 to 1575, using Parker's career as a way into the world of moderate Protestantism. Her wider research interests include the concepts of edification and 'things indifferent' in Elizabethan England and clerical marriage during the Reformation.

Alison Carter is a graduate of the School of Modern European Languages at the University of Durham, where she has recently completed her doctoral thesis. She is interested in the political, religious and intellectual history of post-Reformation France and is currently preparing a monograph on the vernacular works of Catholic theologian René Benoist (1521–1608).

Elaine Fulton is Lecturer in Modern History at the University of Birmingham. Formerly of the University of St Andrews, where she completed her doctorate, she is currently preparing for publication a monograph on Catholic reform in sixteenth-century Vienna. She is also developing a research project on how weather conditions were perceived and understood in early modern Europe.

Mark Greengrass specializes in sixteenth and seventeenth-century religious and intellectual history. He also has scholarly interests in the application of information technology to the humanities. He was the co-founder and director of the Hartlib Papers Project, is the executive director of the John Foxe Project in Sheffield, and is currently the Executive Director of the Humanities Research Institute in the University of Sheffield. The Hartlib Project published a major text and image edition of the important archive of papers of the seventeenth-century man of science Samuel Hartlib (*c.*1600–1662). The Foxe Project is publishing online the famous protestant 'Book of Martyrs', first published in English in 1563. Mark Greengrass also researches and publishes on French history, notably on the first Bourbon king, Henri IV: *France in the Age of Henri IV: The Struggle for Stability in France* (1994). He has recently completed a major study of reforming endeavours in the French Wars of Religion.

Alexandra Kess is working at the Institute for Swiss Reformation Studies at the University of Zurich as a member of the Heinrich Bullinger correspondence project. She has completed a thesis entitled 'Johann Sleidan (1506–1556) and the Protestant vision of history' at the University of St Andrews, shortly to be published as a monograph. She is pursuing a study of the Du Bellay brothers as well as the contemporary reception of the French religious conflict in German lands.

Graeme Murdock is Senior Lecturer in Modern History at the University of Birmingham. His recent publications include *Calvinism on the Frontier, 1600–1660: International Calvinism and the Reformed Church in Hungary and Transylvania* (Oxford, 2000); with Maria Crăciun and Ovidiu Ghitta (eds), *Confessional Identity in East-Central Europe* (Aldershot, 2002); 'Freely Elected in Fear: Princely Elections and Political Power in Early Modern Transylvania', *Journal of Early Modern History* 7 (2003); and *Beyond Calvin: The Intellectual, Political and Cultural World of Europe's Reformed Churches, c.1540–1620* (Basingstoke, 2004).

Luc Racaut is Lecturer in History at the University of Newcastle-upon-Tyne. He is the author of *Hatred in Print: Catholic Propaganda and Protestant Identity during the French Wars of Religion* (Aldershot, 2002). His most recent publications are 'A Protestant or Catholic Superstition? Astrology and Eschatology during the French Wars of Religion', in W. Naphy and H. Parish (eds), *Religion and Superstition in Reformation Europe* (Manchester, 2003) and 'Anglicanism and Gallicanism: Between Rome and Geneva?', *Archiv für Reformationsgeschichte* (forthcoming). His current research concerns printing and Catholic reform in sixteenth-century France.

Michael Riordan is the Archivist of St John's and The Queen's Colleges, Oxford. He is the author of several articles and essays on religion and politics at the Tudor Court, and his contributions to the Oxford DNB include the group article on the Privy Chamber of Henry VIII. He is also active in research on the history of archival thought in the early modern period.

Alec Ryrie is Senior Lecturer in Modern History at the University of Birmingham. His publications on the early history of the Reformation in England and Scotland include *The Gospel and Henry VIII* (Cambridge, 2003); with Peter Marshall (eds), *The Beginnings of English Protestantism* (Cambridge, 2002); and *The Origins of the Scottish Reformation* (Manchester, forthcoming 2006).

Ethan H. Shagan is Associate Professor of History at Northwestern University. His first book, *Popular Politics and the English Reformation* (Cambridge, 2003), won the Whitfield Prize from the Royal Historical Society, the Roland H. Bainton Prize from Sixteenth Century Studies, the Morris D. Forkosch and the Herbert Baxter Adams Prize in European history from the American Historical Association.

Alain Tallon is Professor of Modern History at the University of Paris IV Sorbonne. He has notably published *La France et le concile de Trente 1518–1563* (Rome, 1997) and *Conscience nationale et sentiment religieux en France au XVIe siècle: Essai sur la vision gallicane du monde* (Paris, 2002). His current research concerns the history of early modern Catholicism, mainly in Italy and in France.

Elizabeth Tingle is Senior Lecturer in History at University College, Northampton. She has previously published on the social, economic and religious history of the west of France, particularly Brittany and the Saintonge region. She is currently working on the impact of the sixteenth-century wars of religion on southern Brittany and is preparing a monograph, *Authority and Society in Nantes during the French Wars of Religion*, for Manchester University Press.

Abbreviations

AMN	Archives Municipales de Nantes
ARG	*Archiv für Reformationsgeschichte*
BL	British Library
BNF	Bibliothèque Nationale de France
BSHPF	*Bulletin de la Société d'Histoire du Protestantisme Français*
CS	Camden Society
CCCC	Corpus Christi College Cambridge
CPR	*Calendar of the Patent Rolls Preserved in the Public Record Office*
CR	*Corpus Reformatorum*
EHR	*English Historical Review*
HJ	*Historical Journal*
JEH	*Journal of Ecclesiastical History*
LP	*Letters & Papers, Foreign & Domestic, of the Reign of Henry VIII*
LPL	Lambeth Palace Library
NA	National Archives
PC	*Politische Correspondenz der Stadt Strasbourg im Zeitalter der Reformation*
P&P	*Past and Present*
SCJ	*Sixteenth Century Journal*

Introduction: Between Coercion and Persuasion

Luc Racaut and Alec Ryrie

A book entitled *Moderate Voices in the European Reformation* might be expected to be brief. The reputation of the Reformation era is one of extremism and polarization. It is a period in which the participants in religious disputes were quick to see their opponents as slaves of Antichrist; a period in which the slope leading from doctrinal disagreements down through judicial persecution to religious civil war was dangerously slick. In the traditional narratives of the Reformations, Protestant and Catholic, moderation of any kind is not much in evidence.

This is partly because, in the past, historians of the Reformations have rarely gone out of their way to look for moderation. Both confessional antagonism, and the subtler but more insidious 'lure of symmetry',[1] have led historians to look for clear-cut contests which produce winners and losers. In extremis, this produces a binary worldview in which the job of the historian is that of a referee in the vast arena of history attributing laurels to the victors and infamy to the defeated. The security of historians' employment would thus be guaranteed by the fact that today's winners are often tomorrow's losers. It once seemed to make sense to apply this worldview to the European Reformation. In this view Protestantism clearly emerged as the winner, drafted rather incongruously to act as the midwife of modern rationalism and indeed of capitalism. Meanwhile, obscurantist and tyrannical Catholicism was the loser, standing for 'the world we have lost'.[2] But such easy Enlightenment understandings of what constitutes progress have not survived our loss of faith in the concept of 'modernity'. The consequence has been the emergence of a new historiography of the Reformation: one which is less interested in winners or losers than in the process of conflict, the alternatives that emerged along the way and the roles of those participants who did not manage to leave direct intellectual descendants. The intransigent champions of particular causes now

---

[1] Thierry Wanegffelen, *Une difficile fidélité: Catholiques malgré le Concile en France XVIᵉ–XVIIᵉ siècles* (Paris, 1999), p. 11, n. 1.
[2] Peter Laslett, *The World We Have Lost* (London, 1965). See Helen Parish and William Naphy (eds), *Religion and Superstition in Reformation Europe* (Manchester, 2002) for several important recent attempts to challenge this Protestant-triumphalist view.

seem less interesting than those who were stuck 'in between' confessional totalities.

Some important recent studies have focused on those who chose (or were forced into) such ambiguous positions.[3] This volume seeks to move this debate forward by analysing how individuals and institutions who found themselves in such uncomfortable situations managed the difficult choices they faced. These were choices between resistance and conformity; dispute and concord; persuasion and coercion. It now seems clear that those who, across Europe, had to negotiate such complex problems can tell us more about the state of indecision that characterized Reformation Europe than the traditional narratives of 'winners' and 'losers'. However, this new perspective opens up its own set of problems.

Not least of these is the prospect of a new kind of favouritism: where once we privileged Protestants over Catholics (or vice versa), now we may be tempted to favour 'liberal' approaches to religious disagreement over those which our own age would damn as 'fundamentalist'. From the ecumenical and pluralist perspective of our own age, the vehemence with which the Reformation debates were conducted is more striking than their contents. One respectable but rather forlorn strand of Reformation historiography has long been interested in hunting for those traces of toleration and compromise that can be found. The few serious attempts which were made to reconcile the warring religious parties have received careful attention from scholars.[4] The issue of tolerance and intolerance in the Reformation era has also been the subject of an important collection of essays.[5] Yet such studies inevitably conclude that attempts at compromise failed, and that intolerance was more evident than tolerance: where tolerance existed, it was to be found between the cracks, in the unofficial spaces where what the late Robert Scribner called 'practical rationality' could successfully override theological considerations.[6]

It is becoming clear, however, that 'moderation' in the Reformation era was not as rare a bird as it might once have seemed: merely that it

---

[3] This view is particularly well established for England: for two important recent contributions, see Judith Maltby, *Prayer Book and People in Elizabethan and Early Stuart England* (Cambridge, 1998) and Ethan Shagan, *Popular Politics and the English Reformation* (Cambridge, 2002). For France, see Thierry Wanegffelen, *Ni Rome ni Genève: Des fidèles entre deux chaires en France au XVIᵉ siècle* (Paris, 1997).

[4] Dermot Fenlon, *Heresy and Obedience in Tridentine Italy* (Cambridge, 1972); Peter Matheson, *Cardinal Contarini at Regensburg* (Oxford, 1972); Donald Nugent, *Ecumenism in the Age of the Reformation: the Colloquy of Poissy* (Cambridge, 1974).

[5] Ole Peter Grell and Bob Scribner (eds), *Tolerance and Intolerance in the European Reformation* (Cambridge, 1996).

[6] Robert W. Scribner, 'Preconditions of Tolerance and Intolerance in Sixteenth-century Germany', in Grell and Scribner (eds), *Tolerance and Intolerance*, p. 38.

was well camouflaged. Rather than attempting to impose modern categories – compromise and the 'third way', or tolerance and pluralism – we need to be led by broader and more contemporary understandings of what moderation might mean. It is true that tolerance, in the modern sense, was a rarity in Reformation Europe. As the work of Mario Turchetti has shown, even apparently pluralist approaches such as those represented by the French edicts of pacification were not 'tolerant' in anything like the modern sense.[7] Figures such as Sebastian Castellio, who saw toleration as a virtue, are appealing to modern eyes but eccentric in their context.[8] In contemporary parlance, tolerance was understood to be an evil which might sometimes be necessary – much as we might say that a minor infestation of vermin is 'tolerable'. Moderation, by contrast, was widely understood to be a virtue. Indeed, the Aristotelian principles which were so deeply ingrained in early modern European thought held that moderation was the very principle of virtue. Aristotelian virtues were defined by their position as a mean between two opposed (and extreme) vices.[9]

This understanding of moderation as virtue was in uneasy tension with another defining principle of early modern thought: moral dualism. If historians have looked for winners and losers in the Reformation, this was partly because sixteenth-century Europeans were ready, indeed eager, to understand their world as being polarized between good and evil, between the forces of Christ and Antichrist. Indeed, this was only one symptom of a general willingness to classify the world in dichotomies.[10] Dualism is a recurrent (if problematic) feature of the Christian worldview, with roots not only in the Church Fathers but also in the Scriptures themselves. However, the apparent contradiction between this approach and the Aristotelian 'golden mean' rarely came out into the open. The Aristotelian view merely demanded that virtues position themselves strategically between two extremes. The question of what those extremes should be in any given situation was left to the

---

[7] Mario Turchetti, 'Religious Concord and Political Tolerance in Sixteenth- and Seventeenth-century France', *SCJ* 22 (1991), 15–25.

[8] Hans R. Guggisberg, *Sebastian Castellio, 1515–1563: Humanist and Defender of Religious Toleration in a Confessional Age*, trans. Bruce Gordon (Aldershot, 2003). For a recent example of the appeal of such figures to modern historians, see Perez Zagorin, *How the Idea of Religious Toleration Came to the West* (Princeton, 2003).

[9] See the classic exposition of this theory in the Nicomachean Ethics: *The Complete Works of Aristotle: The Revised Oxford Translation*, ed. Jonathan Barnes (2 vols, Princeton, 1984), vol. 2, pp. 1729–868 (see esp. Book II). We are grateful to Sarah Francis, University of Newcastle, for advice on this point.

[10] Stuart Clark, *Thinking with Demons: The Idea of Witchcraft in Early Modern Europe* (Oxford, 1997).

discretion or creativity of the individual moralist. And indeed, a competent theologian could portray almost any religious position as an Aristotelian mean. This perhaps suggests that the rhetoric of moderation, as it was deployed during the Reformation period, was empty.[11] That the English and French crowns each claimed to be pursuing a *via media* at the turn of the seventeenth century tells us more about their political problems and ambitions than it does about their real religious policies.[12] But even empty rhetorics have a stubborn significance, despite their lack of definition. Moderation remained a virtue which the Reformation era was eager to claim, however implausibly.

Indeed, paradoxically, the claim to be moderate is worthy of historical attention precisely because it was so vacuous. Moderation represented a vacuum that controversialists from all sides strove to fill and define in their own terms. If moderation did exist in the Reformation era, it was not as a political 'centre' in the modern sense. Moderation was not a matter of common sense standing aside from the fray and seeing beyond superficial differences. Rather, the definition of moderation was (characteristically for the Reformation era) lost in a cacophony of voices, each asserting its own brand of moderation.

The essays in this volume are studies in the diversity of moderation in the European Reformation. Between them, they demonstrate the breadth of meanings which were attached to the idea of moderation, and the range of ways in which those caught up in the great religious controversies tried to turn it to their own advantage. For moderation had many layers, and many flavours.

The most obvious meaning for moderation in this period is theological irenicism: a willingness on the part of leading religious figures to listen to their opponents' views and to learn humbly from them.[13] This approach was in short supply in the Reformation period, although it remained a possibility at least until the 1560s. Senior Catholics such as Cardinal Contarini, Archbishop Hermann von Wied of Cologne or even the Cardinal of Lorraine attempted to engage constructively with Protestant doctrine. Senior Protestants such as Martin Bucer and Philip Melanchthon were equally willing to negotiate with their theological

---

[11] See Alec Ryrie, 'Divine Kingship and Royal Theology in Henry VIII's Reformation', *Reformation* 7 (2002), 49–77, pp. 66, 72; and Thierry Wanegffelen's introduction to his *De Michel de L'Hôpital à l'édit de Nantes: Politique et religion face aux Églises* (Clermont-Ferrand, 2002).

[12] Luc Racaut, 'Anglicanism and Gallicanism: Between Rome and Geneva?', *ARG*, forthcoming.

[13] On irenicism, and a careful attempt to distinguish it both from toleration and from *politique* views, see Howard Louthan, *The Quest for Compromise: Peacemakers in Counter-Reformation Vienna* (Cambridge, 1997), p. 9.

opponents. Moreover, while confessional categories remained blurred, national churches could attempt syntheses of varying degrees of coherence. Charles V (in the *Interim*) and Henry VIII both introduced some evangelical practices into a traditional doctrinal structure. These high-profile attempts at cross-confessional reconciliation are not the principal focus of this volume.[14] Modern interest in these subjects has meant that they have received at least their due of scholarly attention. Moreover, all of these attempts at reconciliation are distinguished by their ultimate failure.[15] This may suggest that the study of moderation in the Reformation era is the study of a lost cause. The essays in this volume indicate that that is not the whole truth.

One recent and influential formulation suggests that to be moderate meant to take a stance that was 'neither Rome nor Geneva'.[16] This is a useful reminder that the defined confessional camps into which most Western Christians were eventually sorted were not preordained. Other religious possibilities did exist, especially in the first decades of the Reformation. By the 1560s, however, these possibilities had largely been swallowed up by the expanding and solidifying Protestant confessions, or drawn back into Catholicism. Some theologians did indeed come to use Rome and Geneva as the extremes between which they could find their golden mean – notably those in the emerging English tradition which looked to Richard Hooker. However, for the most part, religious moderation rarely arose from a rejection of confessional identities, or from a consciously even-handed attempt to mediate between them. Such 'moderates' might owe allegiance neither to Rome nor to Geneva, but they would resist being placed in some precarious Alpine perch halfway between. They would be more likely to reject such a dichotomy altogether, finding their own pole in Paris, Vienna or London: they were clear religious identities which rejected Rome, Geneva and (frequently) one another as deluded. The most striking feature of 'moderation', however, is more a matter of mood than of doctrine. 'Moderates' were not lacking in beliefs, but they expressed those beliefs in an irenic fashion: that is, they chose not to confront those with whom they disagreed.

If 'moderation' can be tentatively defined as a willingness to take a non-confrontational approach to religious disagreement, it can be anatomized according to the different motives that lay behind such

---

[14] Although Elizabeth Tingle's essay in this volume touches on one such attempt at conciliation.
[15] The only significant exception to this is the *Consensus Tigurinus* of 1549 between Heinrich Bullinger and Jean Calvin, which itself did more to evade than to resolve the issues at stake. Bruce Gordon, *The Swiss Reformation* (Manchester, 2002), pp. 174–7.
[16] Wanegffelen, *Ni Rome ni Genève*.

approaches. These motives were not necessarily in themselves 'moderate'. One of the most widespread forms of 'moderation' was non-confrontational principally as a polemical tactic. This is the moderation of the religious controversialists who try to win over their opponents by minimizing the scale of the confessional gulf which is to be crossed; and it is the moderation of those who try to blunt the appeal of heresy to their own flocks by borrowing as much of the practice, language and doctrine of the heretics as they safely can. Protestants sometimes adopted this stance, especially early in the Reformation era. Some early English Protestants made valiant attempts to present their gospel in such a way that it might be palatable to their more conservative compatriots, and Geneva used a similar approach more successfully in its absorption of the Vaudois of the Lubéron in the 1540s.[17]

More commonly, however, it was Catholic controversialists who took the risk of engaging their opponents on their own terms. There were good precedents for Catholic attempts to absorb, use and tame criticism in this way. In the twelfth century, potentially dangerous dissident movements had been brought into the Catholic fold through a combination of absorption and usurpation.[18] However, following the advent of the Inquisition in the thirteenth century, the hierarchy was no longer kindly disposed to this approach to heresy. Even in England, where the Inquisition was never established, a theologian such as Reginald Pecock who attempted to confute heresy through vernacular debate risked being charged with heresy himself. Yet as the medieval Inquisition became inoperative in the face of the Reformation crisis in most of Europe, some Catholics returned to these older, more dialectic forms of engagement. Roger Edgeworth in Bristol, for instance, did not merely attempt to answer Protestant criticisms, but also acknowledged that some of those criticisms were reasonable and suggested that they would be acted on. In one Catholic kingdom, Scotland, this kind of constructive engagement with heresy was for a time the hierarchy's policy.[19] This 'moderation' should not be overstated; Edgeworth and the Scottish Catholic reformers were not trying to reconvert Protestants, but

---

[17] Gabriel Audisio, *Les Vaudois du Lubéron: Une minorité en Provence 1460–1560* (Mérindol, 1984); Euan Cameron, *The Reformation of the Heretics: The Waldenses of the Alps 1480–1580* (Oxford, 1984); Alec Ryrie, *The Gospel and Henry VIII: Evangelicals in the Early English Reformation* (Cambridge, 2003), pp. 123–34.

[18] Robert I. Moore, *The Formation of a Persecuting Society: Power and Deviance in Western Europe 950–1250* (Oxford, 1987).

[19] Roger Edgeworth, *Sermons very fruitfull, godly and learned: preaching in the Reformation c. 1535– c. 1553*, ed. Janet Wilson (Cambridge, 1993); Alec Ryrie, 'Reform without Frontiers in the Last Years of Catholic Scotland', *EHR* 119 (2004), 27–56.

to stem the flow of Catholic conversions. And as Alison Carter's work on the French theologian René Benoist reminds us, such 'moderate' Catholics frequently drew on pre-Reformation and pre-confessional texts and traditions.[20] This gave their work a useful veneer of legitimacy and precedent. However, the revival of such material in the explosive context of Reformation Europe had a revolutionary dimension. Eventually, with the adoption of the canons of the Council of Trent, such Catholics as Benoist were made to fall into step, and their experiments were abandoned. This was perhaps sensible, as religious moderation did not in fact have a particularly impressive track record either in winning converts or in preventing defections. However, the polemical logic behind this kind of moderation did not disappear, and it continued periodically to surface.

A second variety of 'moderation' was, again, not strictly non-confrontational: rather, it chose its battles carefully. This was the moderation of Protestants who saw their disagreements with other Protestants as different in kind from the gulf which separated them from Rome. It was moderation as a means to an end: unity against the popish Antichrist. Such people would reject the polarity of Rome and Geneva, wishing to oppose Rome with a coalition of Geneva, Wittenberg, Zurich, Canterbury and – in hope if not in reality – Constantinople. Reformed or 'Calvinist' Protestants were particularly keen to make common cause with their fellow evangelicals against the Pope. This was partly a matter of pragmatic prioritization: Calvinists in Hungary, for example, were eager to make common cause with their Lutheran brethren partly because their common Catholic enemy was a far more serious threat.[21] But theological principles were also at work. Lutherans were strikingly less willing to participate in such projects than were their Reformed brethren. In part, this was because they were more secure in their own lands and did not feel the same need for allies. However, many Lutherans – especially Luther himself – believed the Reformed to be mired as deep in error as the Pope, owing to their rejection of Christ's corporal presence in the Eucharist. By contrast, men such as Martin Bucer and Thomas Cranmer were willing to pursue projects of pan-Protestant unity because they saw Lutherans as being Christians who were in some degree of error, and Catholics as members of Antichrist.[22] 'Moderates' of this school had no interest in compromise with Rome – the devil is to be

[20] See Alison Carter's essay in this volume.
[21] See Graeme Murdock's essay in this volume.
[22] Diarmaid MacCulloch, *Thomas Cranmer* (New Haven and London, 1996); Gordon, *The Swiss Reformation*.

opposed, not met halfway. Yet they were willing to see differences amongst themselves as of secondary importance,[23] much as some in the early Church had feared that doctrinal disagreements between Christians were distracting them from the challenges posed by Jewish and pagan opposition. In its ultimate purpose, then, this is an aggressive 'moderation' – the moderation of the drill sergeant who keeps his troops in step so that they may fight more effectively. Yet much of what conciliation there was between competing Protestant groupings arose from this awareness of having a common enemy. The frequent Catholic taunt that Protestants were hopelessly divided was wounding, and the attempt to blunt it by mitigating those divisions was real.

Almost all Protestants were uncomfortable with the evident fact of their disunity. However, while everyone wanted unity, everyone wanted it on their own terms. It is in the attempts to resolve this problem that we can see another face of 'moderation'. This is the moderation most famously articulated by Philip Melanchthon, who popularized the term *adiaphora*, or 'things indifferent'. *Adiaphora* are those parts of the life of the Church on which it is understood that Scripture gives no authoritative guidance, and on which good Christians can therefore legitimately differ. Those who wish either to foster real religious concord, or to evade disagreements by giving them a veneer of unity, will clearly find this concept valuable. Equally clearly, however, problems of definition arise. Almost all Protestants accepted some variations in liturgy and practice as adiaphorous, matters of local convenience or national preference. Other practices, such as the use of intercession for the dead, were clearly understood by all Protestants to be intolerable. Yet quite where the boundary fell was contentious. Many in the Gnesio-Lutheran tradition were as unhappy with the concept of *adiaphora* as they were with other aspects of Melanchthon's theology, and saw no grounds for compromise with the Reformed Protestants who they understood to be desecrating the Eucharist. Likewise, those Reformed Protestants of a neo-scholastic temper became increasingly fond of the so-called regulative principle, which aimed strictly to forbid any religious practice which was not explicitly commanded in Scripture. Others, however, Lutheran and Reformed, argued for a broader understanding of *adiaphora*, and as far as it goes this is an approach which we can call moderate.

However, even if a particular practice was admitted to be indifferent, the problems had only just begun. Did indifference mean that the practice had no moral content; that it contained both good and evil

---

[23] See Louise Campbell's essay in this volume.

aspects, in balance; or that it could be either good or evil, depending on circumstances and context? It was around the answers to such apparently hair-splitting questions that major religious rifts could form. This was because indifference needed not merely to be defined, but also to be policed. The common early modern fear of the political consequences of any open religious dissent ensured that the Pauline concern for good order was at the forefront of all respectable early modern Christianity. If the concept of *adiaphora* led to variations in practice within the same ecclesiastical structure, good order was seen to be under threat. Ethan Shagan's essay in this volume delineates some of the battle-fronts that had formed in English Protestantism by the 1580s on this issue. The issue was not whether practices such as the use of clerical vestments were indifferent – it was agreed that they were. Rather, such disputes centred on whether decisions about *adiaphora* were to be made collectively, by the Christian magistrate, or individually, by the conscience of the believer. Here moderation itself became the battleground. Those who urged conformity in such matters depicted themselves as moderates, willing to make the compromises which their opponents would not. They were, however, insistent in imposing those compromises on others. Their opponents also claimed the mantle of moderation for themselves, for while they were not willing to alter their own practices they recognized the rights of others to follow their own consciences in other directions. Although the proponents of conscience clearly lost what Shagan calls the 'battle for indifference', they are in many ways closer to the modern meanings of 'moderation'.[24]

In the debates over *adiaphora*, the issues of obedience and good order had a significance which went beyond merely theological questions, and gave rise to other kinds of moderation. In an age when religious discord could have a devastating political impact, politicians of all stripes might have an interest in resolving, containing or evading religious disputes. The term commonly used for such a person is *politique*. This was originally an insult coined by the Catholic League during the French religious wars to refer to their royalist enemies, but it has come to be used – tendentiously – to refer to any who were willing to play down religious differences when it was politically expedient to do so. *Politique* is a term with pejorative undertones, but *politiques* were not necessarily flint-faced Machiavels whose few principles were eclipsed by their hunger for power. It may be that ruling elites were willing to sacrifice religious unity in order to preserve or re-establish a (largely mythical) pre-Reformation concord, while their subjects might be readier to take

---

24 See Ethan Shagan's essay in this volume.

sides against one another regardless of the political consequences. Yet the wish to heal wounds in the body politic was not an ignoble one. (Indeed, many of those princes in the Empire and elsewhere who allied themselves unambiguously with a single confessional group did so as much from a desire to establish civil peace as from religious principle.) If tolerance was an evil in the early modern period, concord and peace were amongst the highest of virtues, and the preservation of concord a worthy political goal. Ideally, it would be achieved by religious uniformity and consistency, but in many cases the attempt to impose this would manifestly do more political harm than good. In this volume, Alexandra Kess argues that Francis I of France was willing to follow inconsistent religious and foreign policies for reasons of political expediency, to the extent of pursuing an alliance with the Lutheran Schmalkaldic League. For the succeeding period, Alain Tallon's essay shows how the Cardinal of Lorraine was prepared to renew the experiment in order to preserve concord within Christendom.[25] Indeed, the French monarchy was only able to pacify the kingdom by putting the idea of equality before the law (introduced by Michel de L'Hôpital) before the age-old identification of the kingdom with one faith.[26] Likewise, the Peace of Augsburg in 1555 provided a legal framework within which the religious divisions of the Empire could exist with a degree of stability. But the success of the *politique* style of moderation was not limited to high politics. *Politique* initiatives and impulses could be just as effective on a small scale. Michael Riordan's essay reminds us that some whom we might call *politiques* were informed by virtues as unspectacular as good neighbourliness.[27] And Elizabeth Tingle's essay describes the surprisingly successful struggle to prevent religious strife in Nantes from breaching public peace, through damping down potentially dangerous flashpoints.[28]

However, the complex motives of *politiques* mean that their apparent 'moderation' can be deceptive. Some *politiques* can in fact be seen to have held unambiguously partisan religious ambitions, but to have judged that those ambitions were best pursued by steady and cautious means. In sixteenth-century Vienna, Protestant worship was permitted for a time, dismaying some Catholic observers. They attributed these policies to *politique* 'weathervanes' who lacked any principles, and to crypto-Protestant 'wolves' at Court who were attempting to undermine

---

[25] See Alexandra Kess's and Alain Tallon's essays in this volume.
[26] Olivier Christin, 'Tolerance and Religion Peace', in *The Cambridge History of Christianity* (Cambridge, forthcoming).
[27] See Michael Riordan's essay in this volume.
[28] See Elizabeth Tingle's essay in this volume.

the Catholic faith. However, as Elaine Fulton argues here, these fears were misplaced. The measure of toleration which the Court permitted to the reformers was given principally in order to preserve Habsburg control and to give Catholicism the space to reform and revive.[29] The English regime of Elizabeth I, Louise Campbell argues, faced similar concerns. One of Elizabeth's advisers noted that a thin-necked bottle is best filled slowly and steadily, for it will reject a sudden flood: the same principle, he suggested, should be followed when trying to fill a stiff-necked people with true religion.[30] This is a 'moderation' which is little more than tactical.

Moreover, while the suspicions of Viennese Catholics may have been misplaced, some of those who played the game of religious moderation in Reformation Europe undoubtedly were 'weathervanes', and there were even a few wolves. Behind the widespread suspicion of *politique* approaches was the fear that they might be providing cover for a more sinister religious agenda. Alexandra Kess's essay shows that some of Francis I's more evangelically inclined courtiers deliberately encouraged and exploited such 'moderation' in order to further their own religious hopes.[31] This is moderation in the service of radicalism. The often justified fear that if *politiques* gave an inch, religious radicals would take a mile served to discredit not only the *politique* approach but religious moderation as a whole.

Finally, moderation was a matter of mood and style as much as of theological and political substance. Many religious leaders of the Reformation era concentrated their attention on their mutual disagreements like a battle casualty fingering his wounds. Some others seem deliberately to have turned their attention away from those wounds: perhaps from a genuine dislike of interconfessional violence or fear of what they might find. Kenneth Austin's essay traces the career of one particularly vulnerable player on the European religious stage, Immanuel Tremellius, who was born and raised a Jew, converted to Catholicism and then again to Reformed Protestantism. Yet despite, or perhaps because of, this explosive personal history, his voluminous writings assiduously avoided controversial matters.[32] Whether from distaste for rhetorical violence, from a wish to be heard rather than shouted down, from a lack of interest in the questions at issue, or merely from a sense that they were living in glass houses, some individuals refused to be drawn into confessional stone-throwing, despite themselves

---

[29] See Elaine Fulton's essay in this volume.
[30] See Louise Campbell's essay in this volume.
[31] See Alexandra Kess's essay in this volume.
[32] See Kenneth Austin's essay in this volume.

having a clear confessional identity. This, too, is a form of moderation and deserves to be recognized as such.

Moderation can be found in the Reformation, but only on the Reformation era's terms. The moderation for which our own age looks would reject coercion in religious matters; it would not merely respect the decisions of the individual conscience, but would insist on their having some measure of validity. It would see religious debate as a matter of dialogue, in which even confrontation is merely an attempt to persuade rather than to browbeat. In an age in which religion could not be privatized without doing violence to the common weal, to the individual believer and to religious truth itself, the use of force and of forceful disagreement in religious matters was inescapable. Coercion and persuasion existed side by side, and it was all but universally understood that this must be so. The moderate voices of the Reformation era are those who inhabited, or tried to inhabit, the space between them. For a range of reasons – some 'moderate' in themselves, others not – they departed from the confrontational, polarizing conventions of early modern religious debate. Some achieved a measure of success through their moderation, and others did not. In either case, however, we would be well advised to listen to the moderate voices of the Reformation, especially if the more strident tones of their brethren threaten to drown them out.

CHAPTER ONE

Diplomacy, Evangelism and Dynastic War: The Brothers Du Bellay at the Service of Francis I

Alexandra Kess

The German Reformation produced an immediate resonance in most parts of Europe. Although Luther's movement would scarcely ever have the same potency away from his German homeland, scholars and clergymen throughout the continent were swiftly aware of the implications of the German movement for their own churches. In France, the impact of Luther's movement was particularly complex. Many in France were already deeply committed to good letters and the fashionable humanist scholarship. Like many in Europe they initially saw in Luther a spokesman and an ally for their own agenda of Church reform. In France, however, critics of Luther were also well entrenched and well organized. Both sides looked with hope to King Francis I. Francis's interest in Renaissance scholarship was well known, but so too was his piety and commitment to traditional religion.

The battle for Francis's support was the focus of a tense Court struggle which lasted over two decades.[1] At first, evangelicals had much cause for optimism, not least in the support of the King's sister Marguerite. Her patronage, her connections to the Meaux circle and her protection of evangelicals were well known, even notorious. Even after the Affair of the Placards in 1534 seemed to have ruined the evangelical cause in France, Marguerite's protection ensured that it would not go entirely unrepresented. This well-known struggle for the control of the domestic reform agenda spilt over into France's relations with her continental neighbours. Those who favoured the evangelical cause at home became increasingly accommodated with the policy of alliance with German evangelicals and forthright opposition to the Emperor. The long-established rivalry between Francis and Charles V meant that this policy could often function as an effective proxy for the more sensitive domestic agenda even when the cause of reform was in the doldrums.

---

[1] On Francis I, see Robert J. Knecht, *Francis I* (Cambridge, 1982); R. Knecht, *Renaissance Warrior and Patron* (Cambridge, 1994).

The central figures in this campaign were a small circle of diplomats and churchmen who strove to promote relations between France and the German states throughout Francis's reign. In particular, a leading role for more than three decades was taken by the family Du Bellay. With Francis I's full consent, the brothers Guillaume and Jean Du Bellay worked towards reform and reconciliation between France and the Protestants of the Empire. They were helped by a staff of reform-minded members of the educated elite in both France and Germany. Throughout Francis's reign, Paris and Strasburg became the headquarters for the struggle to develop an alliance between France and the German Protestants.

The full story of this complex web of negotiations has so far eluded historians' attention. It can be reconstructed through the extant correspondence of those involved – the Du Bellays, Jean and Jacob Sturm, Johann Sleidan, reformers like Melanchthon and Bucer, and the English Court. Guillaume and Jean Du Bellay caught the attention of the French scholar Bourrilly more than a hundred years ago, and Schmidt's biography of Jean Sturm is even older.[2] Johann Sleidan received widespread attention until the early twentieth century, but has never been sufficiently treated.[3] Fine recent work on Francis I, Marguerite of Navarre and the Strasburg politician Jacob Sturm has increased our knowledge of this subject.[4] Additionally, two stages of these negotiations have been explored in articles by Bourrilly and Potter: the diplomatic efforts in 1535 and the French role in the Schmalkaldic War 1546–47.[5]

---

[2]   Victor-Louis Bourrilly, *Guillaume Du Bellay, Seigneur de Langey 1491–1543* (Paris, 1904); V.-L. Bourrilly, 'Johann Sleidan et le Cardinal Du Bellay: Premier séjour de Johann Sleidan en France (1533–1540)', *BSHPF* 50 (1901), 225–45; V.-L. Bourrilly and Nathaniel Weiss, 'Jean Du Bellay, les Protestants et la Sorbonne', *BSHPF* 52 (1903), 97–127, 193–231; *BSHPF* 53 (1906), 97–143; Charles Schmidt, *La Vie et les travaux de Jean Sturm, premier recteur Du Gymnase et de l'Académie de Strasbourg* (Paris, 1855).
[3]   Carl Christian Am Ende, *Vermischte Anmerkungen über den berühmten Geschichtsschreiber Johann Sleidan* (Nuremberg, 1780); Walter Friedensburg, *Johannes Sleidanus: Der Geschichtsschreiber und die Schicksalsmächte der Reformationszeit* (Leipzig, 1935); Adolf Hasenclever, *Sleidan-Studien* (Bonn, 1905); A. Hasenclever, 'Johann Sleidan und Frankreich', *Elsass-Lothringisches Jahrbuch* 10 (1931), 101–22; Theodor Paur, *Johann Sleidans Commentare über die Regierungszeit Karls V. historisch-kritisch betrachtet* (Leipzig, 1843). For more detail on Sleidan and his reception in Germany and France, see Alexandra Kess, 'Johann Sleidan and the Protestant Vision of History' (unpublished PhD thesis, St Andrews, 2004).
[4]   Thomas A. Brady, *The Politics of the Reformation in Germany: Jacob Sturm (1489–1553) of Strasbourg* (Atlantic Highlands, NJ, 1997); T. Brady, *Protestant Politics: Jacob Sturm (1489–1553) and the German Reformation* (Atlantic Highlands, NJ, 1995); Jean-Luc Déjean, *Marguerite of Navarre* (Paris, 1987).
[5]   V.-L. Bourrilly, 'François Ier et les Protestants: Les Essais de concorde en 1535', *BSHPF* 49 (1900), 337–35, 477–95; David L. Potter, 'Foreign Policy in the Age of the Reformation: French Involvement in the Schmalkaldic War, 1544–1547', *HJ* 20 (1977), 525–44.

This essay will try to piece together the puzzle of the rapprochement between Francis I and the German Protestants under the leadership of Guillaume and Jean Du Bellay. The Du Bellays were the political arm of the reform-minded circle around Marguerite of Navarre and the Meaux group. It is difficult to label this group, since it cannot be put firmly into the Catholic or the Protestant camp. The term 'liberal', with all its modern connotations, is problematic. From today's point of view, we might call these people 'evangelicals'. Strict Catholics would have labelled them 'heretics', whereas they would have called themselves 'friends of the Protestants'. But many of them never openly converted to Protestantism, and were later denounced by Calvin as Nicodemites. Likewise, it is difficult to establish whether these moderates were motivated by religious convictions or political opportunism. Such people were recently characterized by Thierry Wanegffelen as *Catholiques critiques*. Wanegffelen showed that the borders between Protestantism and Catholicism, especially in France with its unique concept of the Gallican Church, were far from being clear and finalized before the Council of Trent.[6] For many moderate Catholics, such as the Du Bellay brothers, political and religious peace rather than doctrinal definitions were at the forefront of their agenda. This agenda was to inform Francis's policy towards European Protestants.

I

When Francis I became King of France in 1515, he inherited a monarchy in a constant struggle for power with England, the Pope and the Habsburgs. Charles V's election as Emperor created yet another, more powerful enemy. The ensuing sequence of wars forced Francis I to look for allies, even amongst France's former enemies. His plausible options included the Pope, the Turks, England or the German Protestants. This intricate diplomacy was further complicated by the infiltration of Reformed thought into France. Behind the official antagonism between France and the Empire, a group of moderate theologians and politicians endeavoured to bridge the religious divide. Their motives were not always clear, and often incorporated political reasoning as well as religious convictions.

Guillaume and Jean Du Bellay rose to importance at the French Court during the negotiations concerning Francis's imprisonment by Charles V and the later negotiations about Henry VIII's divorce. The Court they

---

[6] Thierry Wanegffelen, *Une difficile fidélité: Catholiques malgré le Concile en France XVIᵉ – XVIIᵉ siècles* (Paris, 1999), esp. ch. 2.

joined was liberal and open-minded. Francis I, the self-styled Renaissance King, was a keen patron of learning and the arts. Under the influence of his sister Marguerite, Queen of Navarre since 1529, he also came in contact with the evangelical reform movement. In the early 1520s, under Marguerite's wing, reform-minded intellectuals such as Jacques Lefèvre d'Étaples, Guillaume Farel, Michel d'Arande and Gerard Roussel grouped around Guillaume Briçonnet, then Bishop of Meaux. From her prominent position at the Court, Marguerite started an extensive correspondence with Briçonnet and others, read their writings and even invited members of the Meaux group to preach at the Court.[7]

Such reformist agitation at the centre of the French monarchy could not go unnoticed. As early as 1522 this circle caught the attention of the Sorbonne and subsequently had to live under close scrutiny. Marguerite's influence on her brother as well as the involvement of the Du Bellays became a bone of contention for the Paris doctors, especially when many of their planned actions against the Meaux group and other reformers were undermined by the Court.[8] Marguerite's open protection of the Meaux circle and her own evangelical works like the 1533 *Miroir de l'âme pécheresse* ('Mirror of the sinful soul') attracted repeated criticism from the Sorbonne, especially since Francis I ignored and counteracted most of the Sorbonne doctors' attempts to curb what they regarded as heresy at the Court.[9] Marguerite's allies were similarly persecuted by the Sorbonne. In 1530 Jean Du Bellay was accused of heresy, but with the help of Marguerite and the King he was able to clear his name.[10]

Politically, at least, these calls for reform were expressed in the wish to foster a rapprochement with the German Protestants. The German Protestants possessed a powerful attraction on two counts: not only were they a natural ally for those who were more or less openly attracted by Protestant teachings, but such an alliance would also constitute a perfect way to conjure discord for the Emperor. Whilst political connections both within the French Court and between France and Germany have been obscure to historians, they seem to have been clear enough to contemporaries. Already in 1532 rumours circulated that Francis was considering breaking with Rome.[11] Francis's ambiguous policy rapidly

---

7   Déjean, *Marguerite of Navarre*, pp. 149–75; Knecht, *Renaissance Warrior*, pp. 306–13.
8   Bourrilly and Weiss, 'Jean Du Bellay'; Francis M. Higman, 'De l'affaire des Placards aux nicodémites: Le mouvement évangélique français sous François Ier', in F. M. Higman, *Lire et découvrir: La Circulation des idées au temps de la Réforme* (Geneva, 1998), 619–25.
9   See, for example, Knecht, *Renaissance Warrior*, pp. 306–13.
10 Bourrilly and Weiss, 'Jean Du Bellay'.
11 *Correspondance des Réformateurs dans les pays de langue française*, ed. Aimé-Louis Herminjard (9 vols, Geneva, Paris, Basel and Lyon, 1866–97), vol. 2, no. 396.

split the Court into two factions, with the liberal party putting their hopes on Marguerite and the Du Bellays. A conservative pro-Habsburg party assembled around Anne de Montmorency, Grand Master (1526) and constable of France (1538). The suspicions with which traditionalists regarded Marguerite's protégés were reflected by the exaggerated hopes of reformers, illustrated by the large number of works dedicated to Marguerite and Francis I by leading Protestants.[12] In the political arena these hopes were behind the numerous attempts to form an alliance with France against the Emperor. It is within this context that two members of the pro-reform circle at the French Court assumed leading roles: the brothers Guillaume and Jean Du Bellay.

The Du Bellay family was one of the most influential and famous families of mid-sixteenth-century France, closely connected to the royal court.[13] Its most prominent members included the three brothers, Guillaume (1491–1543), Sieur Du Langey, Jean (1492–1560) and Martin (1495–1559).[14] The youngest, Martin, embarked on a military career which earned him leading positions under both Francis I and Henri II. In his last years he compiled a history put together from his own and Guillaume's historical writings. These *Mémoires*, edited by another Du Bellay, René, and first published in 1569, constitute the most important contemporary account of the reign of Francis I.[15]

After studies at the universities of Angers and Paris, Guillaume Du Bellay, the eldest brother, entered diplomatic service and soon became indispensable to Francis I. All his efforts from the late 1520s until the mid-1530s were directed towards arranging an alliance between France

---

[12] For example, Martin Bucer, *S. Psalmorum libri quinque* (1529), dedicated to Francis I's son; Jean Calvin, *Institutiones* (1535), dedicated to Francis I; Wolfgang Capito, *In Hoseam prophetam commentarius* (1528), dedicated to Marguerite; Huldrych Zwingli, *De vera et falsa religione commentarius* (1525), dedicated to Francis I; Zwingli, *Christianae fidei brevis et clara expositio ad regem Christianum* (1531), dedicated to both Marguerite and Francis I. Cf. Bucer's positive report to Luther about the spread of the reformed teachings in August 1530: *Correspondance*, vol. 2, no. 305.

[13] The Du Bellay brothers have received little scholarly attention (unlike their cousin, the poet Joachim Du Bellay). See *Collection complète des Mémoires relatifs à l'Histoire de France*, vol. XVII: *Les Mémoires de Martin Du Bellay*, ed. Claude Bernard Petitot (Paris, 1821) and the entries in *Dictionnaire des Lettres Françaises: Le XVIe Siècle*, ed. Michel Simonin (Paris, 2001).

[14] Their importance was widely acknowledged. In 1555 the translator Claude Cotereau dedicated a book to the Cardinal, praising all three brothers: 'Car chascun voyant que tout ce que nature avoit peu faire en l'homme de parfaict & absolut, l'avoir monstré en vous trois, & que vous esprits & intentions n'auvoient iamais versé, & ne s'emploient que es choses d'extremes magnanimités & grandeurs'. Lucius Columella, trans. Claude Cotereau, *Les Douze Livres de Lucius Iunius Moderatus Columella des choses rustiques* (Paris, 1555), fols ~a2ᵛ–~a3ʳ.

[15] Martin Du Bellay, *Mémoires* (Paris, 1569).

and the German Protestants. During this process he came into close contact with prominent reformers such as Philip Melanchthon, Martin Bucer and Heinrich Bullinger. As a man of letters he also devoted much time to the writing of philosophical, religious and historical works. From 1537 onwards he had to concentrate on the administration of Piedmont and Turin, but still remained in contact with the Franco–German negotiations.[16] It was his brother Jean who continued the diplomatic efforts with the Protestants of the Empire.

Jean Du Bellay decided on a career in the Church, and not least due to Marguerite's influence he became the Bishop of Paris in 1532. In 1535 he was made Cardinal. This elevated position did not prevent him from openly favouring the pro-reform movement that was working towards an alliance with the German Protestant princes and cities. It is perhaps unlikely that he would ever have made the open conversion to Protestantism, but he was certainly one of Wanegffelen's *Catholiques critiques*. His moderate, peace-orientated attitude concerning religion was well known in France and Germany. In 1546, Johann Sleidan described the two brothers to Philip of Hesse:

> Those who now rule at the Court never liked [Guillaume Du Bellay] nor the Cardinal, and this for two reasons. Firstly, because of their great reason and skill, and secondly, because the two brothers have always been inclined and favourable to our nation. Their enemies interpreted this as a proof that they were Lutherans in order to influence the King [Francis I] against them.[17]

The central role of the Du Bellays was closely connected to Francis I. With his death in 1547 the political climate changed. The Du Bellays's star waned, and Jean retreated to Rome.

When in 1536–37 Jean took over the negotiations with the German Protestants, he inherited from Guillaume a large staff of helpers and allies in both Germany and France. These were often recruited from the intellectual elite of German scholars and students in Paris, such as Ulrich Geiger (Chelius), Jean Sturm, the future first rector of the Strasburg academy, and Johann Sleidan, the famous Reformation historian. These men were complemented by a group of French students based in the Empire, among whom were Claude Baduel, Guillaume Bigot and Barnabas Voré, Seigneur de la Fosse. Upon their return to their home country, members of both groups often kept up their old contacts.[18]

---

[16] When informed about Guillaume Du Bellay's death, Charles V is reported to have remarked: 'La plume de Langey m'a trop plus fait la guerre que toute lance bardée de la France!' Bourrilly, *Guillaume DuBellay*, p. 250.

[17] *Sleidans Briefwechsel*, ed. Hermann Baumgarten (Strasburg, 1881), no. 74, p. 133.

[18] Schmidt, *La Vie ... de Jean Sturm*, pp. 12–15.

These diplomatic recruits were supported by two of the most prominent moderate reformers in the Empire, Philip Melanchthon and especially Martin Bucer.

II

It was during Francis's captivity in Madrid after the Battle of Pavia (1525) that the Du Bellay brothers rose to importance and developed into pillars of Francis's reign. After the King returned to Paris, both Jean and Guillaume were engaged in diplomatic missions to Italy and England. Henry VIII had asked Francis for support in his quest for a divorce from Catherine of Aragon; since Charles V was Catherine's nephew, Francis saw political advantage and agreed to help. Both Guillaume and Jean travelled between France, England and Rome to find an agreement.[19]

When in 1531 the Emperor's brother, Ferdinand, was crowned King of the Romans, the German Protestant cities and states met at Schmalkalden to form a defensive league. A letter was dispatched to Francis I to inform him about the formation of the League, outline its aims and ask for support in the call for a general council. Although the 1529 Peace of Cambrai obliged Francis not to interfere in German affairs, he fostered a pan-European anti-Habsburg party while carefully avoiding an open breach of the treaty. France's official response was a neutral, non-committal letter stemming from the traditional Catholic circle around Louise de Savoie, Francis's mother, and Anne de Montmorency. However, simultaneously, the diplomat Gervais Wain was quietly sent to Catholic Bavaria and to Protestant Saxony and Hesse to investigate the situation. The possibility of an alliance with English participation seemed to be cemented by the Treaty of Saalfeld in October 1531, though it ultimately failed due to hesitations on all sides.[20] Yet this did not mean a complete halt to the Franco–German rapprochement; rather it was only the first of a long series of attempts to reach an agreement. The ensuing diplomatic efforts were largely orchestrated by the Du Bellay brothers, with Guillaume taking the lead in the first phase until 1537.

In the spring of 1532 Guillaume Du Bellay embarked on his first mission to Germany to revive the negotiations. His aim was to meet the most important princes and ensure them of France's good will, manifested

---

[19] Knecht, *Renaissance Warrior*, p. 294.

[20] On this early round of negotiations, see Ibid., pp. 293–5; Bourrilly, *Guillaume Du Bellay*, pp. 124–9; Schmidt, *La Vie ... de Jean Sturm*, pp. 6–12.

in Francis's agreement to subsidize the German princes' reconquest of the Duchy of Württemberg from the Habsburgs.[21] In late 1533, Guillaume Du Bellay returned to Germany to represent France at a Diet held in Augsburg in the pursuit of what essentially was an anti-Habsburg policy. Shortly after, Francis and Philip of Hesse, one of the leaders of the Schmalkaldic League, signed the Treaty of Bar-le-Duc in which the French King agreed to finance the restoration of Ulrich of Württemberg.[22]

The true motives underlying Francis's foreign policy in these years seem unclear. Underneath the veil of the peacemaker, Francis seems to have been concentrating on creating as much trouble for the Emperor as possible. At the same time, one should not ignore the strong influence of the evangelical Marguerite on her brother. Throughout these years, Marguerite was constantly associated with those who pressed for a more generous attitude to reformers both at home and abroad. It was Guillaume Du Bellay who officially reintroduced religion into French foreign policy by contacting various reformers in Germany and Switzerland and asking them to draw up reports about the religious situation in France and suggestions for reform. Two amongst these reformers were regarded as among the most moderate in Europe: Martin Bucer and Philip Melanchthon.[23] By the end of the summer of 1534, the majority of these reports had arrived in France, most notably a long report by Melanchthon providing details on various aspects of sacraments and ceremonial.[24]

The ensuing enthusiasm amongst German Protestants and French reformers was suddenly thwarted by the Affair of the Placards on 18 October 1534. This bold display of anti-Catholicism stirred not only the King's bedchamber, but also Paris and subsequently the whole country. French conservatives saw their worst fears confirmed. The situation forced Francis to adopt a strict Catholic line, and the following months were characterized by persecutions of Protestants and a tightening of censorship under the leadership of a triumphant Sorbonne.[25] This in

---

[21] Bourrilly, *Guillaume DuBellay*, pp. 123–48.
[22] *Catalogue des actes de François Ier*, Collection des ordonnances de France, ed. Académie des Sciences Morales et Politiques (10 vols, Paris, 1887–1908), vol. 3, no. 7484.
[23] Bourrilly, *Guillaume Du Bellay*, pp. 177–9.
[24] *Corpus Reformatorum*, ed. Carl Gottlieb Bretschneider (102 vols, Halle, 1834-), vol. 2 (Bad Feilnbach, 1990), nos 1204–5. The collected reports from the reformers who had been contacted were published as *Sententiae Phil. Melanthonis, Martini Buceri, Casp. Hedionis et aliorum in Germania Theologorum de pace Ecclesiae ad virum nobilissimum Gulielmum Bellaium Langaeum* (Paris, 1607).
[25] F.M. Higman, *Censorship and the Sorbonne: A Bibliographical Study of Books in French censured by the Faculty of Theology of the University of Paris, 1520–1551* (Geneva, 1979), p. 34.

turn confirmed the concerns amongst those Protestants in Germany who had distrusted Francis's motives. At the same time, the Emperor and Ferdinand tried to turn the situation to their advantage by pursuing a more lenient policy towards the Protestants in order to restrain them from further attemps to form an alliance with France.

The Placards did not mean a complete reversal of Francis's policy. Despite his former leniency towards evangelicals, Francis had always been careful to maintain his essential loyalty to Catholicism. Nor did the Placards signify the end of a German–French rapprochement or the death of reformism at the French Court. The negotiations with the German Protestants were continued with a new enthusiasm. Again, the Du Bellays and their allies took the initiative and tried to persuade the King to build an alliance with the German Protestants. This is reflected in Francis's apologetic but telling letter to the German princes of 1 February 1535. He adopted a very delicate line, defending his actions against Protestants as directed entirely against sedition, not against religion.[26] In March Jean Sturm sent letters to Bucer and Melanchthon via Barnabas Voré, another agent in the Du Bellays's service. Sturm did not conceal the persecutions in France, but he underlined the influence of the Catholic conservatives and the King's weak will. Yet he hastened to emphasize that Francis was still interested in an alliance and praised the Du Bellays for protecting so many Protestants.[27]

By mid-1535 the situation had much improved. Francis continued to follow the Du Bellays's advice and was increasingly conciliatory towards the Protestants. In June he dispatched an official letter to Melanchthon to invite him for a religious colloquy in France, followed by encouraging letters from both Jean Du Bellay and Jean Sturm.[28] Such a bold move did not escape papal intelligence, and Jean Du Bellay soon reported to Francis that the Pope greatly disapproved of these invitations.[29] In July, the fortunes of the competing factions at Court changed much to the advantage of the reform-friendly party: the conservative chancellor Duprat died, to be replaced by the liberal Antoine Dubourg. During this time Admiral Philip Chabot de Brion, another man well disposed to evangelicals, established himself firmly within Court circles, exploiting the absence of Montmorency, the bastion of religious conservatism at the

---

[26] *Correspondance*, vol. 3, no. 492.
[27] *Correspondance*, vol. 3, nos 498–9. In response, Melanchthon wrote a letter to Jean Du Bellay, expressing his grief over the situation in France, but also underlining his hopes for continued negotiations and praising Du Bellay's efforts: *Correspondance du Cardinal Jean Du Bellay*, ed. Rémy Scheurer (2 vols, Paris, 1969–73), vol. 1, no. 221.
[28] *Correspondance*, vol. 3, nos 512, 515; *Correspondance du Cardinal Jean Du Bellay*, vol. 2, no. 240.
[29] *Correspondance du Cardinal Jean Du Bellay*, vol. 2, no. 283.

French Court. The general improvement in the perspectives of the evangelical party was compounded by the ending of Protestant persecution following the Edict of Coucy in July 1535. Guillaume Du Bellay felt that the time had come to convince the Sorbonne of the advantages of a disputation with the German Protestants.[30] He handed them over a list drawn up from the reports by Bucer, Melanchthon and Caspar Hedio as possible points of debate. However, before they could refuse the request, the negotiations were once again stopped abruptly. Melanchthon informed Francis, Guillaume Du Bellay and Jean Sturm that his lord, John Frederic of Saxony, would not allow him to attend a colloquy in France.[31]

Once again Guillaume Du Bellay did not lose hope. He insisted on attending the assembly of the Schmalkaldic League in December 1535, where he stressed again the French wish for an alliance and defended the integrity of Francis's position.[32] His last mission to Germany in 1536 coincided with the return to a more anti-Protestant policy in France, with the reissuing of the Edict of Coucy and with a renewed attempt by the Emperor and Ferdinand to win over the Protestant princes. Consequently, no agreement was reached, and the princes held to their distrust of Francis's true motives. Du Bellay left Germany disappointed. On the way back to France, still the loyal servant of his sovereign, he had published in Basel a defence of Francis's policy. Other pro-French pamphlets were circulated anonymously.[33] Once more an alliance between France and the German Protestants seemed out of reach. Guillaume Du Bellay now had to concentrate on his role as Governor of Piedmont and Turin and could only occasionally support the negotiations.[34] From then on it was Cardinal Jean Du Bellay who would put all his energy into a renewed effort for an alliance.

---

[30] Bourrilly, 'François Ier et les Protestants' (354–64) provides a transcription of instructions sent to Guillaume Du Bellay specifying his conduct towards various German princes; pp. 340–42 cite parts of Bullinger's report.

[31] CR, vol. 2, nos 1306–8. Melanchthon continued to trust in Guillaume Du Bellay as a peacemaker. In 1540, he dedicated his edition of Xenophon to him, urging him to persist in his striving for peace: CR, vol. 3, no. 2031.

[32] Bourrilly, 'François Ier et les Protestants', 479–94.

[33] Bourrilly, Guillaume DuBellay, pp. 200–226; cf. Guillaume Du Bellay, Literae a legato Christianissimi Regis et serenissimorum ejus liberorum ad principes Electores et aliis sacri Romani Imperii principes (Basel, 1536); anon., Double dune lettre, escripte par ung serviteur Du Roy treschrestien, a ung Secretaire Allemant, son amy, Auquel il respond a sa demande sur les querelles et differens entre Lempereur et ledict seigneur Roy (Paris, n.d.).

[34] In 1537, he published a recueil of letters connected with these negotiations: Exemplaria literarum quibus et Christianissimus Gallorum rex Franciscus ab adversariorum maledictis defenditur (Paris, 1537).

III

The following years brought a temporary standstill for French–German relations. The Franco–Imperial truce of Nice in 1538 heralded a period of peace in which there was no necessity for an alliance with the German Protestants. A period of pro-Imperial, conservative Court policy followed until Montmorency's fall in 1540. These were dour times for the evangelical circle in Paris, but Jean Du Bellay was determined to maintain some contact with the Germans.

The Du Bellays's main German secretary, Jean Sturm, had left Paris for Strasburg in December 1536, but had sent a worthy replacement: Johann Sleidan, the future historian of the Reformation. Once settled in Strasburg, Sturm continued his efforts for the Franco–German alliance, and until the mid-1540s Sturm and Sleidan orchestrated a new round of negotiations under Jean Du Bellay's leadership. In his new post Sleidan seems to have been a pivotal contact between the French Court and the German Protestants. It is immediately clear from surviving correspondence that Sleidan was trusted on both sides.[35]

By 1540, the French Court had become increasingly polarized on the issue of religion. The reformist group around the Du Bellays and Marguerite included Francis's son Charles, Duke of Orléans, Francis's mistress, the Duchess d'Étampes, and Admiral Chabot. This pro-evangelical, anti-Habsburg faction was opposed by a conservative party grouped around Anne de Montmorency, including the future Henri II and the Cardinal of Lorraine, joined also by Cardinal Francis de Tournon and Chancellor Poyet.[36] For several years, the policy towards the German Protestants would rise and fall with the power balance between these two groups.[37] The fall of Montmorency in 1540 as a result of his failure to secure Milan for Francis provided a new chance to revive relations with Germany.

The attempt to solve the religious question at the Colloquy of Hagenau in 1540 presented a welcome opportunity for this. The

---

[35] Martin Bucer wrote in 1539 of the Protestants having a man in Paris who had kept them informed about French affairs, which can only refer to Sleidan: *Briefwechsel Landgrafs Philipps des Großmütigen von Hessen mit Bucer*, ed. Max Lenz (3 vols, Leipzig, 1880–91), vol. 1, no. 34. Sturm apparently agreed: ibid., vol. 1, no. 75; *Politische Correspondenz der Stadt Strasbourg im Zeitalter der Reformation*, ed. Hans Virck et al. (5 vols, Strasburg, Heidelberg, 1898–1933), vol. 2, no. 655.

[36] In 1545, Ulrich Geiger called Tournon 'ein bose, listig Katz': A. Hasenclever, 'Neue Aktenstücke zur Friedensvermittlung der Schmalkaldener zwischen Frankreich und England im Jahre 1545', *Zeitschrift für die Geschichte des Oberrheins* 59 (1905), 224–51, esp. p. 244.

[37] Knecht, *Francis I*, pp. 408–17.

participants included Bucer, Jean and Jacob Sturm of Strasburg and Jean Calvin. The Abbot Lazare de Baïf was sent as Francis's official ambassador, charged with the mission to convince the German Protestants that Francis would not form an alliance with the Emperor.[38] At Jean Du Bellay's insistence, Sleidan accompanied Baïf under the official title of interpreter. Sleidan was charged by Jean and Guillaume Du Bellay to push the issue further and hold secret negotiations with Hesse about a possible alliance.[39] The negotiations went well, and both parties left the colloquy content.

Back in Paris, Du Bellay tried his best to clear the way in order to work towards a successful alliance between France and the German Protestants. On the Protestant side, the matter was complicated by the illegal double marriage of Philip of Hesse. The gravity of this offence forced him to be more submissive to the Emperor, rendering any alliance with France more difficult. This was clear to Du Bellay, who urged Sleidan to accelerate the negotiations and to insist that the German Protestants send ambassadors to Francis I.[40] Sleidan immediately passed the message on to Bucer, drawing attention to the fact that Francis had not ordered a new wave of persecutions of French Protestants.[41] To Jean Sturm he also underlined Francis's innocence regarding the persecutions in France and mentioned that the King did not have problems with the landgrave's double marriage.[42] Meanwhile Tournon and Poyet had managed to bring a diplomat of the Du Bellay camp onto their side, in the person of Barnabas Voré. Voré was sent to Strasburg in order to lure the French Protestants back into France where they would be charged with heresy and punished. Du Bellay discovered the plan and instructed Sleidan to warn the Germans.[43]

New hopes for an alliance between France and the German Protestants were fostered in 1541 by the marriage of Jeanne d'Albret, Marguerite of Navarre's daughter, to the pro-Protestant Duke of Cleves, a relative of the Elector of Saxony.[44] Never since 1535 had an alliance seemed so close. However, the diplomatic effort again failed, due to

---

[38] On Baïf, see V.-L. Bourrilly, 'Lazare de Baïf et le landgrave de Hesse', *BSHPF* 50 (1901), 369–76; Lucien Pinvert, *Lazare de Baïf (1496(?)–1547)* (Paris, 1900).

[39] Schmidt, *La Vie ... de Jean Sturm*, pp. 49–51; Bourrilly, *Guillaume DuBellay*, pp. 284–312; cf. *Briefwechsel*, ed. Lenz, vol. 1, no. 82.

[40] *Sleidans Briefwechsel*, no. 4.

[41] Ibid., no. 6.

[42] Ibid., no. 9, and cf. nos 7 and 10.

[43] *PC*, vol. 3, nos 126, 134.

[44] Despite the outrage of the Emperor, who tried to prevent the marriage and declared Cleves an outlaw, the wedding took place on 14 June 1541. Cleves was in favour of Protestantism but had not yet signed the Confessio Augustana.

hesitation on both sides and the Emperor's pressure on the Protestant princes.[45] A new chance arose with the calling of the Diet of Regensburg for early 1541. Jean Morelet Du Museau, Sieur de Marche-Ferrières, known as a friend of the Protestants, and Johann Sleidan were chosen as France's delegates. After short talks at Strasburg they travelled together to Regensburg.[46] There they met fellow diplomats, theologians and political rulers to conduct negotiations with the Protestants on behalf of France.[47] Yet the mission was unsuccessful. The meetings with Philip of Hesse were fruitless since the Emperor had forced him to agree neither to admit Cleves into the Schmalkaldic League nor to form an alliance with France.[48]

At the French Court, the rivalry between the two factions continued. Having used Voré in 1540 to discredit the reformers, Tournon and Poyet now tried different tactics. They denounced Sleidan for betraying the cause of his own pro-Protestant camp. They claimed that Sleidan had incited the German Protestants to protest against persecution of Protestants in France and thus prevented further negotiations.[49] Both Strasburg and Jean Du Bellay tried their best to defend their colleague, but it fell to a more influential ally, Marguerite of Navarre, to reconcile Sleidan and Francis. Marguerite trusted Sleidan and was able to convince Francis I of his innocence, as she wrote in a letter to Calvin: 'I have received your letter through Sleidan, whom it was not difficult to defend in front of the King, considering the testimonies he has had of his service, in which he puts more faith than any false rumours spread about him'.[50]

The years 1542 and 1543 brought further interruption to the Franco–German negotiations. War was again the cause of the problem,

---

[45] Louis Regnier de la Planche was sent to Saxony and Cleve for new negotiations, but again to no avail: Schmidt, *La Vie ... de Jean Sturm*, p. 52. La Planche, in favour of the Protestants, also served as an ambassador for Marguerite of Navarre, who sent him to England for negotiations: *LP*, ed. James Gairdner and R.H. Brodie (21 vols, London, 1862–1932), vol. 20, no. 942.

[46] *Briefwechsel*, ed. Lenz, vol. 2, no. 115.

[47] *Sleidans Briefwechsel*, no. 13. On 23 May 1541 the German Protestants wrote to Francis expressing their hopes for peace in the church and an end of the suppression of Protestantism in France as well as continued negotiations: *Correspondance*, vol. 7, no. 983.

[48] *Correspondance*, vol. 7, no. 1011, note 6. In a letter to Morelet of 11 February 1541, Philip refused to send a mission to France due to the persecutions there and the Emperor's willingness to make peace with the Protestants: *Sleidans Briefwechsel*, no. 12. However, he conceded that Strasburg or Saxony could send legates to France: *Briefwechsel*, ed. Lenz, vol. 2, no. 117.

[49] *Sleidans Briefwechsel*, no. 14; *PC*, vol. 3, no. 197.

[50] 'J'ay receu vostre letter par Selidanus, lequel je n'ay eu grand peine de justifier envers le Roy, veu les bons tesmoings qu'il a eu de son service, ausquels il a adjousté plus de foy que à tous les Rapports faux qu'on luy eust sceu faire'. *Correspondance*, vol. 7, no. 1017.

this time on two fronts since the Emperor had formed an alliance with Henry VIII, Francis's not so 'good brother'.[51] In Paris, the balance of power shifted again with Admiral Chabot's death in 1543; he was succeeded by Claude d'Annebault, a conservative closely linked to Cardinal Tournon, the greatest enemy of the Du Bellays and their policy.[52] The factional disagreements within the Court had also drawn in Francis's sons. While the future Henri II was strongly linked with the conservative camp at Court, his younger brother Charles, Duke of Orléans, sided with the reform-friendly, anti-Habsburg group. In September 1543 he sent a letter to the Protestant princes expressing 'the great desire we have by the grace of God, that the holy Gospel may be preached throughout the kingdom of France'. He also granted that the Gospel be freely preached in his Duchy of Orléans as well as in the recently conquered Duchy of Luxembourg. Charles's wish was for what had not yet been accomplished to finally become true: an alliance between France and the German Protestants.[53]

Such an alliance was still the aim of Cardinal Du Bellay. Perhaps with the added assurance of the good will of Charles of Orléans, he saw a new and possibly final chance to move towards an alliance with the German Protestants in the Diet of Speyer, which had been called for early 1544. Due to the urgency of the matter he decided to go himself, with François Olivier, president of the parliament, and Sleidan as fellow legates.[54] This mission was a dangerous one. By the time the group had arrived in Nancy, the Emperor had been informed about their mission and was determined to prevent it. Although he refused the French delegates permission to enter Imperial territory, Sleidan was a German citizen and could not be barred from Germany.

Despite threats to his life Sleidan rode on to Speyer to represent France while Du Bellay had an address to the Diet printed, explaining the situation and Francis's position.[55] This short tract agitatedly narrates

---

[51] Knecht, *Renaissance Warrior*, pp. 486–93.

[52] Knecht, *Francis I*, pp. 408–15.

[53] 'Le grant desir que par la grâce de Dieu nous avons, que le sainct Èvangile soit presché par tout le royaume de France'. *Correspondance*, vol. 9, no. 1278.

[54] *Catalogue des actes de François Ier*, no. 13537; Johann Sleidan, *De Statu Religionis et Reipublicae, Carolo Quinto, Caesare, Commentarii* (Strasburg, 1555), book 16.

[55] Sleidan refers to this tract in *Sleidans Briefwechsel*, no. 16. The tract must be *Oraison escripte suyvant lintention du Roy treschrestien ... a tous les estas du sainct empire assemblez en la ville de Spire* (Paris, 1544); cf. also another writing attributed to Du Bellay, *Defense pour le Roy de France Treschrestien, a lencontre des iniures & detractions de laques Omphalius, faicte nagueres en Latin par vng Seruiteur du Roy, & maintenant traduicte en Francois par Simon Brunel* (Paris, 1544), in fact written during the Diet of Worms, again defending Francis's position and positing an alliance between France and the German Protestants.

their journey to Speyer and its abrupt end, when they were severely threatened despite their safe conducts.[56] In its main part Du Bellay used all his powers to convince the German Protestants of an alliance with France. He reminded them of their common history when once they were one people under Charlemagne, their continued friendship throughout the centuries and their common struggle for peace within Christendom. He underlined that Francis had repeatedly tried to join forces with the German Protestants, and wanted to be nothing but 'a loyal friend, a peaceful neighbour, a dear ally and cousin'.[57]

This outpouring of rhetoric was fruitless. The Diet of Speyer completely quashed all hopes of a Franco–German alliance. With their backs to the wall and lured by the prospect of religious toleration, the German Protestants agreed to the Emperor's declaration of war against France despite the protest of many Imperial cities, most notably tolerant Strasburg.[58] The war between the Emperor, England and France was resolved with the Peace of Crépy in September 1544, which was not only supposed to end the continuous warfare between Francis and the Emperor, but also to pave the way to a future alliance with the proposed marriage of Charles of Orléans into the Habsburg family. Crépy crushed Protestant aspirations on two counts: the hopes for religious toleration had not been fulfilled, and since the Emperor was no longer occupied with war against France, the Protestants feared that he would now turn against them. Additionally, in the secret articles of the peace treaty Francis promised not to form an alliance with England and to support the Emperor should he wage a war against the Schmalkaldic League.[59]

The new rapprochement between the Emperor and the King of France brought an inevitable cooling in the latter's relations with German Protestants. The repercussions at Court meant defeat for the reformist circle around Du Bellay and triumph for their enemies. The Du Bellays's influence was declining, and with it the safety of their protégés. Sleidan, who had settled in Strasburg after the Diet of Speyer, along with Jean Sturm and Ulrich Geiger, both still in frequent contact with Jean Du Bellay, were warned that their close relation to France could potentially

---

[56] Du Bellay, *Oraison*, sig. A3ʳ.

[57] Ibid., sigs B3ʳ⁻ᵛ, H6ʳ⁻ᵛ.

[58] On Strasburg's position, see Rodolphe Reuss, *Histoire de Strasbourg depuis ses origines jusqu'à nos jours* (Paris, 1922), p. 135.

[59] On the Peace of Crépy, see Knecht, *Renaissance Warrior*, pp. 492–4. In January 1545 Sleidan informed Jacob Sturm about the secret articles of Crépy: *Sleidans Briefwechsel*, no. 18. Jean-Daniel Pariset states that Sleidan's informant was Jean Du Bellay: 'Les Relations diplomatiques Franco-Allemandes au milieu du *XVIᵉ* siècle' (2 vols, unpublished PhD thesis, Strasbourg, 1979), vol. 1, p. 66.

cause them trouble.[60] Yet the newfound Franco–Imperial friendship and the impending war with the Schmalkaldic League demonstrated the urgent need for new diplomatic efforts.

French foreign policy in 1545 remained ambivalent, despite Crépy. There were several points for Francis to consider at this juncture, not least that a truce with the Emperor had never before lasted very long. If the Peace of Crépy failed, it would be difficult to work towards an alliance with the German Protestants, since they would once more doubt Francis's true motives. A pact with the German princes was in itself a difficult affair: it certainly helped stir up more troubles for Charles V within the Empire. On the other hand it would be detrimental for France if Charles were to take up arms and defeat the Schmalkaldic League while it was an ally of France. In any case, an alliance with the 'heretic' English and Germans would most certainly damage France's relations with the papacy. Hence French diplomacy remained ambiguous, officially adhering to the truce while unofficially arranging for a new round of negotiations with the German Protestants. It is hard to establish whether France's motives were of a merely political nature or rather orientated towards a general moderation and peace as advocated by the Du Bellays. At their instigation, renewed negotiations with the German Protestants were in progress from at least April 1545.[61]

For the Schmalkaldic League, the situation was equally difficult. Despite more severe persecutions of Protestants in France they were forced to continue their diplomatic relations with France since a declaration of war by the Emperor against them was looming. Their objective was to prevent France and England from siding with the Emperor, and at best win their support in case of an Imperial attack. The Schmalkaldic League therefore had to ignore their growing reservations regarding French policies and work out a way forward. It was suggested that their legates would act as mediators to end the war between France and England and settle the question of Boulogne. During the summer of 1545 preparations for these meetings went ahead. There were to be two groups of delegates. The first, composed of Jean Sturm, Johann von Nidbruck and Christoph von Venningen, was to travel to France, whereas Sleidan, the marshal of Hesse Ludwig von Baumbach and Philip von Nidbruck were to negotiate with the English. In the end, all parties were to meet in Northern France for communal negotiations. Such a mission, difficult in itself, was even more fragile when considering that at the same

---

[60] PC, vol. 3, no. 448; Sleidans Briefwechsel, no. 16.
[61] On 13 April 1545 Sleidan reported the arrival of French legates in Strasburg: Sleidans Briefwechsel, no. 22; cf. no. 28.

time both France and England were negotiating with the Emperor out of fear that the other party would form an alliance with him.[62]

On 28 August 1545, Sleidan and his companions, the Hesse marshal Ludwig von Baumbach and Philip von Nidbruck, left Strasburg. After meeting with their fellow legates sent to France and the French at Amiens, they arrived at Windsor on 19 September.[63] In France, the situation had changed again with the unexpected death of Charles of Orléans on 9 September 1545, which effectively annihilated the terms of Crépy since the proposed Habsburg–Valois marriage was now void. It also destroyed any hopes the Protestants in both France and Germany had invested in Charles; now the scene was set for the conservative Dauphin Henri.

Given the circumstances, it is not surprising that the negotiations between France, England and the German Protestants conducted at Ardres and Calais with parallel missions to the respective courts proved difficult. Neither France nor England would make concessions concerning their disagreements over Boulogne and the marriage of Mary, Queen of Scots.[64] After meetings with Henry VIII, William Paget and others, the delegates sent to England travelled to Calais in mid-October to attend the main negotiations.[65]

Unfortunately, despite the Protestants' efforts the different parties could not come to any agreement. As the negotiations broke off, each party blamed the other and expressed general discontent. The English had heard rumours 'that in the King of Romans's Court it was advertised out of France that the French King used the Protestants to practise a peace with us, and found them but beasts, although they were commended to him for men of wit'.[66] Paget remarked to Henry VIII that the German legates were 'such sheep'.[67] Sleidan, the leader of the delegation to England, was soon accused of misrepresenting France's policy and thereby of having prevented a successful outcome of the negotiations.[68]

Again, nothing had been accomplished, and an attack by the Emperor against the Schmalkaldic League seemed inevitable. The German Protestants tried frantically to convince France to support their cause, but failed. In July 1546 the Emperor declared war on the

---

[62] *LP*, vol. 20, nos 48, 58, 239, 381; *PC*, vol. 3, no. 604.

[63] For their itinerary, see *Sleidans Briefwechsel*, pp. 87–9.

[64] *LP*, vol. 20; *PC*, vol. 3, no. 637; vol. 4(i), nos 680–84, 686–9; Hasenclever, 'Neue Aktenstücke zur Friedensvermittlung der Schmalkaldener'.

[65] *Sleidans Briefwechsel*, nos. 44–65; *LP*, vol. 20, nos 836, 856, 942, 984, 1011, 1014.

[66] *LP*, vol. 20, no. 128.

[67] *LP*, vol. 20, no. 917.

[68] *Sleidans Briefwechsel*, nos 69, 71; V.-L. Bourrilly, 'Deux nouvelles lettres de Johann Sleidan', *BSHPF* 55 (1906), 212–19.

Schmalkaldic League.[69] Yet negotiations with France continued, while Jean Du Bellay tried to support their cause from within the French Court. He even wrote to the English to urge them to help the German Protestants alongside a French initiative, arguing that otherwise the evangelical cause would be lost.[70]

Francis himself was still willing to form an alliance with the German Protestants, but only in return for Henry's VIII full support, the return of Boulogne and the Imperial Crown.[71] While the war raged, negotiations wavered between hope and despair. In November, Admiral d'Annebault let one of his messengers know that under no circumstances was the alliance with the Emperor to be broken.[72] Around the same time, Jean Sturm, who had been sent to France to rally support, was promised financial support by Francis.[73] Only a month later the English ambassador Wotton reported good news: 'The Queen of Navarre is sent for, and therefore the Protestants' matter is likely to prosper'.[74] As so many times before, all efforts were in vain. The Schmalkaldic War continued, and with the death of Henry VIII on January 1547 and that of Francis I in March 1547 the hopes for a pro-Protestant, anti-Habsburg coalition came to an end.

IV

The accession of Henri II meant the ultimate end of a moderate policy towards Protestants, both within France and in Germany, and the return of ultra-Catholicism to the Court. The time of men such as Jean Du Bellay was over. The Cardinal realized this himself and retired to Rome. Henri would occasionally seek Protestant support for his policy, but only when it suited him; at no time would he allow evangelical sentiments as near to the Court as Francis had done. With the Peace of Augsburg in 1555 the German Protestants no longer needed an alliance with France. Moreover, their closest ally, Jean Du Bellay, the Cardinal of Paris, was now gone.

---

[69] On the Schmalkaldic War and France's involvement, see H. Baumgarten, 'Zur Geschichte des Schmalkaldischen Kriegs', Historische Zeitschrift 36 (1876), 26–82; Potter, 'Foreign Policy'.

[70] LP, vol. 21, no. 457.

[71] Baumgarten, 'Zur Geschichte des Schmalkaldischen Kriegs', 69. With Brandenburg, Palatine and Saxony the Protestants already had three out of seven electoral votes, and would possibly have counted on the vote of Hermann von Wied, the evangelical Archbishop of Cologne, too. It seems unlikely, though, that they would ever have seriously considered deposing Charles V.

[72] Potter, 'Foreign Policy', p. 542.

[73] Schmidt, La Vie ... de Jean Sturm, p. 69.

[74] LP, vol. 21, no. 638.

The policy of accommodation between France and the German Protestants pursued energetically over three decades thus seems to have had few tangible results. This, however, is only part of the story. Although the negotiations between Francis and the German princes came to no discernible result, all sides, friend and foe, were very much aware that at different moments this radical departure in policy was a real possibility. In France, conservative forces had constantly to guard against such a shift in policy, and it was an ever-present danger to Charles V as well. For those associated with the evangelical cause, however loosely, the pursuit of a Protestant alliance offered a way forward even when the prospects for domestic reform seemed bleak. The need to keep this option open was a good reason for avoiding the whole-hearted persecution of evangelicals that might otherwise have followed the Affair of the Placards in 1534. In this sense, the attempts at an alliance with the German Protestants under the leadership of the Du Bellays, rather than radical reform, were possibly the best if not the only option for moderation and religious peace under Francis I. Such a policy could be supported by Protestants, evangelicals and *Catholiques critiques* alike. Naturally, political and religious motives would often merge. The tactics and motives of those who pursued such subtle diplomatic strategies were not always understood or approved of, even by those whose cause they sought to assist. No one was more scathing than Jean Calvin about evangelicals who had elected to remain in France rather than follow his example and take exile abroad. Such Nicodemites, as he described them, were constantly vilified in Protestant polemic. Indeed, the attack on Nicodemism was one of the leading themes of Protestant religious literature of that period. In retrospect, however, it is easy to recognize the value of highly placed friends at a Court where studied ambiguity was for the King an important instrument of policy even while his central commitment to Catholicism was never in doubt.

CHAPTER TWO

A Diagnosis of Religious Moderation: Matthew Parker and the 1559 Settlement

Louise Campbell

Over the centuries the Elizabethan religious settlement of 1559 has been the subject of much debate. In the past historians focused on the questions of what kind of religious settlement Elizabeth and her advisers wanted following her accession in November 1558, and how close the settlement achieved in parliament in the spring of 1559 was to the settlement they had envisaged. Were the queen and her advisers held back by Catholic opposition in the House of Lords or were they pushed too far in a Protestant direction by proto-puritans in the House of Commons?[1] Regardless of whether the regime and the queen got the settlement they wanted, historians seem unanimous in their description of the settlement; it was a *via media*, a moderate religious settlement implemented by the embodiment of moderation, Archbishop Matthew Parker. From the first weeks of Elizabeth's reign her chief ministers William Cecil and Nicholas Bacon were determined that Parker, their old associate, would become the new archbishop of Canterbury. The regime was fortunate that Cardinal Pole, the previous Archbishop, had died 12 hours after Mary I in the evening of 17 November 1558; for Pole, a staunch Catholic, would have presented a difficult problem for the new regime. The candidate chosen to be the new archbishop would signify to the world the nature of Elizabethan religious policy Historians, from John Strype in the eighteenth century to William Haugaard in the twentieth, seem united in believing that the key to Parker's appointment as archbishop in 1559 was his

---

[1] The traditional view that the most sustained pressure on the regime in 1559 came from Catholic opposition in the House of Lords in 1559 was challenged by John E. Neale, *Elizabeth I and her Parliaments, 1559–1581* (London, 1953), which proposed that Protestant pressure in the House of Commons pushed the regime in a more radical direction. Neale's thesis has been debunked by Norman L. Jones in *Faith by Statute: Parliament and the Settlement of Religion, 1559* (London, 1982).

moderation.[2] Surprisingly, however, despite the almost universal use of the term 'moderate' there has been little discussion of what 'moderate' in this context really means. This essay will attempt to diagnose the kind of religious moderation found in Matthew Parker and the religious settlement of 1559. The treatment of 'moderation' by historians of the Elizabethan Settlement and the problems arising from the different ways in which moderation has been handled will be explored to begin with. Then three symptoms of moderation in this context will be examined, before finally turning to Matthew Parker and his appointment as archbishop of Canterbury.

I

The authors of the mass of literature on the religious settlement have handled moderation superficially and with ambivalence. On the one hand they have praised men like Parker for their moderate behaviour in religious affairs, which they demonstrate was necessary in securing and implementing the settlement. On the other, they have used moderation as a measure of religious devotion: moderate Protestants, on this view, were not as hot as puritans and not as Protestant as they could have been, nor as committed to the complete godly Reformation as perhaps they should have been. The kind of moderation described by Parker's biographers, while being a thoroughly laudable quality, seems to have been one nevertheless tinged with timidity in comparison with wholehearted Protestantism. Parker's failure either to join the Marian exiles in Europe or to be consumed by the flames of Marian martyrdom was supposedly symptomatic of his religious moderation. The liberal use of 'moderate' as an epithet for the Protestantism of the 1559 settlement as well as for the personal beliefs of a variety of leading Elizabethans has rendered it a term whose use and understanding are fraught with difficulties. An analysis of the literature on the settlement shows that 'moderate' is used principally to indicate a set of beliefs located midway between the poles of Rome and Geneva: the *via media*. While this kind of moderation may have made sense politically, as Wilbur Jordan remarked in his study of religious toleration 'middle courses do not inspire particularly warm enthusiasm'.[3]

---

[2] John Strype, *The Life and Acts of Matthew Parker* (3 vols, Oxford, 1821), vol. 1, p. 2; William P. Haugaard, *Elizabeth and the English Reformation: The Struggle for a Stable Settlement of Religion* (Cambridge, 1968), pp. 33–5.
[3] Wilbur K. Jordan, *The Development of Religious Toleration in England* (London, 1932), p. 86.

In his treatise of 1834 John Henry Newman set down his concept of the Anglican *via media*. Newman exclaimed, 'The glory of the English Church is, that it has taken the *VIA MEDIA*, as it has been called. It lies *between* the (so called) Reformers and the Romanists.'[4] An article critical of 'this idol of the early Tractarians' in *The Church Times* in 1881 defined 'viamedialism' as 'a scheme whereof one party is asked to believe a little more, and the other a little less, than what they conceive to be true'.[5] However, historians have seemed keen to transpose this High Church concept of a *via media* into the Elizabethan period, and so Archbishop Parker has often been treated as a moderate tentatively treading the tightrope of the middle way between Catholicism and hotter Protestantism, endeavouring to form 'a party strong enough to bridge the gap between Protestants and Catholics' or using his tact and wisdom to steer a course between the extremes of papists and puritans whilst managing to 'preserve the catholicity of the Church'.[6] Parker's moderation supposedly reflected the lukewarm version of Protestantism peddled by the early Elizabethan regime; a brand of belief dissatisfying to many Marian exiles who felt the Elizabethan Church was 'but halfly Reformed'.[7] Only recently have historians begun to grapple seriously with the *via media* concept, challenging the traditional interpretation and putting a positive gloss on moderation.[8] Diarmaid MacCulloch points out that men like Archbishop Thomas Cranmer would have been horrified at this idea of compromising between true religion and the Antichrist, and has further argued that the idea of a *via media*, as expressed by Newman, is anachronistic when looking at the Tudor Church.[9] MacCulloch suggests persuasively that the idea for an English *via media* developed around the time of Richard Montague's remark in 1624 that 'the gap against Puritanisme and Popery' should be filled by the Church of England, which surely implies that Montague felt the Church had not previously done this.[10] The path followed by Parker and the Elizabethan

---

[4]   John H. Newman, '*Via media* 1834', in his *The Via Media of the Anglican Church* (2 vols, London, 1877), vol. 2, p. 20.

[5]   *The Church Times* 19 (1881), p. 128.

[6]   William P.M. Kennedy, *Archbishop Parker* (London, 1908), pp. vii–viii; Edith W. Perry, *Under Four Tudors: Being the True Story of Mathew Parker and Margaret* (London, 1964), p. 115.

[7]   Victor J.K. Brook, *A Life of Archbishop Parker* (Oxford, 1962), pp. 344–5.

[8]   Andrew Pettegree, *Marian Protestantism: Six Studies* (Aldershot, 1996), pp. 129–50; Dewey D. Wallace. Jr., '*Via media*? A Paradigm Shift', *Anglican and Episcopal History* 72 (2003), 2–21.

[9]   Diarmaid MacCulloch, *Thomas Cranmer: A Life* (London and New Haven, 1996), p. 617; D. MacCulloch, 'Richard Hooker's Reputation', *EHR* 117 (2002), 773–812, pp. 773, 790.

[10]   MacCulloch, 'Richard Hooker's Reputation', p. 790.

regime was not a middle way between Rome and Geneva, but an attempt to unite Protestants against the Church of Rome without compromising their own faith.[11]

As a measure of commitment to Protestantism, 'moderate' has been endowed with negative undertones; its meaning has, at times, metamorphosed from a term describing the position between Rome and Geneva into a synonym for *politique*.[12] Yet using the term *politique* to refer to people in early Elizabethan England is as anachronistic as calling evangelicals in Henrician England Protestants; the term originated during the Wars of Religion in France in the 1570s.[13] Confusing the term *politique* with 'moderate' has also masked the genuine evangelical credentials which people like Cecil, Bacon and Parker revealed in their early careers. Parker fraternized with early evangelicals in 1520s Cambridge and his promotion in 1535 to become one of Anne Boleyn's chaplains confirms his evangelical inclinations.[14] While Parker acted as chaplain to both Henry VIII and Edward VI, he made his name at Cambridge University; he became master of his old college, Corpus Christi, in 1544, and served as Vice-Chancellor of the University twice in that decade. In Edwardian Cambridge he struck up a friendship with the irenic German reformer Martin Bucer, who was Regius Professor of Divinity there, and Parker preached Bucer's funeral sermon in March 1551. Following the accession of Mary I Parker lost the mastership of Corpus on account of his religion and his other preferments for being a married priest. As Andrew Pettegree has recently observed those, like Parker, who forsook continental exile did not necessarily do so because of any lukewarm Protestant convictions.[15] Parker's decision to remain in Marian England may have been influenced by an arrangement he made with Corpus Christi College in the autumn of 1553.[16] Parker emerges from his early career as a committed evangelical academic who promoted humanist educational reforms.

Parker was a product of the same classically steeped humanist world as Cecil and Bacon and their early careers hold the keys to their

---

[11] MacCulloch, *Thomas Cranmer*, p. 617.

[12] Jordan, *Development of Religious Toleration*, pp. 88–9; Conyers Read, 'Walsingham and Burghley in Queen Elizabeth's Privy Council', *EHR* 28 (1913), 34–58, pp. 36–7; C. Read, *Mr Secretary Cecil and Queen Elizabeth* (London, 1955), pp. 127, 134; Robert Tittler, *Nicholas Bacon: The Making of a Tudor Statesman* (London, 1976), p. 55.

[13] *Oxford English Dictionary*, 2nd edn, ed. J.A. Simpson and E.S.C. Weiner (20 vols, Oxford, 1989), vol. 12, p. 35.

[14] Eric W. Ives, 'Anne Boleyn and the Early Reformation in England: The Contemporary Evidence', *HJ* 37 (1994), 389–400, pp. 390–91.

[15] Pettegree, *Marian Protestantism*, p. 88.

[16] I intend to discuss this possibility in my forthcoming doctoral thesis.

aspirations and actions at the beginning of Elizabeth's reign. Winthrop Hudson's thesis of the 'Cambridge connection' illuminates the course of events and promotions in 1559, revealing the employment by the early Elizabethan regime of many of the old 'Athenian' tribe which had surrounded John Cheke (a close friend of both Parker and Cecil).[17] Stephen Alford has reconstructed ably the 'Athenian' mental world, showing how classical concepts infused the thoughts and actions of men like Cecil and his brother-in-law Nicholas Bacon, whose motto 'moderate things endure' (*mediocria firma*) was taken from a Senecan tragedy.[18] The friendship between Bacon and Parker probably dated back to early 1520s Cambridge, when they both attended Corpus Christi College, and developed further over the years as Parker turned to Bacon for his expert legal opinion on various matters. Like Parker and Cecil, Bacon remained in England during Mary's reign spending his spare time pursuing intellectual interests.[19] Professor Collinson's examination of Bacon's 'mediocrity' and the *via media* reveals the differences in the understanding of moderation between early Elizabethans and modern historians. Early Elizabethan moderation was inspired by the idea of the Aristotelian golden mean rather than a notion of finding a middle way between two extremes, such as Rome or Geneva.[20] Aristotle implied the mean was equal to an amount which was appropriate for the circumstances, not necessarily therefore, a point midway between two extremes.[21] Early Elizabethan religious moderation was about having the appropriate amount of Protestantism, avoiding the excessive scrupulosity of Geneva, to defeat the Popish Antichrist. In many respects this kind of moderation seems to have been a highly subjective and self-fashioned condition. Those who considered themselves 'moderates' were perhaps so only from their own point of view.

How can this strain of religious moderation be recognized: what are the symptoms? First, this kind of religious moderation was concerned with maintaining Protestant unity against Rome, centred around the idea of *adiaphora*. In the 1559 parliament Catholics cogently criticized Protestants for their disunity in practices and their constant bickering; the idea of *adiaphora* countered this attack conveniently. Protestant practice could vary across Europe as rites and ceremonies were 'things

---

[17] Winthrop S. Hudson, *The Cambridge Connection* (Durham, NC, 1980).
[18] Stephen Alford, *The Early Elizabethan Polity: William Cecil and the British Succession Crisis, 1558–1569* (Cambridge, 1998), pp. 14–24; Patrick Collinson, 'Nicholas Bacon and the Elizabethan *Via media*', *HJ* 23 (1980), 255–73, pp. 258–61.
[19] Tittler, *Nicholas Bacon*, pp. 56–7.
[20] Collinson, 'Nicholas Bacon and the *Via media*', 257, 261.
[21] William F.R. Hardie, *Aristotle's Ethical Theory*, 2nd edn (London, 1982), pp. 134–5, 145.

indifferent' and were not of necessity to salvation. The 'Cambridge connection' emphasizes this aspect of moderation: Hudson demonstrates convincingly that rather than being connected by theological concerns, the 'Athenians' instead identified with the irenicism of Martin Bucer.[22] Second, religious moderates exhibited a concern for the maintenance of the stability of the commonwealth.[23] This kind of moderation was tightly bound up with obedience to the Crown: stability in religious affairs was essential for the stability of the realm. Religious moderates allowed the government to prescribe the pace and method of Reformation and to decide adiaphorous matters in order to maintain the stability of the commonwealth. Finally, religious moderation also had more personal symptoms, being endowed with humanist rhetoric and a concern for seemly behaviour: opponents, including Catholics, should be listened to politely and then persuaded calmly of their errors. Like the other forms of moderation, this was not new in 1559. Cardinal Wolsey had successfully used a strikingly similar policy towards suspected Lutherans in the 1520s, while humanists from Erasmus to Vives had detailed the kind of language and behaviour appropriate to religious debate, prescribing the rules of rhetoric to be followed.[24] This aspect resonated with university men from a humanist milieu such as Parker, Bacon and Cecil.

II

The idea that without unity and concord 'noe common wealth can longe endure and stande' was at the forefront of the minds of the men such as William Cecil who shaped the policies of the early Elizabethan government. It permeated the advice treatises offered to the regime by Protestants in the winter of 1558–59.[25] However, in parliament in March 1559, Archbishop Heath's speech against the Supremacy Bill skilfully employed the imagery of disunity, warning that those who accepted the royal supremacy risked drowning 'in the waters of scisme, sectes and divisions'.[26] The disputes of the Marian Protestants, most famously amongst the English exile congregation at Frankfurt, had provided

---

[22] Hudson, *The Cambridge Connection*, p. 42.
[23] Jones, *Faith by Statute*, p. 159.
[24] Craig W. D'Alton, 'The Suppression of Lutheran Heretics in England, 1526–1529', *JEH* 54 (2003), 228–53; Erika Rummel, *The Confessionalization of Humanism in Reformation Germany* (Oxford, 2000), pp. 123–5.
[25] *Proceedings in the Parliaments of Elizabeth I, 1558–1581*, ed. T.E. Hartley (3 vols, Leicester, 1981–1995), vol. 1, p. 51.
[26] Ibid., pp. 12–13.

Catholic opponents of religious change with ample ammunition for their cause, enabling them to portray Catholicism as being 'more stedfast' and 'agreable with ytselfe'.[27] To counter this Catholic attack, the early Elizabethan regime sought to unite Protestant exiles with each other and with those who had remained in Marian England using the concept of 'things indifferent'. The brand of unity they were suggesting, however, was not a 'mingle mangle', a *via media* between Rome and Geneva, but a Protestant irenic unity against the Romish Antichrist.[28] This symptom of religious moderation appeared among the propositions to be debated at the Westminster Disputation.

At Easter 1559, the regime organized a disputation at Westminster between eight Catholics and eight Protestants, ostensibly to end diversity in opinions by reducing the realm to godly and Christian concord, but primarily as part of the regime's plan to discredit ardent Catholic opposition to the settlement, whilst generating support for their religious policies, so preparing the way for the introduction of separate supremacy and uniformity bills into parliament after Easter.[29] Three propositions were to be debated at Westminster: that it was contrary to the Word of God, and the practice of the primitive Church, to use in public prayers and the administration of the sacraments a language unknown to the people; that every provincial Church could establish, change or abrogate ceremonies and ecclesiastical rites 'wherever it may seem to make for edification'; and that it cannot be proved in Scripture 'that ther is in the Masse offred vp a Sacrifyce propiciatory for the quicke and the deade'.[30] The Protestants never got the opportunity to defend the last two propositions at Westminster, as disagreements between the Catholic disputants and the adjudicator Nicholas Bacon resulted in the dissolution of the conference on the second day.

The second proposition was designed to counter the Catholic claim that Protestantism was neither steadfast nor agreeable with itself, and also to persuade Protestants to unite together around the concept of *adiaphora*. A copy of the prepared answer of the Protestants to the second proposition survives in the Parker Library at Corpus Christi College, Cambridge. Their answer began by defining rites and ceremonies as things that 'neither expressely neither by necessarie

---

[27] Ibid., pp. 27–8.
[28] BL Cotton MS Julius F.vi, fol. 167ᵛ.
[29] Jones, *Faith by Statute*, p. 123.
[30] *The Zurich Letters. comprising the correspondence of several english Bishops and others with some of the Helvetian Reformers during the early part of The Reign of Queen Elizabeth*, ed. Hastings Robinson (2 vols, Parker Society, Cambridge, 1842–45), vol. 1, pp. 10–11; *The declaracyon of the procedynge of a conference begon at Westminster the laste of March 1559* (London, 1559), unpaginated, in CCCC MS 121, no. 21.

deducion or consequence are commaunded or forbidden in the Scriptures, but are thinges of their owne nature indifferent'.[31] They claimed that 'all Ecclesiasticall Rites and Ceremonies are thinges which apperteine vnto ordre and decencie' and were not of necessity to salvation.[32] Therefore, national churches could determine the order to be followed according to local conditions, thereby allowing for variation in Protestant practice across Europe. The proposition on rites and ceremonies which was to have been considered at Westminster in 1559 was repeated in Elizabethan doctrinal statements from the 11 Articles in the early years of the reign to the 39 Articles of Religion. Article 33 of the Edwardian 42 Articles stated, 'It is not necessary that traditions and ceremonies be in all places utterly like.' When the articles were revised in 1563, this article was expanded with the assertion that 'every particular or national Church hath authority to ordain and change and abolish ceremonies, or rites of the Church ordained only by man's authority, so that all things be done to edifying'.[33] However, the problem of who had the authority to decide which rites and ceremonies were edifying and so could be retained for order's sake would dominate the 1560s and would divide those who emphasized obedience to the queen in such matters from those whose consciences would not allow them to conform.

III

The second manifestation of religious moderation in the 1559 settlement was the regime's attempt to control the pace of religious change towards Protestantism. While contemporary observers recognized that the accession of Elizabeth sounded the death knell for Marian Catholicism, the regime appeared keen to restrain any Protestant overenthusiasm for the inevitable change in religious policy, and caution was the keynote of those who offered advice to the regime. Historians have identified the anonymous 'Device for the alteration of religion' and lawyer Richard Goodrich's 'Divers points of religion contrary to the Church of Rome' as the most significant of the four extant treatises of advice presented by Protestants to the regime.[34] A recurring theme in these treatises was that

---

[31] CCCC MS 121, p. 197.

[32] Ibid., p. 198.

[33] *Documents of the English Reformation*, ed. Gerald Bray (Cambridge, 1994), pp. 349–50, 304–5. Article 33 of 1563 was renumbered as Article 34 in the 1571 revision.

[34] Jones, *Faith by Statute*, pp. 20–25; N. Jones, 'Elizabeth's First Year: The Conception and Birth of the Elizabethan Political World', in Christopher Haigh (ed.), *The Reign of Elizabeth I* (Basingstoke, 1984), 27–53, pp. 32–3.

of proceeding with caution in religious affairs, summed up most memorably by Armagill Waad, author of the third treatise, the 'Distresses of the commonwealth':

> Glasses with small necks: if you powre in to them any licor sodenly or violently will not be so fylled, but refuse to receive that same that you would powre in to them howbeit, if you instill watter in to them by a littill and littill they are soone replenisshed.[35]

The regime had to keep Protestant enthusiasm firmly under control and to direct the pace at which it flowed through such a small-necked glass as the Elizabethan commonwealth. Sudden or violent changes could cause an overflow of opposition to the changes, resulting in instability. Waad warned that 'great cunnyng, and circumspection' were needed 'boothe to reforme Religion and to make vnite betwene the subjectes', not only because of the reaction of foreign princes and the Pope, but especially because of the danger of altering religion at the beginning of a reign.[36]

In his memorandum of 17 November 1558, the day Mary I died, William Cecil jotted a reminder to 'consider ye condition of ye prechar at powles cross and to [sic] that no occasion be gyven by hym to stirr any dispute towchyng the governance of ye realme'. The following day he decided that William Bill, Elizabeth's almoner and an old Athenian, would deliver the inaugural sermon of the reign.[37] However, Bill's sermon on 20 November provoked an angry response the following week from Bishop Christopherson of Chichester, who condemned Bill as seditious and heretical.[38] To avoid further controversies being played out in the nation's pulpits in the run-up to the first parliament, the Elizabethan regime silenced the pulpits until parliament had 'moved in matters and ceremonies of religion' with the proclamation of 27 December 1558 prohibiting unlicensed preaching and regulating ceremonies.[39] The only sermons to be heard were those delivered in London by men considered learned and discreet by the regime – including Matthew Parker, who preached two sermons in February 1559.

To preserve the stability of the commonwealth Cecil and his allies intended that the queen, with counsel from her ecclesiastical commissioners, would determine which things were necessary for order's

---

[35] NA SP 12/1, fol. 150ᵛ.
[36] Ibid.
[37] NA SP 12/1, fol. 3ʳ; NA SP 12/1, fol. 4ʳ.
[38] *Zurich Letters*, vol. 1, p. 4.
[39] *Tudor Royal Proclamations*, ed. P.L. Hughes and J.F. Larkin (3 vols, New Haven, 1964–69), vol. 2, pp. 102–3.

sake, and they expected all loyal Protestants to obey.[40] Their position was to be modified when the queen took a slightly different line, believing the decision was hers alone; while the reaction of Edwin Sandys (the first Elizabethan Bishop of Worcester) to the order to retain the ornaments and ceremonies of the second year of the reign of Edward VI encapsulated the differences between the understanding of *adiaphora* of the former exiles, the regime and the queen. Sandys explained to Matthew Parker that 'our gloss upon this text is that we shall not be forced to use them but that others in the meantime shall not convey them away, but that they remain for the queen'.[41] However, men like Sandys would soon find themselves constrained to enforce things of indifference against their own personal inclinations as the regime and Parker insisted that obedience to the queen should take precedence over individual consciences.

In his closing speech to the 1559 parliament on 8 May Lord Keeper Nicholas Bacon warned that the hinderers of religious uniformity would receive 'sharpe and severe correccion', especially those:

> that subtillye by indirecte meanes seeke or procure the contrarye. Amongst thease I meane to comprehende aswell those that be to swifte as those that be to slowe, those, I say, that goe before the lawe or beyond the lawe, as those that will not followe. For good governaunce cannot be where obedience fayleth and both theise alike breaketh the rules of obedience.[42]

Bacon's parliamentary rhetoric was far from new, having been employed in the Henrician parliaments of the 1540s.[43] It also echoed the observations in the 'Device for the alteration of religion': those who cried 'cloked papestrye' in response to the Elizabethan Settlement were to be repressed as severely as the papists themselves.[44] However, his rhetoric did not mean that the regime wished to cleave a course between these stumbling blocks; proceeding moderately did not preclude the

---

[40] Article 13 of the Act of Uniformity (1° Elizabeth c. 2) stated that the ornaments of the second year of Edward VI would be retained until other order be taken 'by the aucthorite of the Quenes Majestie, withe the advise of her Commissioners ... for [Ecclesiasticall Causes,] or of the Metropolytan of this Realme'. *Statutes of the Realm*, ed. T.E. Tomlins (11 vols, London, 1819), vol. 4, p. 358.

[41] *Correspondence of Matthew Parker, D.D. Archbishop of Canterbury*, ed. John Bruce and T. Perowne (Parker Society, Cambridge, 1843), p. 65.

[42] *Proceedings in the Parliaments of Elizabeth I*, p. 51.

[43] Collinson, 'Nicholas Bacon and the *Via media*', 255–6; D. MacCulloch, 'Henry VIII and the Reform of the Church', in his *The Reign of Henry VIII: Politics, Policy and Piety* (Basingstoke and London, 1995), 159–80, p. 175; G.W. Bernard, 'The Making of Religious Policy 1533–1546: Henry VIII and the Search for the Middle Way', *HJ* 41 (1998), 321–49, p. 345.

[44] BL Cotton MS Julius F.vi, fol. 167ᵛ.

establishment of a 'fully' Protestant settlement. The regime was only too well aware of the various potential threats to stability and order, especially when the question of the succession remained open. Although the regime's restraint was understandable to the returning exiles, John Jewel (newly returned from the continent and soon to become Bishop of Salisbury) voiced their fears in January 1559 when he hoped the regime would not act 'with too much worldly prudence and policy in the cause of God'.[45] As the year progressed Jewel had to admit that despite the queen favouring 'our cause', she was 'wonderfully afraid of allowing any innovations' and by November 1559 he noted the 'slow-paced horses retard the chariot' of Reformation. It was no easy feat, grumbled Jewel, 'to drag the chariot without horses, especially up hill'.[46] The Elizabethan regime was determined that the 1559 settlement would not be overtaken by intemperate zeal, no matter who was trying to whip up speed.

IV

Enmeshed with the concern for stability of the commonwealth was the idea that for unity and concord in religion one should act in an orderly, seemly manner: the third symptom of moderation. Protestant innovations were to be executed with decorum: an overzealous or unseemly preacher could easily disturb the stability of the commonwealth. Parker reminded Cecil of this in November 1559, remarking disapprovingly: 'God keep us from such visitation as Knox have attempted in Scotland; the people to be orderers of things.'[47] The disorderly, violent implementation of the Scottish Reformation inspired by the preaching of John Knox was simply not a model to be esteemed in England, while Knox, particularly due to the publication of his *First Blast of the Trumpet against the Monstrous Regiment of Women*, became the epitome of the kind of immoderate Protestantism Elizabeth wished to avoid. The Elizabethan regime exhibited this symptom of religious moderation in its exhortations to the members of the 1559 parliament; Lord Keeper Bacon's speeches at the opening and closing of the parliament were riddled with references to the necessity of orderly behaviour in parliament. On 25 January the Lords and Commons were ordered optimistically to 'flee from all manner of contentious reasoninges and disputacions' in their consultation of weighty matters, in which they were also to eschew 'all contentious, contumelious or

---

[45] *Zurich Letters*, vol. 1, pp. 7–8.
[46] Ibid., pp. 10, 55, 45.
[47] *Parker Correspondence*, p. 105.

opprobrious wordes, as hereticke, schismaticke, papist'. Such terms, thundered Bacon, were 'the causers, continuers and increasers of displeasure, hate and malice' and 'utter enemyes to all concorde and unitie, the very marke that you are now to shoote at'.[48]

The returned exiles and the regime were keen to portray the behaviour of Catholic opponents of the settlement as intemperate and immoderate, a threat to the stability of the commonwealth. John Jewel dubbed John Christopherson 'that brawling Bishop of Chichester' after hearing of Christopherson's response to William Bill's Paul's Cross sermon following Elizabeth's accession; and Jewel judged Bishop White's sermon at the funeral of Mary I 'a most furious and turbulent discourse'.[49] But according to (heavily biased) Protestant observers, the pinnacle of inordinate Catholic behaviour occurred during the Westminster Disputation of Easter 1559. Professor Norman Jones has described the confusion over the order of the debate at Westminster, suspecting both the regime and the Catholic party of equivocation.[50] The official printed version of the disputation begins by noting that the conference was broken up by the 'default and contempt' of certain bishops. The regime insisted that Archbishop Heath of York and his party had requested particularly that they be allowed to give their opinions in writing, in Latin, and it was agreed that they would dispute first, followed by the Protestants' response, before submitting the books of their arguments to the Privy Council. The debate was held before the Privy Council and both Houses of Parliament, whose request that the debate be in English 'for the better satisfaction and inhabling of their owne judgments' was agreed upon by both parties.[51] However, when the parties gathered on Friday, 31 March 1559 Bishop White of Winchester alleged there had been a misunderstanding, and although they were ready to dispute, their book was not yet finished. Nevertheless they were allowed to proceed, the official account referring disparagingly to Dr Cole, dean of St Paul's, as the one appointed as the 'vtterer of their minds'.[52] In John Jewel's extremely partial account of the disputation, Dr Cole was portrayed rather comically as the antithesis of moderation and seemly behaviour. Cole harangued his opponents, 'stamping with his feet, throwing about

---

[48] *Proceedings in the Parliaments of Elizabeth I*, vol. 1, pp. 34–5.

[49] *Zurich Letters*, vol. 1, pp. 6–7.

[50] Jones, *Faith by Statute*, pp. 123–7.

[51] *The declaracyon of the procedynge of a conference*. The draft of this, containing alterations in Cecil's hand, is at NA SP 12/3 fols 166ᵛ–173ʳ; another version (NA SP 12/3 fols 163ʳ–164ᵛ) was signed by the Privy Council.

[52] *The declaracyon of the procedynge of a conference*. In the draft of the official account (NA SP 12/3 fol. 170ᵛ) Cecil amended the description of Dr Cole from 'the prolocutor' to the 'vtteror'.

his arms, bending his sides, snapping his fingers, alternately elevating and depressing his eyebrows', all in all a performance, Jewel sneered, that would make one exclaim 'Poh! Whoreson knave!'[53]

In contrast, Robert Horne read the Protestant answer distinctly, 'with so much moderation as only to treat upon the matter in dispute, without wounding our opponents'. The official version claimed Horne persuaded the audience with his oration, to the chagrin of the bishops who demanded the right to reply – a claim given some credence by a remark from the Catholic Venetian commentator Il Schifanoya.[54] The disputants were told to reconvene on Monday, 3 April, with the bishops kicking off proceedings with their response in writing to the second proposition. However, arguments over the order of proceedings halted the debate and resulted in the Bishops of Winchester and Lincoln being incarcerated in the Tower of London. The official account singles out these bishops as those who 'most obstinatly both disobeied common auctority and varied manifestly from their owne order', due to their refusal to adhere to the order previously agreed upon. Even those sympathetic to the bishops gave the impression that bishops White and Watson acted rather obstreperously being 'inflamed with ardent zeal for God'.[55] The actions of the eight unfortunate Catholic disputants were described officially as indiscreet and irreverent; through their 'dysorder, stubbernes and selfe wyll' they had frustrated the godly purpose of the Queen.[56] Christopher Haigh hints that the imprisonment of bishops White and Watson was vital to the success of the Uniformity Bill by way of reducing the number of potential opposing votes in the Lords.[57] The Uniformity Bill was passed on 28 April by 21 votes to 18 in the Lords and came into effect on 24 June 1559; the third draft of the Supremacy Bill was passed on 29 April. The regime had secured its Protestant settlement, portraying those who offered opposition to the settlement as immoderate menaces to the stability of the realm.

---

[53] *Zurich Letters*, vol. 1, p. 14.
[54] Ibid., p. 15; *The declaracyon of the procedynge of a conference*; *Calendar of State Papers and Manuscripts, Relating to English Affairs, Existing in the Archives and Collections of Venice*, Vol. 2: 1558–1580, ed. R. Brown and G.C. Bentinck (London, 1890), p. 65.
[55] *The declaracyon of the procedynge of a conference*.
[56] Ibid.
[57] C. Haigh, *English Reformations: Religion, Politics and Society under the Tudors* (Oxford, 1993), p. 241.

V

During the summer of 1559 the regime followed a two-pronged policy of implementing the religious settlement through a visitation of the country, and through cajoling Catholics into taking the Oath of Supremacy; it appears that they expected a number of Marian bishops to conform.[58] Therefore the new archbishop of Canterbury not only had to be acceptable to Elizabeth, with her old-fashioned evangelical convictions, and to those who had experienced continental Protestantism at first hand in their period of Marian exile, but also to those Catholic bishops the regime hoped to retain. Matthew Parker appears to have been the sole candidate for the job. However, he did not want it.

Parker's *nolo episcopari* was understandable: he must have wondered over what kind of Church he was going to be expected to officiate. The tone of Parker's letters in 1559 to Bacon, Cecil and the queen, in which he desperately tried to prove his unsuitability for Canterbury, belies the fact, recognized by the regime, that Parker had been an astute university politician in the reigns of Henry VIII and Edward VI. His sagacity was unwittingly revealed in his letter to Bacon in March 1559. Parker prayed that Bacon and Cecil should bestow the archbishopric of Canterbury well, listing the qualities the candidate should possess, before examining exhaustively the reasons why he could not be considered for the position. Parker hoped they would choose neither an arrogant nor a fainthearted man. An arrogant man:

> shall discourage his fellows to join with him in unity of doctrine, which must be their whole strength; for if any heart-burning be betwixt them, if private quarrels stirred abroad be brought home, and so shall shiver them asunder, it may chance to have that success which I fear in the conclusion will follow.[59]

Despite lamenting 'that I am so basely qualified inwardly of knowledge', Parker had identified astutely one of the main concerns of the regime and one of the main criticisms directed at Protestantism by Catholics in the parliament of 1559: that of incessant infighting.[60] Parker had little sympathy for those who would threaten Protestant unity and concord. In 1551 he had voiced his distaste for those who were 'so depelye framed in there opinion' that they had frustrated the attempts of Martin Bucer to reach a concord and instead offered 'there lyffes and goodes, and jeoperde sowle and all, in maintenance and defense of there iudgemente': the issue

---

[58] NA SP 12/4 fol. 133ʳ.
[59] *Parker Correspondence*, p. 57.
[60] Ibid., p. 70.

at stake here was one far from adiaphorous, the nature of Christ's presence in the Eucharist.[61] Parker's stance on *adiaphora* reflected the position taken by Bacon and Cecil. However, the prospect of being the primate expected to unite Protestantism understandably held little appeal for Parker, for whom quiet scholarly pursuits were infinitely more desirable.

The second kind of man to avoid, reasoned Parker, was the fainthearted man, who 'should be too weak to commune with the adversaries, who would be the stouter upon his pusillanimity'.[62] Not only was Parker politically aware but his comment suggests that he was painfully aware of his own limitations and the constraints of his mild character. Historians emphasize the importance of Parker's moderation to explaining his appointment as archbishop in 1559. Indeed, it is impossible to study Parker without being bombarded by references to his 'great prudence and moderation';[63] his 'piety, soberness, moderation and integrity';[64] his 'kindness, moderation, [and] conciliation'.[65] However, by conflating Parker's conciliatory character and his religious beliefs historians have misunderstood Parker's moderation. Like Cecil and Bacon he was concerned with Protestant unity and maintaining order and stability, but while Parker's mild nature did not dilute his commitment to Protestantism, it did affect his efforts to get Catholics to conform to the settlement; which six months after his letter to Bacon was exactly what Parker, as archbishop-elect, found himself doing.

In the late summer and autumn of 1559 the regime made use of Parker's perceived skills of persuasion, sending a variety of Catholics to him to be convinced of the error of their ways. The rhetoric of temperance and moderation employed by the regime throughout 1559 accurately reflected their priorities. The regime envisaged an episcopal bench on which stay-at-homes, émigrés and a few venerable Catholics were seated next to each other, headed by the uniting figure of Matthew Parker. Parker's Marian retirement had been free from involvement in divisive disputes and likewise he was not involved in the Westminster Disputation: surely points which the regime felt could make him seem like a more credible figure to the Catholics whom they wanted to persuade to comply quietly with the settlement. In late August Parker received the first of those Catholics the regime wanted to conform. The

---

[61] Matthew Parker, *Howe we ought to take the death of the godly* (London, [1551]), *A Short–Title Catalogue of Books Printed 1475–1640 revised*, ed. W.A. Jackson, J.F. Ferguson and K.F. Pantzer (London, 1986), no. 19293, sigs E8ᵛ–F1ʳ.

[62] *Parker Correspondence*, p. 57.

[63] Strype, *Life of Matthew Parker*, vol. 1, p. 2.

[64] Henry N. Birt, *The Elizabethan Religious Settlement* (London, 1907), p. 250.

[65] Perry, *Under Four Tudors*, p. 181.

Privy Council sent Richard Smith, a former reader of Divinity at Oxford who had been apprehended on his way to Scotland, to Parker and Edmund Grindal, Bishop-Elect of London, with instructions for them to:

> use such measures as you think meet to persuade him to be an obedient subject, and to embrace the doctrine established; whereunto if he shall shew himself conformable, then we pray you to signify the same unto us ... Otherwise, if he be obstinate and will not shew himself as he ought, then we pray you to let us also understand from you the same, to the end order may be given for his further proceeding with, according to the laws.[66]

Parker and Grindal reported back their success three days later, having 'spent some time in conference with him'.[67] In an undated letter Smith thanked Parker for his charitable treatment and promised to conform. He went on to describe his sureties, who included his dearly beloved nephew, and promised ominously, 'I shall never breake that bonde.' However, Parker's triumph was ephemeral. Smith was a slippery character with a record of insincere recantation and bond-breaking, so it was with an air of resignation that Parker jotted on Smith's letter, 'notwithstanding this earnest promise and bond yet this good father fled into Paris such was his faythe'.[68] Smith died in Douai in 1563.

The regime made concerted efforts to persuade certain Catholic bishops to accept the religious settlement but with little success.[69] In particular, they worked hard to persuade Cuthbert Tunstall, Bishop of Durham since the 1520s, to conform to the settlement. After seeing the iconoclastic actions of the 1559 visitors Tunstall informed Cecil, 'my conscience will not suffer me to receyve and allowe any doctryne in my diocesse other then catholike'.[70] Yet despite Tunstall's firm stance, the regime still fostered the hope of his conformity, issuing a commission to the bishop on 9 September 1559 for Parker's consecration. But 18 days later the Privy Council sent Tunstall to Parker for Parker to have conference with him 'in certain points of religion wherein he is to be resolved'. Tunstall seems to have been deprived of his bishopric the following day. However, hope was still entertained of his reconciliation: 'a thyng for my part much desyered', mused Cecil.[71] On 2 October Cecil

---

[66] *Parker Correspondence*, pp. 72–3.
[67] Ibid., pp. 73–4.
[68] CCCC MS 119, pp. 111–12.
[69] Only Anthony Kitchin, Bishop of Llandaff, and possibly Thomas Stanley, the obscure Bishop of Sodor and Man, conformed to the settlement. See Haugaard, *Elizabeth and the English Reformation*, p. 36.
[70] NA SP 12/6 fols 50ʳ–51ʳ.
[71] *Parker Correspondence*, p. 77; NA SP 70/8 fol. 9ᵛ.

told Parker that 'the comfort that ye give of the Bishop of Durham's towardness' was much liked, but again Parker's optimism had been misplaced, as by 5 October he admitted defeat, much to the sorrow of Elizabeth and her chief minister. 'The recovery of such a man' as Tunstall, lamented Cecil, 'would have furthered the common affairs of this realm very much.'[72] When such attempts at reconciliation ended in failure the regime treated many with restraint: one foreign Catholic observer expressed surprise that 'the Queen, notwithstanding her perversity in religion, has not yet shown any disposition to deal rigorously with the ... churchmen who have refused to take the oath of obedience or deny the Catholic religion, but has merely deprived them of their offices and benefices'.[73]

Tunstall died in the care of Parker on 18 November 1559 at the age of 85 and Parker contributed towards the expenses for his burial in Lambeth parish church.[74] Of the ten Catholics sent to Parker mentioned in the *Parker Correspondence* in the autumn of 1559, eight remained obdurate, and the fates of Edward Chamber from Abingdon and Matthew, vicar of Howe in Kent, remain unclear.[75] While Parker may have failed to persuade any of those who we know were sent to him to conform, he did gain a reputation for his clemency.[76] Perhaps Bacon should have paid more attention to Parker's veiled warnings about appointing a fainthearted man to Canterbury. Although Victor Brook charitably suggests that perhaps the regime only sent to him the most obstinate Catholics, it seems more likely that Parker was too accommodating a character to use persuasion alone to get Catholics to conform.[77]

VI

Religious moderation in early Elizabethan England was a subjective and complex condition. However, it does not refer to the personal religion of the queen. From her analysis of Elizabeth's letters Susan Doran draws a persuasive picture of an evangelical leaning queen whose beliefs were

---

[72] *Parker Correspondence*, pp. 77–8.
[73] *Calendar of State Papers relating to English Affairs preserved principally at Rome ... 1558–1571*, ed. James M. Rigg (London, 1916), pp. 14–15.
[74] Charles Sturge, *Cuthbert Tunstal: Churchman, Scholar, Statesman, Administrator* (London, 1938), pp. 327–8.
[75] Brook, *Archbishop Parker*, p. 75. They were sent to Parker between 27 August and 9 November 1559: see *Parker Correspondence*, pp. 72–3, 75–7, 96–7, 103–6.
[76] CCCC MS 119, p. 109; MS 114b, pp. 855–6.
[77] Brook, *Archbishop Parker*, p. 75.

'frozen in the religion of her youth',[78] and scholars have hinted that Elizabeth needed to be steered firmly towards the kind of Protestant settlement Cecil had in mind in 1559; in particular, that she had to be persuaded of the need to remove altars.[79] Having old-fashioned evangelical sympathies did not make Elizabeth a 'moderate' Protestant in the way that 'moderate' was understood following her accession. Rather than being situated in the middle of a sliding scale between hotter Protestantism and Catholicism, religious moderation in early Elizabethan England was a way of behaving, a way of dictating the pace of change, the direction of which could only be towards Protestantism and away from the follies of popery. Elizabeth's obsession with her supremacy and her determination to enforce a rigid conformity to the 1559 settlement illuminate her lack of 'moderation'. Her static attitude to *adiaphora* appears out of step with the sentiments of the 1559 settlement; the Westminster disputants argued how indifferent ceremonies could become corrupt and the ornaments proviso of the Act of Uniformity authorized the taking of further order in such an event.[80] However, Elizabeth would not entertain alterations to the settlement even to avoid Protestant divisions and it looks likely that the 'moderates' underestimated Elizabeth's conservatism and had to work hard to get her consent for the 1559 religious settlement.[81]

Indeed Cecil and his allies seemed to make a number of miscalculations in 1559. It seems that they had underestimated the opposition of the Catholic bishops to the settlement; that they had misunderstood Elizabeth's conception of the royal supremacy and her religious idiosyncrasies; and that their rhetoric of maintaining Protestant unity and concord, keeping order and stability, and acting temperately was going to be difficult to practise in the real world, where one person's 'thing indifferent' was another's pernicious stumbling-block.[82] Although a similar policy was successful in the suppression of Lutheran heretics in

---

[78] Susan Doran, 'Elizabeth I's Religion: The Evidence of Her Letters', *JEH* 51 (2000), 699–720, p. 720.

[79] Alford, *Early Elizabethan Polity*, p. 218; P. Collinson, 'If Constantine, then also Theodosius: St Ambrose and the Integrity of the Elizabethan *Ecclesia Anglicana*', in his *Godly People: Essays on English Protestantism and Puritanism* (London, 1983), 109–33, pp. 128–30; P. Collinson, *Elizabethan Essays* (London, 1994), p. 109; Inner Temple Library, Petyt MS 538/38, fols 29^r–31^r; LPL, MS 2002, fols 107^r–110^v.

[80] CCCC MS 121, pp. 119–200, 216–17; *Statutes of the Realm*, vol. 4, p. 358 (Act of Uniformity, 1° Elizabeth c. 2).

[81] Interestingly, Parker recalled in 1571 that 'her Highness would not have agreed to divers orders of the book' (the Act of Uniformity) until the inclusion of the ornaments proviso. *Parker Correspondence*, p. 375.

[82] See Ethan Shagan's essay in this volume.

the 1520s, the 'softly-softly' approach of using scholarly persuasion to cajole Catholic bishops in Elizabethan England to conform, with hindsight, appears doomed to failure.[83] Despite his earnest protestations Parker's close friends had felt he would be robust enough to dispute with Catholics and persuade them of their errors; that he would be a credible figure to unite together fractious Protestant interests because he embodied a kind of moderation consistent with their own. On paper Matthew Parker looked like the perfect candidate to fill the position of archbishop of Canterbury. Indeed Bacon told him: 'If I knew a man to whom the description made in the beginning of your letter might more justly be referred than to yourself, I would prefer him before you; but knowing none so meet, indeed I take it to be my duty to prefer you before all others.'[84] Many Parkerian scholars have shared Bacon and Cecil's optimism about Parker's suitability for Canterbury, yet by the end of 1559 Parker had failed spectacularly to persuade the high profile Catholics sent to him to conform, and the controversy over the Queen's determined retention of a crucifix in the Chapel Royal was bitterly dividing the bishops-elect. It was no wonder that Parker remarked on his memoranda roll on 17 December 1559, the day of his consecration as archbishop: 'Alas! alas! O Lord God, for what times hast thou kept me. Now am I come into deep waters, and the flood hath overwhelmed me.'[85]

The strain of religious moderation whose symptoms have been examined in this essay was neither a *via media* between Rome and Geneva nor a lukewarm Protestantism. Instead, it was an elitist condition, compelling those afflicted to strive for Protestant unity and concord through obedience to the queen and compromise over 'things indifferent': things which were supposed to be decided upon by the queen with counsel, and which would need to be re-examined periodically. The moderation found in Matthew Parker and the religious settlement in 1559 embodied a generational attitude to conformity, compromise and obedience fashioned from the fluidity of the early English Reformation. It was a condition that seemed outmoded by the 1560s.

---

[83] D'Alton, 'Lutheran Heretics', p. 253.
[84] *Parker Correspondence*, p. 68.
[85] Ibid., p. x.

CHAPTER THREE

A Mini-'Colloquy of Poissy' in Brittany: Inter-confessional Dialogue in Nantes in 1562

Elizabeth Tingle

The Colloquy of Poissy of September 1561 is well known to historians of the French Reformation. Presided over by the Queen Mother and Regent, Catherine de' Medici, and the young King Charles IX, the Colloquy was a reforming council of the French Catholic Church and a forum for debate between Catholic and Protestant theologians led by the Cardinal of Lorraine and Theodore Beza. Catherine and her advisors hoped that a compromise would be found between the two confessions which would help to heal the religious divisions within the French kingdom. Ultimately it was hoped to reunite all French people under the Gallican Church; in short, to mediate a religious settlement without military conflict.[1] This attempt at compromise failed. The doctrinal positions of the parties were fixed, particularly over the nature of the Eucharist, and as David Nugent comments, there was no psychological readiness for agreement on either side.[2] A second Colloquy of January 1562, following the Edict of toleration of Saint-Germain, likewise foundered. By April, France had tumbled into civil war between Protestant and Catholic factions.

The Colloquy of Nantes is less well known. In July 1562, the Royal Governor of Brittany, Jean de Brosse, Duke d'Étampes, called a conference at the chateau of Nantes. The colloquy was held over two days and took the form of a formal disputation between two Protestant pastors of Nantes, Antoine Bachelard and Philip de Saint-Hilaire, and the Doctor of Theology, Jacques du Pré, before the Governor, his household and invited notables. The guests were chosen from amongst the religious orders of Nantes, several noble families from the *comté*, and the leading military officers of the Governor. In particular, the presence

---

[1]   Robert J. Knecht, *The French Civil Wars* (London, 2000), pp. 78–9; David Potter, *The French Wars of Religion: Selected Documents* (Basingstoke, 1997), pp. 11–12.

[2]   David Nugent, *Ecumenism in the Age of the Reformation: The Colloquy of Poissy* (Cambridge, MA, 1974); also cited in Potter, *French Wars of Religion*, p. 12.

of the d'Avagour brothers and of two cousins, de la Muce-Ponthus and Jean de Rieux, was important. The former two families were Protestants and possible clients of François d'Andelot, brother of Admiral Coligny, whose wife had brought him estates in the *comté* of Nantes. Rieux may have been a relative of D'Andelot's wife. There were four areas of disputation: the nature and organization of the Church, methods of worship, sources of truth and the sacraments.[3] At seven o'clock on the second evening the conference was closed, with an agreement to continue the debate in writing. Nothing was resolved, however, for civil war disrupted life in western France from the late summer of 1562 and in any case the theological divisions between the two parties were too firmly entrenched. The Protestants' rejection of the established Catholic Church order and prophetic tradition for a scripturally based worship and ministry, and above all their denial of the real presence in the Eucharist, divided them clearly and emphatically from the Catholic position. As at Poissy and Saint-Germain, the conference illustrated the hard lines that had been drawn between members of the two confessions.

The historian of Protestantism in the Nantais, Roger Joxe, called the colloquy held in the city 'a private meeting, of little significance'.[4] By 1564, when du Pré's account was published, the dialogue seemed to have been doomed to failure from its outset:

> Briefly, it is not possible to convince [the Protestants] ... because they will not listen, they will not be corrected by any church authority – which in any case they do not accept – nor are they moved by persuasion, because they have been subverted ... For this reason, conference and dispute with heretics cannot be turned to any profit or for the comfort of the Church.[5]

Indeed, René Benoist, in his prologue to du Pré's pamphlet, claimed that the doctor had, by the grace of God, 'carried glorious victory'.[6] The conference confirmed that Catholics were the true Christians, and from their point of view it showed clearly the deceits perpetrated by ignorant, false ministers.

---

[3] An account of the conference was published two years later by Jacques du Pré, with an introduction by René Benoist, who was also present. Jacques du Pré, *Conferences avec les ministres de Nantes en Bretaigne: Cabanne et Bourgonnière* (Paris, 1564). A description and evaluation of the conference, with details taken from the pamphlet, can be found in Bernard Varigaud, *Essai sur l'histoire des Eglises Réformées de Bretagne (1535–1808)* (3 vols, Paris, 1870–71), vol. 1, pp. 100–101. On Benoist, see Alison Carter's essay in this volume.

[4] Roger Joxe, *Les Protestants du comté de Nantes XVIème–XVIIème siècles* (Marseille, 1982), pp. 79–80.

[5] Du Pré, *Conferences avec les ministres de Nantes*, pp. 7–8.

[6] Ibid., p. 4.

Yet this hard-line view was not the predominant sentiment in 1562. Du Pré recognized that at the time, thanks to d'Étampes's 'wise and prudent government, we have been maintained and continue in peace and tranquillity, without there having arisen any sedition at all in the duchy of Brittany'.[7] Du Pré stated that the conference was held in the hope that the Protestants would recognize their errors. Failing this, if they would not give up their opinions, a formal disputation would reveal plainly to a wider audience where the truth really lay, and thus at least convince waverers to support the Catholic rather than the Protestant cause. Both sides were willing to participate in the discussions. Raoul Le Maistre later observed that du Pré was anxious not to appear churlish in refusing to parley with the Protestants when they were so insistent upon meeting him. This was in spite of the peril in which he placed himself, from God and from men, in seeming to show heresy some sympathy by taking it seriously.[8] While the Protestant pastors were at first afraid to enter into an open – Catholic – forum, asking for discussions in secret, they trusted in d'Étampes's neutrality and the debate passed off 'modestly and tranquilly'.[9] Rather than an incidence of no importance, doomed to failure, the Nantes Colloquy was an unusual attempt at irenicism and dialogue in a single province at a time when confessional warfare had already broken out in much of the French kingdom.

One reason for the attempt at irenicism in Nantes may have been the distinctive nature of Protestantism in Brittany. The development of the Calvinist Church and the scale of inter-confessional violence were not always the same in the Breton towns as in the rest of northern France. Philip Benedict has suggested recently that the structure and experience of the early Protestant churches in Brittany might be particular to the province.[10] The origins of organized Calvinism here were rural and noble, becoming urban only in its second phase, after 1560. Further, the Church quickly developed and retained a particularist regional identity. From 1559–60, provincial synods with representatives of all the Breton congregations were held annually, except in periods of military conflict, and their decisions were adhered to by the whole community.[11] The

---

7 Ibid., p. 2.
8 Raoul Le Maistre, *Original des troubles de ce temps Discourant briefvement des Princes plus Illustres de la tres-ancienne et tres-illustre famille de Luxembourg* (Nantes, 1592), pp. 214–15.
9 Du Pré, *Conferences avec les ministres de Nantes*, p. 3.
10 Philip Benedict, 'La Chouette de Minerve au crépuscule: Philippe Le Noir de Crevain, pasteur sous Louis XIV, historien des Eglises réformées du XVIe siècle', *BSHPF* 146 (2000), 335–66, p. 356.
11 Jean-Yves Carluer, 'Deux synodes provinciaux bretons au XVIe siècle' in *BSHPF* 135 (1989), 329–51.

pastors of different Breton Reformed churches regularly visited each others' churches and identified with each other; once in exile, in La Rochelle after 1585, Breton Protestants set up their own church, consistory and services.[12]

Inter-confessional relationships within Breton urban communities did, however, mirror those of other French towns, although there were local nuances and changes over time. If we take the example of Nantes, where one of the largest Breton Reformed churches was founded, we find events and processes that parallel those of towns such as Rouen, Troyes and even Paris. A clandestine Calvinist community is known from early 1560, uncovered in a judicial enquiry that followed the Conspiracy of Amboise, a failed *coup* which had assembled its forces in Nantes in that year.[13] The formal gathering of the Nantes church, in September–October 1560, opened the public phase of Protestant activity. In October 1560, there was a street dispute between a theologian of the *collège* of Saint John and several Protestants, over the display for sale of a picture of Moses and the Tablets of the Law, in which images rather than idols were condemned.[14] Meetings and professions of faith became more open in the winter of 1560–61, with some Catholic retaliation. In February 1561 Protestants returning from a *prêche* outside the city walls threw stones at a Catholic Church where Mass was being held, precipitating a riot and several casualties; in June there was an incident during the feast of St John the Baptist, when Huguenots threw water and hurled abuse at those dancing around the traditional bonfires.[15] In July there was an armed demonstration of Protestants through Nantes, followed by violent reaction and counter reaction: forced rebaptisms of Protestant babies; militant Calvinist services held in the suburbs; the burning of a Protestant bookseller's house.[16] Finally, in December, a barn used for Protestant meetings at Le Pressoir, outside of the city, was burnt down.[17] There was abuse and aggravation in the streets. Name-calling and threats were frequent. By the summer of 1561, the locksmith Jean Bras-de-fer went about the city armed, accompanied by three or four

---

[12] Benedict, 'La Chouette de Minerve au crépuscule', p. 356.

[13] Varigaud, *Essai sur l'histoire des Eglises Réformées*, vol. 1, pp. 34–9.

[14] A printed edition of the seneschal's report and a facsimile of some of the documents produced during the enquiry are reproduced in B. Varigaud, *Essai sur l'histoire des Eglises Réformées*, vol. 1, pièces justicatives, pp. xi–xv.

[15] The deposition of witnesses in the judicial enquiry which followed are printed in Dom Philip H. Morice, *Mémoires pour servir des preuves à l'histoire ecclésiastique et civile de Bretagne* (3 vols, Paris, 1746, reprinted 1974), vol. 3, pp. 1275–86.

[16] Varigaud, *Essai sur l'histoire des Eglises Réformées*, vol. 1, pp. 72–4.

[17] Letter from the lieutenant of Nantes to d'Étampes, 24 December 1561, printed in Morice, *Mémoires pour servir des preuves*, vol. 3, p. 1297.

journeymen, threatening to chastise anyone who told him to attend Mass. One Friday morning, the wife of Vincent Vilaine saw Bras-de-fer and a small party returning to the city from a suburban prayer meeting; she shouted at them from her upper storey window 'what a fine company we have here, returning from their sermon!' Bras-de-fer aimed his pistol at her and made threats.[18]

Yet what is noticeable about Nantes is the relatively low number of large-scale incidents and the relatively small amount of bloodshed in the city, compared to other communities. There was aggravation between confessions but disorder was short-lived and did not spill over into a bloody culture of retribution, apart from a period in late July and August 1561. Rouen experienced around nine 'incidents' in 1560–61; Nantes, three or four, excluding the plotting of the Conspiracy of Amboise.[19] How might this be explained?

An important factor underlying attempts at inter-confessional dialogue, at the French royal court and in Brittany, was the concept of conciliarism within the Catholic Church at this time. Alain Tallon has argued that in the mid-sixteenth century, the King, his counsellors, *parlementaires*, bishops and theologians, and most educated Frenchmen believed that 'a good and holy council' for the reform of the Church and the reunification of all Christians was the 'supreme solution for all the religious conflicts that tore Europe apart'.[20] Since the fifteenth century ideas of reform through a Church council were thought to be the best means of ending religious crisis and of reconciling Christians with each other. As early as 1534, it was thought possible to reach an agreement with Lutherans through dialogue in a council, a view which informed Franco-Papal discussions about the re-opening of the Council of Trent after 1560. It was hoped that German Protestants would attend, engage in dialogue with the Catholic Church, and that some of the decrees blocking their re-entry into the Church would be repealed.[21] Elsewhere in this volume Tallon argues that a significant section of the royal court and episcopate thought that the religious discord that broke out within the French kingdom after 1559 could be resolved by concord and the reabsorption of the Reformed sect into the Gallican Church through a policy of moderate reform.[22] At the Estates General of Blois of 1560,

---

[18] Witness deposition of July 1561. Morice, *Mémoires pour servir des preuves*, vol. 3, pp. 1275–86.

[19] P. Benedict, *Rouen During the Wars of Religion* (Cambridge, 1980), p. 58.

[20] Alain Tallon, *La France et le Concile de Trente (1518–1563)* (Rome, 1997), pp. 2–3.

[21] Ibid., pp. 3, 284, 547. See Alexandra Kess's essay in this volume.

[22] P. Benedict, '"Un roi, une loi, deux fois": parameters for the history of Catholic-Reformed coexistence in France, 1555–1685', in Ole P. Grell and Bob Scribner (eds), *Tolerance and Intolerance in the European Reformation* (Cambridge, 1996), 65–93, p. 69.

clergy and laity pressed for a council to re-establish religious unity, where each group would make some contribution to debates.[23] The Queen Mother was moved to call a French council under the pressure of events in France in 1561, and because of the slowness of opening of the general council of the Church in Trent, to which France had not yet appointed a delegation. The aims were to find means of pacifying the kingdom, to draw up a programme to bring to Trent and if the latter failed to be held, to design reforms for the Gallican Church to promote religious unity.[24] For these reasons, a Colloquy met at Poissy at the same time as the Estates General met at Orléans, in September 1561. Discussions about reforms of ecclesiastical structures and abuses were overshadowed, however, by the invitation of Reformed Church pastors to present their views. The churchmen present at the conference were scandalized by Beza's theology, and feared for the total loss of France to heresy.[25]

Despite the failure of Poissy to achieve its organizers's aims, certain elements of the royal council and ecclesiastical establishment maintained hope for a conciliar solution to religious problems. The Cardinal of Lorraine attended a colloquy with Lutherans in the Court of Christopher of Württemberg in Savern.[26] The Queen Mother also persisted in her dialogues with Calvinists and organized a new conference at Saint-Germain held from 27 January to 11 February 1562. Her decision finally to accept freedom of worship for Protestants in the Edict of Saint-Germain of 17 January was not because of an abandonment of the ideal of concord. Rather, it was an attempt to achieve civil peace through temporary toleration and religious compromise. The hope of reunification through conciliation remained. It was the belief of the moderates around de' Medici that 'the dissidents had only left the Roman Church because of abuses ... They would return when these were corrected. In the meantime, freedom of worship ... was a transitory political expedient to restore order.'[27] Many still spoke of the national council that would achieve these ends. In practice, however, hope in conciliarism was overtaken by events themselves.[28]

The Royal Governor of Brittany in 1562, the Duke d'Étampes, seems to have shared Michel de L'Hôpital's views that 'conscience is of such a nature that it cannot be forced but must be ... persuaded by real and

---

23 Tallon, *La France et le Concile de Trente*, pp. 286–7.
24 Ibid., p. 294.
25 Ibid., pp. 304–6.
26 Ibid., pp. 311–12, 328ff.
27 Ibid., pp. 325, 328.
28 Jean Lecler, *Histoire de la tolérance au siècle de la Réforme* (Paris, 1995), p. 451.

sufficient reasons'.[29] Although a Catholic, d'Étampes was seen by both Catholic and Protestant commentators as having no particular antipathy towards the Reformed religion, in contrast with the Guise family.[30] D'Étampes's inclinations seem to have been for peace, order and a measure of freedom of conscience, with close relatives given over to Calvinism (two sisters-in-law and possibly his wife).[31] His personal inclination towards moderation, and a belief in the use of persuasion and reason, were also sustained by events within his *gouvernement*. As discussed above, the nature of the Calvinist Church and the scale of inter-confessional violence were different in Brittany than in the rest of northern France. Nor was particularism confined to Calvinists. The Catholic Church had long retained a specific, regional identity and some autonomy from the wider Gallican Church. By the Contract of Union of 1532 the French Crown agreed to maintain the separate status of the Breton Church and to appoint only Bretons to ecclesiastical benefices in the province. Brittany remained a *pays d'obédience* formally outside the provisions of the Concordat of Bologna, although the Crown often broke its promises and the Pope extended some of the Concordat's provisions to the province in 1555. Further, there was a noticeable Breton flavour to Catholicism. For example, early episcopal reforms including parish registers were introduced in the fifteenth century; there were distinctive saints' cults and a genre of devotional writing. The provincial estates in the sixteenth century frequently remonstrated to the Crown about infractions to Breton Church privileges, and saw a separate Church as one of the liberties of the duchy.[32] These echoed Gallican conceptions of the Liberties of the French Church, although with a stronger commitment to the role of the papacy, as an upholder of provincial rights, than in the rest of France. The late conciliarism of

---

[29] Michel de L'Hôpital's speech to the Assembly of Clergy, 1 September 1561, quoted in Lecler, *Histoire de la tolérance*, p. 459.

[30] Jean Crespin, *Histoire de Martyrs Persecutez et mis à mort pour la verité de l'Évangile* (3 vols, Toulouse, 1885–89), vol. 3, p. 335; H. Morice and Charles Taillandier, *Histoire ecclésiastique & civile de Bretagne* (3 vols, Paris, 1756, reprinted 1974), vol. 2, p. 287; Philippe Le Noir, *Histoire Ecclésiastique de Bretagne depuis la Réformation jusqu'à l'Édit de Nantes*, ed. B. Varigaud (Nantes, 1851), p. 83.

[31] Joxe comments that d'Étampes had too many kin and friends in the Huguenot camp to be hostile to them: *Les Protestants du comté de Nantes*, pp. 35–6. Varigaud claims that d'Étampes's sister-in-law, Madame de Cany, was a correspondant of Calvin: Varigaud, *Essai sur l'histoire des Eglises Réformées*, vol. 1, p. 8.

[32] Details of Brittany's ecclesiastical history can be found in Alain Croix, *La Bretagne aux XVIe et XVIIe siècles: La Vie – la mort – la foi* (2 vols, Paris, 1981); A. Croix, *L'Âge d'or de la Bretagne 1532–1675* (Rennes, 1993); *Histoire religeuse de la Bretagne*, ed. Guy Devailly (Chambray, 1980); *Le diocèse de Nantes*, ed. Yves Durant (Histoire des diocéses de France 18: Paris, 1985).

d'Étampes was born out of hope that confessional rivalry in Brittany might be reduced or contained sufficiently to avert war in the province.

Tallon argues that an important party in the French episcopacy in 1560–61 considered that the way to defeat Protestantism and to restore religious harmony in the kingdom was to reform the Gallican Church, bringing all parties back into its fold.[33] Such a view may have appealed to a section of the Breton clergy and lay elites in the early 1560s and is an issue that needs further investigation. Odet de Châtillon urged modification of practices, of images, of the language of prayer and the taking of communion in both kinds. The Cardinal of Lorraine favoured greater autonomy for national churches, wherein each individual church would remain in communion with Rome but would settle on liturgical formulations and even on aspects of dogma that best suited its situation. The Colloquy of Nantes might be seen as a particularist attempt to tackle the religious problems of the province, independent of the French situation, by both Catholic and Protestant groups who felt themselves to have a special Breton tradition. To transpose Tallon's arguments to Brittany, separate agreement with Protestants might have enabled the Breton Catholic Church to reassert its autonomy from that of France. Further, a Breton settlement, albeit temporary and expedient, might suit the needs and interests of both confessional groups while a national solution was being fought out. Defence of the Liberties of the Breton, as with the Gallican, Church offered the best prospect of achieving religious unity.

A second strand of explanation for the relative lack of violence in Brittany lies in the distinctive nature of Breton Protestantism in the early 1560s. The nature and tactics of Nantes' Calvinist community was important. The reasons for this are complex. The Protestant population in the city was always a minority, somewhere between 5 and 10 per cent of the population in early 1562. They were certainly visible people, in their behaviour and their distinctive styles of worship, and were concentrated in certain parts of town, the port parishes of Saint-Nicolas, Saint-Saturnin and Sainte-Croix. But the community was never large enough to overwhelm the town, while the great mix of different peoples in this large port city perhaps facilitated a certain acceptance of diversity. Second, because of its minority status, from the second half of 1561, the Protestant community made increasing resort to legal authorities and official resolution of conflict. In September 1561, after the riot that

---

[33] A. Tallon, 'Gallicanism and Religious Pluralism in France in the Sixteenth Century', in Keith Cameron et al. (eds), *The Adventure of Religious Pluralism in Early Modern France* (Bern, 2000), 15–30, pp. 22–3; Tallon, *La France et le Concile de Trente*, p. 313.

destroyed his home, the bookseller Maurice Papollin appealed to the Governor and town authorities for compensation for his losses. D'Étampes ordered the town council to make recompense. After objections on the grounds that it would encourage others in their heresy, the council agreed to collect contributions from the public, on condition that Papollin live as a Catholic in future and hold no more assemblies in his home.[34] In the same month, Nantes' Protestants lobbied the Estates of Brittany to request the King for churches where they might publicly worship.[35] In November, they were partly successful, for d'Étampes's Lieutenant-General, the count de Martigues, allowed them the use of Le Pressoir outside the city walls for worship.[36] Finally, Protestants were, on the whole, peaceful people, even if armed. There were only one or two recorded incidents of window breaking, no known iconoclasm and no physical attack on priests as at Troyes and Rouen. The small and increasingly legalistic nature of Nantes' Protestantism perhaps contributed to a hope that civil conflict along French lines might be avoided in Brittany, if the basic objectives of the community could be met through discussion and conciliation with the province's governors.

The nature of municipal government in Nantes in the late 1550s and early 1560s also helped to limit confessional strife, in at least four ways. First, until the creation of a municipal *corps et communauté* in 1565, the city was administered by royal judicial officers and a *Conseil des bourgeois*. The *Conseil des bourgeois* was a weak institution, lacking independent judicial authority. Traditionally, the *Conseil* had some social and economic responsibility in the city, over markets and traders, prices, poor relief and sanitation for example. In 1560, an edict of Francis II established a corporate municipality at Nantes, with a mayor, aldermen and police court, but because of objections from other privileged groups, notably the *prévôt*, the seneschal and the Governor of the chateau, René de Sanzay, the municipality was not formally constituted until 1565. The lack of police and judicial authority prevented the *Conseil* from initiating independent policies in the city, for decision-making and executive functions had to be carried out in consultation with the royal judicial and military officers. As these groups had their own interests and were closely tied into royal policies, any anti-Protestant activities of the city administration were limited. For example, in the autumn of 1561, the clergy and municipality united in

---

[34] AMN, BB4 Délibérations et assemblées des Conseils des bourgeois 1555–1564, fols 292, 294.

[35] L'Abbé Nicolas Travers, *Histoire civile, politique et religieuse de la ville de Nantes* (3 vols, Nantes, 1837), vol. 2, p. 359.

[36] Le Noir, *Histoire Ecclésiastique de Bretagne*, p. 75.

their efforts to condemn public Protestant preaching and prayer meetings in Nantes. Without a direct means of enforcing their policy, this prohibition remained a dead letter.

Second, any actions taken against heretics in Nantes were frustrated by the fragmented and competing nature of urban justice in the city. As in many other regions of France, there was no clear judicial apparatus for prosecuting heresy; when one institution attempted to do so, it was challenged by others. The Catholic Church's campaign against Protestantism was rarely successful because its jurisdiction over heresy was contested. In June 1558, Bishop de Crequi arrested several Protestants at Le Croisic and brought them for trial to Nantes; the accused appealed to the *parlement* and were eventually released by this court.[37] De Crequi wrote to the Cardinal of Lorraine in October 1560: 'I would like to know the King's wishes and those of yourself, because I have been given no jurisdication.'[38] Within the royal courts themselves there appears to have been a reluctance to convict, even sympathy for the Reformed community. In November 1560, the lieutenant-general of Brittany, Bouillé, wrote in frustration to d'Étampes: 'I see that those who are said to be of the religion are so well supported and loved by so many people that I do not know anyone in the region who will ... take any action against them. On the contrary, many people excuse their actions ... Too many!'[39] A case against two Genevan booksellers in 1561–62 exemplifies these points. In July 1561, at the instigation of Vicar-General de Gand, using the authority of the Bishop's Court of the *régaire*, a consignment of books was seized and two booksellers from Geneva were arrested in Nantes. One of them, Girard, was imprisoned in the Bishop's gaol. De Gand argued that the consignment contravened royal edicts; the Genevans appealed to the *parlement* for their liberty and restitution of their goods. To the outrage of de Gand, the *parlement* ordered him to be incarcerated for interrogation for three months and gave the investigation of the case to *conseiller* Michel d'Essefort, then Robert du Hardaz, both of whom were suspected Protestants.[40] The case was resolved by the release of Girard a year later, but without restitution of his merchandise.

Third, the issue of heresy was time and again relegated to second place in disputes over authority between the different institutions of Nantes, especially between the *Conseil des bourgeois* and the Governor of the chateau, Sanzay. This limited the effectiveness of any stance against the

---

[37] Joxe, *Les Protestants du comté de Nantes*, p. 46.
[38] Varigaud, *Essai sur l'histoire des Eglises Réformées*, vol. 1, pp. 57–8.
[39] Cited in Joxe, *Les Protestants du comté de Nantes*, p. 71.
[40] Varigaud, *Essai sur l'histoire des Eglises Réformées*, vol. 1, p. 97.

Reformed. Even the Royal Governor d'Étampes could be frustrated. In February 1560, he failed to have the *parlement* of Brittany publish orders forbidding inter-confessional disputes, because, he was told, the King had not ordered the *parlement* to do so and d'Étampes could not do so on his own authority.[41] In December 1561, Protestants desecrated the Cathedral of Nantes, in retaliation for the burning down of their site of worship at Le Pressoir. For once the *Conseil des bourgeois* and the military Governor agreed a course of action. Sanzay reinforced the King's orders to guard against sedition; the *Conseil* agreed an augmentation of the watch and guard of the city gates by the inhabitants; orders were given to prevent Protestants from assembling and vagabonds were to be expelled from the city. But then the *Conseil* and royal judicial officers fell into dispute; the *Conseil* passed a motion of no confidence in the judge of the *présidial* court of Nantes and took the decision to use only the *prévôt's* court. The meeting fell to recriminations and denials between different members of the city's governing groups.[42]

Fourth, the men of the *Conseil* disliked heresy but they had an equal distaste for disorder and tumult. A growing number of historians of Reformation cities show how aversion to internal disorder was the prime cause of de facto toleration. Robert Scribner has argued this for Erfurt and Lorna Abray for Strasburg: 'toleration was never the policy of choice but always one taken to stave off a larger disaster'.[43] Especially feared in Nantes was the impact of an open and provocative Protestant presence on trade with Spain. The bourgeois were in the process of negotiating an important treaty, arranging mutual trading privileges with merchants from Bilbao and other northern Spanish ports. Royal Spanish disapproval of heresy might cause a rupture in these arrangements.[44] Also, Protestant plots and manifestations of militancy were bad but they were rarely as dangerous to lives and property as rampaging Catholic mobs. To be too repressive was to provoke greater disorder than that which was being quelled, and turbulence might be noticed elsewhere.

Above all, public disorder caused by heresy persecution and sectarian passions brought unwelcome royal attention to and greater intervention in town affairs. The *Conseil* and the bourgeois played down disorder and

---

[41] Ibid., vol. 1, p. 37.
[42] AMN, BB4 Délibérations et assemblées des Conseils des bourgeois 1555–1564, fol. 302ᵛ; AMN, GG 642 La Religion réformée 1560–1575.
[43] Robert Scribner, 'Civic Unity and the Reformation in Erfurt', *P&P* 66 (1975), 28–60; Lorna Abray, *The People's Reformation: Magistrates, Clergy and Commons in Strasbourg 1580–1598* (Oxford, 1985); quote from Muriel McClendon, *The Quiet Reformation: Magistrates and the Emergence of Protestantism in Tudor Norwich* (Stanford, CA, 1999), p. 31.
[44] Joxe, *Les Protestants du comté de Nantes*, p. 56.

heresy, to avoid attracting outside attention and to limit royal interference in town affairs, especially by the King's military governors.[45] After the images affair of October 1560, the seneschal moved quickly to prevent sedition and to reduce royal scrutiny of the city's affairs. He appealed to the *parlement* of Brittany to sanction emergency measures at the town gates, organized armament provision for the watch and guard, and four *conseillers* of the *parlement* were to aid the ordinary judicial officers of Nantes in keeping order.[46] However, Lieutenant-General Bouillé successfully appealed to the King for authority to disarm the inhabitants of the town, as the authorities could not be trusted to prosecute heretics. Instead of the citizen militia, he asked for two companies of gendarmes to guard the walls and gates of the city, in contravention of the city's privileges of self-defence.[47] The main concern of the bourgeois of Nantes was to safeguard local privileges from royal interference and to limit the authority of the King's agents in the city. To these ends they 'fell back on a policy of containment which they hoped would keep things more or less under control'.[48]

Some historians have claimed that town councils were reluctant to prosecute heretics in their midst because of shared humanist values of civic ecumenism. Mark Konnert explains the low levels of conflict and violence in Châlons-sur-Marne by the devotion of the civic elites to ideals of urban solidarity and integrity, and by a commitment to a civic agenda. Councillors shared some humanist ideals of education and reform, which overrode the religious division within the city.[49] Work by Tim Watson on Lyons has also revealed a humanist and civic agenda shared by many members of the city's elite, Catholic and Protestant, at least before 1562.[50] There emerged in some cities a practical secularization and de facto toleration of Protestants. Elaine Fulton's essay on Vienna in this volume shows that practical irenicism occurred all over western and central Europe. Here, the Holy Roman Emperors of the later sixteenth

---

[45] This was a common urban response. See McClendon, *Quiet Reformation*, p. 63; David Nicholls, 'The Nature of Popular Heresy in France', *HJ* 26 (1983), 261–75, p. 263.

[46] Anon., *Narration Sommaire de ce qui est advenu en la ville de Nantes par ceulx que l'on a prétendu conspirateurs contre la majesté du Roy nostre sire et souverain seigneur* (1560, reprinted Nantes, 1860).

[47] Varigaud, *Essai sur l'histoire des Eglises Réformées*, vol. 1, p. 62; Charles Mellinet, *La Commune et la milice de Nantes* (5 vols, Nantes, 1841), vol. 3, pp. 163–6 cites extensively from Bouillé's letters to d'Étampes and de' Medici.

[48] An observation also made of Lyons' city council: Tim Watson, '"When is a Huguenot not a Huguenot?" Lyon 1525–1575', in K. Cameron et al. (eds), *Adventure of Religious Pluralism*, 161–76, p. 172.

[49] Mark Konnert, 'Urban Values Versus Religious Passion: Châlons-sur-Marne during the Wars of Religion', *SCJ* 20 (1989), 387–405, pp. 387, 403.

[50] Watson, '"When is a Huguenot not a Huguenot?"', pp. 161–76.

century allowed nobles the right to open Lutheran churches on their estates, and even gave over a room in the Viennese *Landhaus* for Protestant worship, in order to maintain peace and their own authority within their territories.

In Nantes, there was certainly much day-to-day coexistence. Catholic and Protestant lived cheek by jowl, each knowing who the other was. It was impossible for each confessional group to separate itself from the other. Guillemette Bonyveau and her family, Catholics, lived as lodgers in a house owned by the Protestant Penmaingeon. Bonyveau informed against Penmaingeon in a judicial enquiry into Calvinism in July 1561, and feared the landlord's violence against her should he find out. Marie Robouan, Catholic, was a servant in the household of the Protestant weaver Michel Pertuis. She observed him receiving Calvinist visitors, with whom he would withdraw to have private conversations.[51] Neither the Church nor the civic authorities sought the physical extirpation of Protestants themselves. There were no executions of heretics in the city in the period and few casualties of sectarian violence (two or three before 1562). While the authorities sought to limit the legal and public toleration of Protestantism, the Reformed minority was left alone so long as it was quiet, orderly and unthreatening in its behaviour.

But the leading bourgeois of Nantes did not have an ecumenical view. Reformed ideas were viewed with disdain. In December 1560, the *Conseil* wrote to the King asking that Huguenots be disarmed and expelled from the city and county. In April 1561, they requested that the *parlement* of Brittany publish confirmation of the Edict of Romorantin so that the Nantais had greater authority to prevent illicit assemblies and the right to prosecute heresy in the *présidial* court.[52] There were denunciations and expulsions of suspected heretics from municipal government. In August 1561 the procurator of the *Conseil*, Jehan de Luc, was dismissed because of his sympathy with the Reformed cause; and in December, the *Conseil* asserted its suspicion of a number of judicial officers, including the chateau Governor Sanzay and a number of the city's sergeants, who were told that they were no longer trusted to pursue heretics.[53] The Edict of Saint-Germain of January 1562, granting legal toleration to Protestant worship in noble households and outside walled towns, was met with dismay. On 6 March the *Conseil* designated 12 men to lobby the royal court against

---

[51] Morice, *Mémoires pour servir des preuves*, vol. 3, pp. 1283–4.
[52] In May, 12 inhabitants were appointed to prevent seditions and assemblies, linked with this act. Travers, *Histoire … de la ville de Nantes*, vol. 2, p. 357.
[53] AMN, GG 642 La Religion réformée 1560–1575.

the edict's application in Nantes.[54] As they remonstrated to the King in November 1561, the bourgeois 'never made nor required to be made a church other than the churches built and made according to the ... Roman Church'.[55] In practice, however, civic unity was pursued by the bourgeois of the *Conseil* and the city's judicial officers. The elite sought to dampen conflicts between citizens before great upheaval broke out. They did not articulate support for heresy at any time, but they rarely imprisoned heretics for long, and Catholics were also punished for disorder: the clergy involved in the burning of Le Pressoir were arrested and still being held in April 1562. Privileges and economic well-being were of greatest concern. As David Nicholls has remarked for Tours, in Nantes 'at no stage was religion deemed more important than politics'.[56]

Finally, the prerogative of action against heresy lay with the King. Without royal sanction, the civic and military authorities in Nantes were reluctant to act. The Conspiracy of Amboise was important here. The rebels had met in the city in February 1560 and had fled through the county when the *coup* failed.[57] The loyalty of Nantes' citizens had been cast into some doubt. They were henceforth anxious to show their fidelity. This could be difficult, for royal religious policy was contradictory and confusing. The Crown's failure to act effectively against heresy was resented, and puzzled the civic elite. In the midst of the troubles of July 1561, the seneschal Le Maire wrote to d'Étampes for advice: 'I am greatly perplexed because we do not understand the King's wishes as to how we should proceed in these circumstances ... I wish only to do the best that I can in this case.'[58] But there was no questioning of the royal prerogative. The *Conseil* was obedient to royal commands and anxious to act within the law, enforcing royal edicts and ordonnances even where these were unpopular. Rather, the unclear and apparently incomprehensible royal religious policy shifts confused civic elites as to which line to follow. Because they were reluctant to come to any clear conclusion or execute their own policy, they adopted a stance of limited containment or of doing nothing at all.[59]

An anti-Protestant campaign was thus not possible in Nantes. There was neither institutional framework nor ideological unity to underpin a

---

[54] AMN, BB4 Délibérations et assemblées des Conseils des bourgeois 1555–1564, fols 323^v–324^r.

[55] Ibid., fol. 298^v.

[56] D. Nicholls, 'Protestants, Catholics and Magistrates in Tours, 1562–72: The Making of a Catholic City during the Religious Wars', *French History* 8 (1994), 14–33, pp. 1, 33.

[57] Le Maistre, *Original des troubles de ce temps*, p. 149; Travers, *Histoire ... de la ville de Nantes*, vol. 2, pp. 354–5.

[58] Morice, *Mémoires pour servir des preuves*, vol. 3, p. 1275.

[59] Watson, '"When is a Huguenot not a Huguenot?"', p. 172.

consistent campaign against the Huguenot Church. What transpires from the municipal registers is a real hatred and rhetorical condemnation of heresy, but a tacit and grudging toleration of Protestantism in practice, provided that individuals were quiet, private and discreet in their religious affairs. There was no active rooting out of Protestants, except following 'emotions'. There were no expulsions from the town and no serious official attempt to prevent the public worship at Le Pressoir, unlike towns such as Troyes or Toulouse. Nantes resembles Châlons-sur-Marne, where Konnert argues that city councillors would have preferred a totally Catholic city, but order was a higher priority.[60] As in Tours, Nantes' urban government was more 'concerned with consolidating its own authority, especially corporate municipal status, than challenging religious policy and defying the Crown'.[61]

The attitude and policies of the Royal Governor the Duke d'Étampes were also important in maintaining a relative tranquillity in Nantes. He was largely conciliatory in his treatment of the Protestant community and their claims to public worship. The Governor's religious policies in Brittany combined a close obedience to royal legislative measures with moderate application on the ground, although it was difficult to steer a course through the contradictions of Crown policy shifts. D'Étampes did not seize upon the weakness of the Crown to seek semi-sovereign authority in his province. Rather, his actions were those of a man constantly faithful to the Crown, whose aims were peace and order. Likewise, his Lieutenants-General, Martigues and Bouillé, although antipathetic towards heresy and greatly frustrated by the constraints upon their powers to act, were notable for their adherence to royal policy, even where they found it misguided, and for constant communication with their superiors. In May 1560, d'Étampes responded to the anger raised in Nantes by the appearance of Protestant placards in the city by exhorting the population not to take part in illegal assemblies.[62] After the images incident of October of that year, he quickly released those arrested for heresy and sedition, merely detaining the leaders and ordering the others not to leave town.[63] At intervals, he urged the citizens of Nantes to live in unison and friendship, to take no

---

[60] Konnert's interpretations of the councillors' motives are less convincing for Nantes, however: that they were inspired to toleration by humanist ideas, that there was devotion to civic unity and that there was an absence of confrontational social groups, a large working class or a conservative sovereign court. Konnert, 'Urban Values Versus Religious Passion'.

[61] Nicholls, 'Protestants, Catholics and Magistrates in Tours, 1562–72', p. 33.

[62] Joxe, Les Protestants du comté de Nantes, p. 54.

[63] Ibid., p. 69.

part in sedition and not to assemble contrary to the edicts of the King.[64] In the autumn of 1561, d'Étampes forced coexistence upon a reluctant *Conseil des bourgeois*.

In August a Catholic riot had destroyed the house of the bookseller Maurice Papollin, as discussed above. The case shows how d'Étampes blamed the bourgeois of Nantes for not maintaining order, contrary to his previous commands, and he ordered them to make amends with Papollin. One party was of the opinion that Papollin was the cause of his own misfortune and that he deserved nothing – to compensate him would be to encourage others in heresy. A second party suggested that a deputation should go around the city to ask for donations, so that compensation should not come out of city funds. In the end, the *procureur des bourgeois* visited the 'citizens and inhabitants of the town' to ask their views; the majority stated that they would give alms to Papollin out of charity, 'so long as he was content with his losses ... and that in future he lived as a Catholic, following the edicts and commandments of the King'.[65] D'Étampes's attempts to secure religious coexistence in his government was one of his responsibilities as the King's Viceregent in Brittany, and important in securing his authority and position among all groups.

When civil war erupted in France in the spring of 1562, d'Étampes found that his province was in a rare position. In March, the massacre at Vassy that sparked the outbreak of war in the rest of the kingdom had no parallel in Brittany. There was little or no violence there, although confessional positions began to harden. Up river, in Tours, Protestants seized the town in April, then were defeated and massacred by royal forces and local Catholics in July.[66] In the neighbouring provinces of Normandy and Poitou, campaigning began. To the north of Nantes, in the small towns dominated by Protestant seigneurs, Guérande, Blain and la Roche-Bernard, arms were taken up and defences strengthened – these strongholds were maintained as Protestant refuges throughout the first and subsequent wars – but even here the peace was not broken. In Nantes, defensive measures were stepped up. In April the civil militia augmented the watch and guard of the walls and gates and a survey was made of the provisions held in the town in case of attack. The water-gate of Port Maillard-Briand, leading directly from the city onto the Loire,

---

[64] For example, a letter of 19 May 1561 to the *Conseil des bourgeois*, cited in Travers, *Histoire ... de la ville de Nantes*, vol. 2, p. 357.

[65] AMN, BB4 Délibérations et assemblées des Conseils des bourgeois 1555–1564, fols 292ʳ–294ʳ.

[66] Nicholls, 'Protestants, Catholics and Magistrates in Tours, 1562–72', pp. 15–17.

was closed, with all river craft forced to alight at the quays of Richebourg or La Fosse, outside the city walls.[67] But here again, a tense calm prevailed.

How might d'Étampes best maintain the peace of his province? Observations of the war in other regions of northern France would have shown that two of the main sources of conflict were the Calvinist minorities within cities, who might seek to take the town for their own party, and the Protestant nobility of the surrounding countryside, who might raise troops to pursue Huguenot war aims. If these two groups rose in Brittany, war would immediately follow. To keep the peace, d'Étampes ordered that the Nantes Protestants be unmolested and retain the position given to them by the Edict of January. The Church continued to meet outside the city walls, partly protected by noble participation.[68] Calvinists were forbidden to enter the city bearing arms, except for gentlemen, but d'Étampes ensured that toleration continued. Attempts by the Cathedral chapter to prevent the sale of Reformed literature, and of the *Conseil* to prevent preaching, effectively failed. The July colloquy was aimed especially at Protestant nobles and the urban Church. Its aims were to try to convince Catholics and Protestants that peace was possible. In particular, the Protestant nobility of the *comté*, many of them clients of Rohan and d'Andelot, may have been under particular pressure to join the Huguenot party. D'Étampes sought to assure both confessions that his role, as Breton overlord, was to ensure coexistence and that he took responsibility for the protection of both groups. While waiting for a national solution, d'Étampes was following Catherine de' Medici's ideas at Poissy, applied to the quasi-autonomous Breton context. He hoped to encourage provisional toleration and reconciliation within the duchy's borders, based on patronage and clientage networks, a provincial neutrality from a national problem, to mediate a settlement without involvement in a 'foreign' war.

But the clouds of war were gathering ever closer and in July d'Étampes and his nephew Martigues were ordered to gather their forces and fight against rebels in lower Normandy. The Governor's absence allowed the local authorities to treat the Protestant community with increasing harshness. In August a royal order arrived commanding Protestant ministers to leave Brittany within 15 days, on pain of death; in Nantes there was some violence, partially recorded, along with abjurations.[69] In the autumn much of the Protestant community fled to

---

[67] AMN, BB4 Délibérations et assemblées des Conseils des bourgeois 1555–1564, fol. 330^{r-v}.

[68] Crespin, *Histoire de Martyrs*, vol. 3, p. 335.

[69] Varigaud, *Essai sur l'histoire des Eglises Réformées*, vol. 1, pp. 108, 111–12.

nearby Blain, a fortified town held by the Calvinist Rohan family. In the summer of 1562, positions in Brittany crystallized. War hardened the lines between Catholic and Protestant on the ground, while the reconvened Council of Trent began to pronounce on fundamental doctrines such as the Eucharist, which defined clearly the boundaries between heresy and orthodoxy.

So did irenicism fail in Nantes and the *comté nantais* and did the humanist dream of dogmatic conciliation vanish?[70] Do we see here another failure at compromise and negotiation, as at Poissy itself? To a large extent, the answer must be yes. But even with the possibilities for persecution created by the conflict, a small Calvinist community remained in Nantes throughout the war, holding meetings in private houses; there were no massacres or mass expulsions. After the first war ended, Nantes' municipal authorities followed a consistent policy until 1585: Protestantism was tolerated if it was a private creed, if there was no overt public presence such as a formally-constituted, legal church where public worship took place, and if individuals complied, broadly, with the public culture of the town.[71] The municipality did – broadly – uphold the royal edicts of toleration, although forcing Protestants to go as far outside the city walls to worship as possible. There was no St Bartholomew's day violence in Nantes, despite orders from the Royal Governor Montpensier to kill all Calvinists. Religious war did not break out within the boundaries of Brittany until 1589, and then the causes were the rehabilitation and then succession of a Huguenot claimant to the French throne rather than the presence of Protestants in the duchy itself. Perhaps in a small way, d'Étampes's attempts at compromise and negotiation did not entirely fail.

In Nantes, toleration of Protestantism and a policy of religious moderation were political acts not expressions of cultural values. Several of the essays in this volume suggest that moderation was part of a search to maintain political authority, and a strategy to prevent civil disorder. Fulton argues that the Holy Roman Emperors permitted the legal coexistence of Protestants and Catholics to ensure their authority over all sections of the Austrian nobility. In England under Elizabeth I, Campbell argues, the maintenance of civil order was a strong motive in the 'moderate' settlement of 1559, to avoid the disorder wrought in Scotland by rapid religious change. In France itself, the royal policy of religious

---

[70] Le Cler, *Histoire de la tolérance*, p. 451.

[71] For details on the struggles between the *Conseil des bourgeois* and the Protestant community over the siting of a reformed site of worship, see Penny Roberts, 'The Most Crucial Battle of the Wars of Religion? The Conflict over Sites for Reformed Worship in Sixteenth-Century France', *ARG* 89 (1998), 247-66.

toleration, culminating in the Edict of Saint-Germain of 1562, was also a response to growing threats to royal authority begun with the Conspiracy of Amboise and increasing sectarian unrest in the cities of the kingdom in 1560. It was an attempt to pacify disaffection, a temporary expedient while the affairs of the Church were put in better order. The policy failed in many parts of France, however, as religious positions hardened and polarized, culminating in war.

However, Brittany and its largest city, Nantes, were different. There were sectarian tensions and a great antipathy towards heresy among the majority of the population, but violence was limited. One reason was the nature of Nantes' society: as a diverse port city it had a tradition of toleration of 'foreign' minorities of Spaniards, Irish and Germans among others, so long as they were peaceful and orderly people. Second, and more importantly, the municipality was concerned to extend its own authority and to prevent interference in city affairs from outside agencies, particularly the Crown and its local representatives. This was best served by keeping order within the city, preventing sedition through de facto toleration of a range of opinions so long as their adherents kept the peace. This found echo in Governor d'Étampes's quasi-feudal view of his role as overlord of all Bretons, in which his own authority and the royal power that he represented were best served by compromise with and protection of all subjects, whatever their confession – a view that perhaps conditioned royal policy itself. Authority was best protected through the maintenance of order, and its successful conservation required a level of give and take from the different parties. Moderation was born out of necessity and not desire.

CHAPTER FOUR

Immanuel Tremellius and the Avoidance of Controversy

Kenneth Austin

Immanuel Tremellius (*c*.1510–80) made a significant contribution to the religious and intellectual culture of the sixteenth century. He enjoyed a long and prestigious career as a teacher of Hebrew in various Reformed universities and academies of northern Europe, his scholarship was highly regarded by his contemporaries, and he corresponded with many of the leading figures of the period.[1] Moreover, his writings, and in particular his translation of the Bible, which has been described as 'one of the classical works of the Reformation',[2] ensured that his influence extended through to the eighteenth century.[3] This was all the more remarkable given the complexity and the potential awkwardness of his religious background. Tremellius had been born a Jew and spent at least the first 20 years of his life as an adherent of Judaism; thereafter he spent a number of years at least nominally as a Catholic, before he finally came to embrace Calvinism in early 1542. The successes of his career were thus achieved despite the stigma of being a double convert. It is the contention of this essay, moreover, that his career would have been by no means as successful had it not been for the implementation of a subtle strategy in which his actions were characterized, above all, by a desire to avoid, or at least to minimize, controversy wherever possible.

---

[1] The historiography relating to Tremellius is surprisingly limited. Two biographies do exist: Friedrich Butters, *Emanuel Tremellius, erster Rector des Zweibrücker Gymnasiums* (Zweibrücken, 1859) and Wilhelm Becker, *Immanuel Tremellius: Ein Proselyntenleben im Zeitalter der Reformation* (Breslau, 1887). Both are extremely short, poorly referenced and devote at least as much time to the general European context as they do to Tremellius' career. There were no substantial treatments of Tremellius in the twentieth century. See, most recently, Kenneth Austin, 'From Judaism to Calvinism: The Life and Writings of Immanuel Tremellius (1510–1580)' (unpublished PhD thesis, St Andrews, 2002).

[2] David de Sola Pool, 'The Influence of Some Jewish Apostates on the Reformation', *Jewish Review* 2 (7–12) (May 1911–March 1912), pp. 327–51, 340.

[3] Thirty-four editions of Tremellius's Old Testament were published between the late sixteenth and early eighteenth centuries. The majority of these were supplemented by a New Testament translated either by Tremellius (from the Syriac) or Theodore Beza (from the Greek), or indeed by both translations printed together.

This essay will explore two separate, but related, areas that illustrate a number of the key elements of the strategy Tremellius adopted. The first of these is his relationship with Jews and Judaism. As a Jewish convert, he might have been expected both to attack his former brethren as a means of proving the authenticity of his conversion, and to have been the victim of prejudice himself from Christians who refused to accept it. In fact, Tremellius' attitude to the Jews was at worst neutral; he seems to have envisaged their ultimate conversion through persuasion rather than coercion, and authored one work which could well have served that end. His views of Judaism were more positive, however, and rested primarily on the intellectual benefits it could contribute to Christian understanding. Nonetheless, he remained conscious of the precarious nature of his position and made sure never to push this too far. This careful combination of factors ensured that Tremellius encountered far less prejudice than one might have envisaged for a Jewish convert who continued to involve himself thoroughly with Hebraic sources.

The essay will move on to look at the nature of Tremellius' adopted faith. Although he was never the most ardent or outspoken member of the Reformed faith, there seems little reason to consider that his religious convictions were anything other than genuine, or that his conversion had been false. The work of Howard Louthan and Robert Evans relating to a central European context is instructive here.[4] Louthan, in his recent work *The Quest for Compromise*, looked at the careers of four individuals whose work at the imperial Court of Maximilian II (1564–76) in Vienna reflected ideals of religious compromise and moderation, which he termed 'irenicism'.[5] He argued that this movement, whose roots are to be found in the Christian humanism of Erasmus, 'became more distinct as the middle ground between the Catholics, Calvinists and Lutherans began to disappear in the second half of the sixteenth century'.[6]

These ideas had already been touched upon by Evans in his monograph on the intellectual world of Rudolf II, Maximilian's successor as Emperor.[7] He wrote, 'the irenical movement owed its very strength to the heightened confessional tensions which it found so repellent; its significance was ... as an abstraction, an attitude of mind, which found little practical outlet, save in the world of the academic and

---

[4] I am grateful to Elaine Fulton who first drew my attention to these works.

[5] Howard Louthan, *The Quest for Compromise: Peacemakers in Counter-Reformation Vienna* (Cambridge, 1997), especially pp. 1–10.

[6] Ibid., p. 9.

[7] Robert J. Evans, *Rudolph II and His World: A Study in Intellectual History, 1576–1612* (London, 1973).

the artist'. He portrayed irenicism as an attempt to evade the tightening religious antagonisms 'by calling on intellectual reserves which the practical world would not admit'. He suggested that two of the main alternatives were an inner religious solution which could be reconciled with Catholic observances, and what he calls a 'lukewarm Calvinism'.[8]

In many ways, Tremellius may best be considered as a 'lukewarm Calvinist'. He rose to prominence in the second half of the sixteenth century and was clearly an academic of the kind identified by Evans. More importantly, he typified this emphasis on moderation and tolerance. While some of this may simply be attributed to a natural instinct towards self-preservation, it is also apparent that there was a more positive and irenic spiritual agenda underlying Tremellius' career, evident in his attitudes towards both Jews and Christians. He may have been naturally disposed to this outlook, but, more significantly, I would argue, this ought also to be seen as the product of a range of experiences of his early life in Italy, and the particular environment in which Tremellius came to adopt his mature religious outlook. The attitudes formed in that part of his life would stay with him throughout the rest of his career.

I

Before moving on to deal with these main themes, it is important to begin with a brief sketch of Tremellius' career, to contextualize the discussion which follows. Immanuel Tremellius, or Tremellio,[9] was born as a Jew in the Italian city of Ferrara, where he spent the first 20 years of his life.[10] In around 1530, it is believed that he headed to Padua where he pursued a course in classical studies at the university, although his religion would have meant that he was unable to matriculate.[11] Towards the end of that decade, Tremellius converted from Judaism to a Catholicism which was probably quite evangelical in character. In the summer of 1541, he obtained his first teaching post at the rich and influential monastery of San Frediano at Lucca: he was responsible for instructing the inhabitants of that house in Hebrew. Although he was only there for about a year,

---

[8]   Ibid., p. 92.
[9]   Immanuel Tremellius was presumably the name he adopted on his conversion to Christianity; his original name is not known.
[10] For further detail see Austin, 'From Judaism to Calvinism', pp. 10–66.
[11] On Jewish admission to universities, see Maria Rosa di Simone, 'Admission' in *A History of the University in Europe*, ed. Hilde de Ridder-Symoens (4 vols, Cambridge, 1997), vol. 2: *Universities in Early Modern Europe (1500–1800)*, pp. 285–325 especially pp. 294–5.

this was long enough for Tremellius to complete the second major step in his religious development: he moved on from evangelical Catholicism to Reformed Protestantism.

The revival of the Roman Inquisition in the summer of 1542, however, obliged Tremellius to leave Italy; he spent the next four decades carving out a career as a highly respected Hebraist in a number of the most prestigious educational establishments in northern Europe. He taught in the academies or universities of Strasburg (1543–47), Cambridge (1549–53), Hornbach (1558–60), Heidelberg (1561–76) and Sedan (1577/8–80). In addition, he served as tutor to the three young children of the Duke of Zweibrücken (1555–58), as well as undertaking short diplomatic missions on behalf of the French town of Metz,[12] Elizabeth I of England and Frederick III, the Elector Palatine. He was also responsible for a number of significant works of Christian Hebraica, including translations into Latin of the New Testament from Syriac, which he published in 1569, and of the Old Testament from Hebrew, which he produced in conjunction with Franciscus Junius, and which was first published in four volumes between 1575 and 1579. This last work came to be widely regarded as the best Protestant Latin version of the Bible to emerge from the early modern period.

II

Tremellius' two conversions undoubtedly constituted a pivotal period in his life. The transition from Judaism to Reformed Protestantism brought with it significant ramifications for his life as a whole: his first conversion obliged him to break his ties with the Jews, while the second necessitated his departure from his homeland. He spent the remainder of his career in exile, travelling around northern Europe, always at least in part as an outsider, never sharing a first language nor a religious or cultural heritage with those he encountered. Given the importance of these events as regards his subsequent career, they ought to be considered in a little more detail.

The dating and exact circumstances of the first part of his life, however, are elusive despite the apparent involvement of two distinguished cardinals. The first of these was Reginald Pole, a cousin of Henry VIII and a future candidate for the papacy. In *De Antiquitate Britannicae*, a history of the 70 archbishops of Canterbury, first

---

[12] In 1544, while in Strasburg, Tremellius married Elisabeth, a woman from Metz. She had been married already and brought with her at least one daughter from that previous marriage.

published in 1572, and probably written by, or at least under the auspices of, the then holder of that office, Matthew Parker, the following incident is recorded:

> Immanuel Tremellius, a most learned man, often came to the gathering of evangelicals around Reginald Pole and the company of Antonio Flaminio. And he was converted [*conversus fuit*] from his Jewish stubbornness to Christ in the household of Pole, and was taught doctrines against the Pope; he also consumed evangelical doctrines, and moreover he was baptized by Pole and Flaminio within Pole's household.[13]

Less than a decade after this work was published, Cardinal Alessandro Farnese, who went on to become Pope Paul III in 1534, was also implicated in Tremellius' conversion. His involvement is mentioned in an anonymous work of 1581, the *Specularius contra Genebrardum*, which was written to defend Tremellius' translation of the New Testament from Syriac into Latin against allegations of plagiarism made by, among others, Gilbert Genebrard, the renowned professor of Hebrew at the Sorbonne.[14] In the dialogue, the character of Tremellius is made to say: 'the renowned Cardinal of Rome, Farnese ... took me, by birth a Jew, fifty years ago, into his household, when I first passed over [*transivi*] to the Christians, drawn by a sure religious knowledge: and he illuminated that doctrine of truth'.[15] These extracts prompt as many questions as they answer. Both sources seem to describe a general movement from Judaism to Christianity; yet it can hardly be imagined that Tremellius made the same conversion twice! Furthermore, neither extract provides a date or a location for the events they describe; nonetheless, there are clues which allow a tentative chronology to be proposed. The source relating to Farnese suggests that the encounter happened 50 years before the dialogue was written in 1581, but at such a distance, we cannot be certain how much of an approximation this was; Rome would certainly have been the most likely location for Farnese's residence throughout that period. If the mention of Flaminio is correct in the second source, the events relating to Pole could only have occurred in the winter of

---

[13] [Matthew Parker], *De Antiquitate Britannicae Ecclesiae & Privilegiis Ecclesiae, cum Archiepiscopis eiusdem 70* (London, 1572), p. 410. The inclusion of the anecdote relating to Tremellius in this work is discussed in Thomas F. Mayer, *Reginald Pole: Prince and Prophet* (Cambridge, 2000), p. 55, n.

[14] [Tremellius], *Specularius, Dialogus perneccessarius, quo se Immanuel Tremellius purgat ab illis criminiationibus, quas Gilbertus Genebrardus Theologus Parisiensis divinarum & Hebraicarum literarum Professor Regius, ipsi in Chronographia, seu universae historiae speculo intulerat* (Neustadt an der Haardt, 1581).

[15] [Tremellius], *Specularius, Dialogus pernecessarius*, pp. 10–11.

1541/2. Pole only moved to Viterbo from Padua in September 1541, and it was there that he was joined by Flaminio. If Tremellius followed him there, he cannot have remained there long, as he must have been in Lucca by early 1542 at the latest.

For our purposes here, these respective contributions are perhaps less important than the fact that this part of Tremellius' religious development was closely associated with Farnese, Pole and Flaminio. Pole and Flaminio were among the leading figures of the rather nebulous group of reform-minded Italians known as the *spirituali*. Efforts to define the beliefs of this group of 'evangelicals' are fraught with difficulty, not least because the intellectuals and churchmen of which it was comprised regarded individual freedom in these matters as paramount. Nonetheless, as Gleason has argued, among the most commonly held aspects were an interest in the reform of the Church and a belief in justification by faith.[16] As Paul III, Farnese showed himself to be sympathetic to ideas of Church reform, and to these evangelicals in particular: he promoted men like Pole, Gasparo Contarini and Gregorio Cortese to the office of Cardinal, and then encouraged their involvement in Church reform, most famously in producing the *Consilium de emendanda ecclesiae* of 1537. It was in the company of such men, then, that Tremellius first encountered Catholicism.

Consequently, the next step in Tremellius' religious development, on to Reformed Protestantism in the Lucchese monastery, was not as great a leap as it might have been. In addition, there were also more tangible connections. It was most likely on Pole's recommendation that Tremellius gained his post as teacher of Hebrew in the monastery of San Frediano: he presumably recommended Tremellius to Peter Martyr Vermigli. Moreover, Flaminio and Peter Martyr had been members of the same group around Juan de Valdés in Naples in the later 1530s. Indeed, it has been argued that both these men headed north through Italy at the end of that decade with the explicit intention of spreading the evangelical message of the Naples circle.[17] More generally, Peter Martyr was another leading figure within the *spirituali*.

According to his friend and biographer Josias Simler, through the winter of 1541 and 1542 Peter Martyr daily interpreted passages from

---

[16] Elisabeth G. Gleason, 'On the Nature of Sixteenth-century Italian Evangelism: Scholarship, 1953–1978', *SCJ* 9 (1978), 3–25, replying to Eva-Maria Jung, 'On the Nature of Evangelism in Sixteenth-Century Italy', *Journal of the History of Ideas* 14 (1953), 511–27. See also Paolo Simoncelli, *Evangelismo italiano del cinquecento* (Rome, 1979); William V. Hudon, *Marcello Cervini and Ecclesiastical Government in Tridentine Italy* (De Kalb, IL, 1992).

[17] Massimo Firpo, *Tra alumbrados e «spirituali». Studi su Juan de Valdés e il Valdesianesimo nella crisi religiosa del '500 italiano* (Florence, 1990), pp. 135–6.

the Epistles of St Paul and the Psalms in accordance with his evangelical views.[18] In addition, writings of Philip Melanchthon, Martin Bucer, Heinrich Bullinger and Jean Calvin are all believed to have been read within his circle.[19] The impact of this programme was immediate and profound: 18 of the fellows of San Frediano, including Tremellius, followed Peter Martyr in leaving the Catholic Church. Of course, the revival of the Roman Inquisition in the summer of 1542 in part forced their hand: the religious ambiguity which had characterized Italian evangelism until this point was no longer possible. Confessional lines began to harden rapidly. Nonetheless, it was of considerable significance that Tremellius underwent his most formative religious experiences before this transformation had fully occurred: the lessons he learned in the 1530s and early 1540s did much to shape his career in exile.

III

It hardly needs to be affirmed that early modern Christendom was deeply anti-Semitic. From approximately AD 1000, relations between Christians and Jews had become increasingly characterized by tension and even violence.[20] The Crusades brought with them the slaughter of more than 100 000 Jews, and those who remained were subject to progressively more repressive legislation.[21] From the thirteenth century onwards, the Jewish populations of Europe were driven into exile: from England in 1290, France in 1315, Austria in 1421 and Spain in 1492.[22] As Friedman remarks, 'The elimination and isolation of Jews had the desired effect: the year 1500 saw fewer Jews in western and central Europe than at any point in the previous 1000 years.'[23] Despite the wide-ranging contribution of the Jews to the culture of the Renaissance, moreover, such sentiments did not diminish during the sixteenth century.[24] Jewish

---

[18] Josias Simler, *Oratio de Vita et Obitu Clarrissimi Viri et Praestantissimi Theologi D. Petri Martyris Vermilii...* (Zürich, 1563), fol. 8ᵛ.

[19] Philip McNair, *Peter Martyr in Italy: An Anatomy of Apostasy* (Oxford, 1967), p. 231.

[20] Jerome Friedman, *The Most Ancient Testimony: Sixteenth-century Christian-Hebraica in the Age of Renaissance Nostalgia* (Athens, OH, 1983), p. 16 ff.

[21] Ibid., p. 17.

[22] Ibid.

[23] Ibid., p.18.

[24] See Moses A. Shulvass, *The Jews in the World of the Renaissance* (Leiden, 1973) for a consideration of the principal areas of this contribution. On anti-Semitism, see Achim Detmers, '"Sie nennen unseren Retter Christus einen Hurensohn und die göttlicher Jungfrau eine Dirne": Heinrich Bullinger Gutachten zur Duldung von Juden 1572', in Alfred Schindler and Hans Stickleberger (eds), *Die Zürcher Reformation: Ausstrahlungen*

converts, particularly those whose conversion had been voluntary, were regarded with anxiety and distrust, because of the suspicion that their conversion was merely superficial, and a means of gaining rights or opportunities unavailable to them as long as they remained Jews.[25]

For this very reason, many Jewish converts to Christianity in the later Middle Ages sought to prove the authenticity of their conversion by immediately attacking Jews. As Newman writes, 'the majority of Jewish apostates proved themselves a source of great vexation to their erstwhile comrades'.[26] Peter Alphonso, Samuel of Morocco and others wrote polemics against Judaism in the early twelfth century.[27] Among the best known Jewish apostates in the thirteenth and fourteenth centuries were Nicholas Donin, Paul Christian and Joshua ha-Lorki; all three assisted the Dominicans in their assault on Jewish books by identifying those parts of Talmudic and rabbinic works which were contrary to Christian belief.[28] Still other converts encouraged the ritual murder charge and took part in burnings of the Talmud.[29]

Tremellius, on the other hand, seems largely to have adopted a policy of studied neutrality. As far as we know, he cut all ties with the Jews of Europe from the point of his conversion. There is no evidence to suggest that he returned to the community in Ferrara in which he had spent his childhood and youth; nor are there any grounds for believing that he had any contact with Jews in northern Europe once in exile. Despite skills as a diplomat, moreover, he seems never to have been called upon to mediate in cases involving Jews, nor to have represented their interests. Although he based his career on working with Hebrew, and occasionally even rabbinic, sources (or perhaps because of that fact), he does not appear to have resorted to making anti-Semitic statements to prove his orthodoxy.

Of course, the readiness of converts from Judaism to attack their former brethren was closely tied to the environment in which they

---

und Rückwirkungen (Berne, 2001), 229–59; Jerome Friedman, 'Sebastian Münster, the Jewish Mission, and Protestant Anti-Semitism', *ARG* 70 (1979), 238–59; Steven Rowan, 'Luther, Bucer and Eck on the Jews', *SCJ* 16 (1985), 79–90.

[25] See, for instance, Salo W. Baron, *A Social and Religious History of the Jews* (18 vols, New York and London, 1969), Vol. XIII: *Inquisition, Renaissance and Reformation* esp. pp. 64–158; Stephen Haliczer, 'The First Holocaust: The Inquisition and the Converted Jews of Spain and Portugal', in S. Haliczer, *Inquisition and Society in Early Modern Europe* (London and Sydney, 1987), pp. 7–18; Henry Kamen, *The Spanish Inquisition: An Historical Revision* (London, 1977), esp. pp. 3–43, 214–29.

[26] Louis I. Newman, *Jewish Influence on Christian Reform Movements* (New York, 1925), pp. 370–71.

[27] Ibid., p. 371.

[28] Ibid., p. 306.

[29] Ibid., p. 371.

found themselves: if they met with a sympathetic reception, there would be less need for self-justification. It would certainly be tempting to suggest that a confessional distinction may be made in this regard. In the sixteenth century, the best known apostates, including Tremellius, found employment in Protestant areas. Matthew Adrian was elected professor of Hebrew at the trilingual college of Louvain;[30] in April 1520, Martin Luther managed to persuade the University of Wittenberg to hire Adrian as its first professor of Hebrew.[31] Michael Adam, a converted Jew who found his way to Zurich, helped Leo Jud in the preparation of his Latin Bible.[32] Philip Ferdinand, a Polish Jew, born in about 1555, taught Hebrew first at Oxford and then, from 1596, at Cambridge.[33] None of these figures felt the need to disparage other Jews.

Nonetheless, it would be misguided to conclude from this that Protestants had a significantly more enlightened attitude towards apostates, or that Jewish converts only resorted to activities of this kind in Catholic areas. The reality is rather more complicated. In the Middle Ages it is possible to identify certain apostates, such as Martin of Lucena, who remained friendly to the Jews, and others who remained neutral.[34] Moreover, anti-Jewish sentiment was by no means exclusive to one confession; allegations of Judaizing were almost universal. Johann Reuchlin was accused of Judaizing because of his involvement in Hebrew studies, while Carlstadt attacked Philip Melanchthon on the same grounds. Martin Luther and Jean Calvin were both subjected to charges of Judaizing, and used the term themselves to accuse a range of other figures.[35]

In fact, perhaps the most revealing piece of evidence as regards Tremellius' attitude to his former co-religionists is his translation of Calvin's catechism into Hebrew, which he produced in 1554. In the preface to this work, he began by accepting that in producing such a work, 'I am not unaware ... that I may well incur the displeasure of many'; nevertheless, this was not enough to dissuade him from what he felt was a valuable project. He continued: 'the Jewish nation nowadays has a hostile attitude to our religion, because they do not read what we say for or against them ... But they are more receptive to things written

---

[30] Gareth Lloyd Jones, *The Discovery of Hebrew in Tudor England* (Manchester, 1983), p. 181.
[31] Robert Wakefield, *On The Three Languages* [1524], ed. and trans. G. Lloyd Jones (New York, 1989), p. 28.
[32] Newman, *Jewish Influence*, p. 508.
[33] Henry P. Stokes, *Studies in Anglo-Jewish History* (Edinburgh, 1913), pp. 209 ff.
[34] Newman, *Jewish Influence*, p. 370.
[35] Ibid., pp. 617–22.

in Hebrew.'[36] It was his belief that a large part of the Jewish aversion to Christianity was founded on ignorance; by providing a clear statement of Christian beliefs in their own language, therefore, he believed they might be led to accept that truth, much in the same way that he had done himself.[37] Clearly, there are echoes in this of the evangelical efforts of Protestantism more generally: the emphasis placed on providing access to the Scriptures in local vernaculars relied on exactly the same belief in the truth of these texts which would be clear to any who were exposed to them. At the same time, of course, there were rather more obstacles for the Jewish readers of Tremellius' work to overcome for that end to be achieved.

Indeed, the extent to which Tremellius' work was genuinely intended to serve missionary purposes is debatable. Jerome Friedman, whose seminal study surveys Christian Hebraica throughout this period, certainly believes that it was. He describes this catechism as the 'only ... missionary treatise from the entire sixteenth century [that] was open, friendly and sincere in its desire to convert Jews to Christianity. This same treatise was the only such Christian-authored work absolutely avoiding any and all anti-Semitic denigration.'[38] The absence of anti-Semitic sentiment is certainly exceptional, but it should also be appreciated that Tremellius did not attempt to accommodate the Jews with special arguments: he simply presented a straightforward summary of Christian (and in this case, specifically Calvinist) belief. Furthermore, the fact that this work was published with vowel points, a feature which would have been unnecessary for Jewish readers, would suggest that this work was primarily intended for a Christian audience, perhaps as a text of proven orthodoxy for Calvinists learning Hebrew to practise their translation skills.[39] Finally, the slightly patronising tone of the lines quoted above about the prejudices of the Jews against Christian works would hardly have endeared him to that readership.

Nonetheless, even if this work was unlikely to provide as many converts as Friedman seems to envisage, what is most important for our purposes here is that Tremellius avoided engaging in polemic against the Jews in a context where that was absolutely the norm. The fact that he was not prepared to resort to this, despite the precarious

---

[36] Tremellius, *Initatio electorum Domini: est versio Hebraica catechismi Jo. Calvini* (Paris, 1554), p. 2.

[37] Ibid., pp. 2–3.

[38] Friedman, *The Most Ancient Testimony*, p. 250.

[39] I am grateful to Stephen Burnett for this suggestion, and for discussing the issue further with me.

nature of his position, must be seen as part of a larger strategy. It is evident that Tremellius envisaged conversion of other Jews by persuasion rather than coercion. While one might suggest that he could have done more to facilitate this plan, both in terms of making this specific work more suited to that audience, and by producing more works with that intention, it is undeniable that he provided a positive image of Christianity for Jews, and might, in the longer term, have had greater success in what he was hoping to do. This impression is confirmed by his career. Apart from his conversion itself, there was nothing which he did or wrote which would have aggravated Jewish hostility towards him.

Tremellius' attitude to Judaism and Jewish learning as a whole was rather more positive, although even here he continued to exercise restraint. As we have already seen, his career rested on the use of Hebraica: he taught Hebrew and Old Testament studies for almost 40 years, and his writings reflect exactly the same interests. His translations of the Old and New Testaments were made from Hebrew and Syriac respectively. He also produced a translation into Latin of Jonathan ben Uzziel's paraphrases of the 12 minor prophets in Chaldaean,[40] and a Chaldaean and Syriac grammar.[41] His intentions in producing this range of works are clear: he wanted to make Hebrew sources available to a Christian audience that could not otherwise understand them, and to provide the necessary tools for the most enthusiastic to continue the same enterprise themselves.[42]

Yet all of these were relatively acceptable works. On a handful of occasions, Tremellius moved into slightly more dangerous territory. As we will shortly see, for instance, he became involved in editing the Talmud, with deleterious consequences. More generally, it is apparent that he continued to use rabbinic sources throughout his career. The clearest evidence for this is a series of notes made by a student who attended Tremellius' lectures on Isaiah in Heidelberg. In these notes, it becomes very clear that he was heavily indebted to rabbinic sources. For instance, on Isaiah 38:2, Tremellius referred to both David Kimhi and Abraham ibn Ezra, two of the most influential medieval Jewish

---

[40] Tremellius, *Ionathanae Filii Uzielis, Antiquissimi & summae apud Hebraeos authoritatis Chaldaea paraphrases in duodecim minores Prophetas, per Immanuelem Tremelium [sic], Theologiae Doctorem & Professorem latine reddita* (Heidelberg, 1567).
[41] Tremellius, *Grammatica Chaldaea et Syra* (Geneva, 1569).
[42] Tremellius did not produce a Hebrew grammar, presumably because his son-in-law, Antoine Chevallier, had done so in 1561. In fact, Tremellius wrote a prefatory letter in Hebrew to that earlier work, again indicating his interest in increasing knowledge of the Semitic languages among Christians.

commentators, in support of his interpretation of that verse.[43] These two, in particular, are cited with considerable regularity throughout the remainder of the manuscript. Interestingly, however, Tremellius' treatment of the same text in his published version of the Bible contains no such references. Yet that is not to say that he did not make use of them. Indeed, Lloyd Jones has drawn attention to the manner in which the Authorised Version of the Bible of 1611 incorporated various rabbinic traditions in its translation as a direct result of the use of Tremellius' translation.[44] Rather, it would appear that while Tremellius never doubted the value that Hebrew and rabbinic sources could provide, he was sufficiently sensitive to the mood of the times, and would sometimes be more covert in using such sources when he felt their open use might be too controversial.

After all, Tremellius must have anticipated hostility from Christians because of his conversion and his former association with Jews. It was clearly an association from which he could never fully escape: he is described as being of Jewish descent in sources which date from at least three decades after his conversion. This again highlights contemporary sensitivity to this issue. The reality of the situation into which Tremellius was moving is shown, for instance, by a letter which Pierre Viret wrote to Guillaume Farel from Berne in November 1547, explaining why he was unable to find employment for Tremellius as Jean Calvin had asked him to:

> As for Tremellius, I do not really know what I can reply to you. There is no post for him here, and if there were, there are many good and learned men who ought not to be neglected. At the moment, moreover, the Jews and Italians are badly spoken of in Berne.[45]

As if it were not bad enough that Tremellius had a Jewish background, he was also Italian, which only compounded the prejudices of northern Europeans against him.

On the other hand, however, Tremellius' Jewish origins seem only occasionally to have caused him sufficient trouble to have left any traces in the sources. In addition to Viret's letter just mentioned, I have found only three instances where this issue may have been problematic. Several nineteenth-century Tremellius scholars suggested that this was one of the reasons why he did not enjoy his post as rector of the Academy of Hornbach. However, as so often in the historiography relating to

[43] Columbia University, New York, X893 B476, *Observata ex Immanuelis Tremellii lectionibus in Jeschaiam Prophetam et in Hoscheam Joelem et Amosum Emmanuel Tremellius*, fol. 2ᵛ.
[44] Jones, *Discovery of Hebrew*, pp. 50–52.
[45] Pierre Viret to Guillaume Farel, 24 November 1547, *Calvini Opera* 12, no. 969, 621.

Tremellius, this seems to be a conjecture which has become part of the tradition of his life; there does not seem to be anything more substantial in the sources from the time.[46]

A second reference to this theme comes from the anonymous work known as the *Specularius contra Genebrardum* mentioned above. Throughout this dialogue, the character of Genebrard refers to Tremellius as an 'unlearned Marrano'.[47] Marranism was a term used by Christians, especially in the Iberian context, to refer to Jewish converts who, despite public conversion, continued to worship as Jews in secrecy. As we have already seen, false converts were viewed with particular hostility in this period. Yet the accusation of Marranism against Tremellius in this work sounds rather too much like a stock charge: it is never elaborated upon, and seems simply to be an insulting form of address. In any case, as it seems most likely that this work was written either by Tremellius or one of his close supporters, we cannot be sure that Genebrard said anything of the sort; indeed, he is made to look more foolish by his having to resort to stereotypical insults in the absence of more compelling arguments. At the very least, however, this does again emphasize how deeply engrained anti-Semitic sentiment was in the culture of the sixteenth century. Religious converts, of whatever persuasion but especially between Judaism and Christianity, always ran the risk of having that conversion challenged, simply as a means of undermining them in other respects.

Third, Tremellius encountered a degree of hostility towards the very end of his life, as a result of his role in censoring certain books of the Talmud on behalf of the printer Johann Froben. According to Tremellius, this undertaking had been arranged while he was still in the employment of the Elector Palatine; Froben had passed through Heidelberg at the time of the Frankfurt book fair, and enlisted the Hebraist's services for this highly skilled task. Although he had not done much work on this, and none of it had yet been published, Tremellius had, by 1579, heard sufficient criticism of his actions that he was prompted to contact Theodore Beza in the hope that he might be able to resolve the situation. Tremellius wrote:

> As for the Talmud, this is the third or fourth complaint that, to my great regret, I have heard: I wish in truth that I had never lain hands on it. God knows that this [i.e. his work on the Talmud] has not

---

[46] Philip C. Heintz suggested in 1816 that Tremellius failed to win the respect of the pupils at the Academy of Hornbach while rector. This idea was picked up by Butters, *Emanuel Tremellius* (p. 22) who hypothesized that Tremellius may have encountered anti-Semitic and anti-Italian prejudice there. Becker, *Immanuel Tremellius*, p. 30, endorsed this explanation. At the root of all this, however, was simply the fact that Tremellius's successor at Hornbach was admonished to impose better morals and order on the academy.

[47] [Tremellius], *Specularius, Dialogus pernecessarius*.

been intended to confirm an error or blasphemy, nor in any way to obscure the truth.[48]

Rather, he continued, he had been asked by Froben to 'remove what would be considered blasphemous and contrary to the Christian faith, which I was happy to do'.[49]

It is salutary to notice that even in his late sixties, after a distinguished career serving Christian purposes, his involvement in this enterprise could so quickly bring criticism. Evidently he could never entirely escape this form of prejudice, even when his intentions, as he explains them, were entirely honourable. His reaction is even more revealing. Almost as soon as he was aware of dissenting voices, he approached Beza to ask for support of what he had done, while simultaneously backing away from the project. His conviction of the value of the Jewish sources for a Christian audience inclined him to keep working with them, even though he was acutely aware of how vulnerable this made him as a converted Jew. Whenever controversy arose, however, he preferred to back away rather than to defend his position at any great length; more generally, he sought to act with considerable tact and diplomacy, as a means of disarming opposition to what he was doing even before it could properly organize itself.

IV

The next section of this essay will look at the nature of Tremellius' assumed religion. Two separate aspects are of relevance here: his conversion, and his behaviour thereafter. Unsurprisingly, especially given the uncertainty surrounding Tremellius' first conversion, and his failure to talk about it himself, one of the most obvious questions posed by his career is whether it was genuine. Indeed, at least in some respects, the confessional use made of Tremellius' beliefs came to be as significant as the beliefs themselves. Following Tremellius' death, certain Catholic writers suggested that he had renounced his Christianity on his deathbed, preferring to die as a Jew. The original accusations do not survive; the earliest mention of the charge comes from a work of 1616 by Jacques Cappel, a professor of theology at the Academy of Sedan in France, the institution in which Tremellius had ended his life. Cappel wrote: 'Messers Remand and Fernier felt no shame in writing that [Tremellius]

---

[48] Tremellius to Theodore Beza, September/October 1579: Theodore Beza, *Correspondance de Théodore de Bèze*, ed. Hyppolyte Aubert et al. (Geneva, 1960-), no. 1373, p. 194.
[49] Ibid., p. 195.

recanted and died as a Jew.'[50] This accusation, however, seems to be little more than confessional point-scoring: by calling into question Tremellius' very adherence to Christianity, these Catholics were seeking to undermine his contribution to the Reformed faith as a whole. In addition, it may have helped to explain his rapid abandonment of Catholicism: by contending that he continued to harbour an adherence to Judaism, his transition from Catholicism to Protestantism became entirely superficial and academic.

Needless to say, Tremellius' fellow Protestants were quick to endorse his commitment to his adopted faith. Johann Grynaeus, in his *Apothegm Morientum*, claimed that Tremellius' dying words were 'Vivat Christus, pereat Barabas' ('let Christ live, let Barabas die'):[51] an obvious allusion to Pontius Pilate's famous offering of freedom to a prisoner. Tremellius chooses Christianity, represented by Christ, over Barabas who presumably represents his Judaism. Yet one can hardly imagine that Tremellius would have said such a thing; only the challenge to his orthodoxy, which itself came after his death, can have prompted such a reaffirmation. More compelling, perhaps, is the evidence of Tremellius' will, which was written only a couple of months before his death. In that, apparently, not only did he leave 30 *écus* to the poor of Sedan, the town in which he died, but he also offered thanks to God for having drawn him away from Judaism, and for having led him to know Jesus Christ.[52]

Even when one leaves aside the confessional polemic, the possibility that Tremellius's conversions were in some way career-motivated remains. He did, after all, enjoy a prestigious career of the sort which would not have been open to him had he remained a Jew. Against this, however, one has to remember that especially at the point in Tremellius' life at which he converted from Judaism, there was no guarantee that he would enjoy such a successful career; indeed, at the time of his first conversion, he had not yet held a single teaching post. Even if he did have high-placed patrons, such as Farnese and Pole, they could not be relied upon to provide for his career in the longer term, especially once he had left Italy.[53]

---

[50] Jacques Cappel, *Les Livrées de Babel, ou l'Histoire du Siege Romain* (Sedan, 1616), p. iii.

[51] I have been unable to trace this work, which is quoted, for instance, in Paul Colomies, *Italia et Hispania Orientalis ... Vitae* (Hamburg, 1730), p. 111.

[52] The will itself has apparently not survived, but its contents are discussed in Cappel, *Les Livrées de Babel*, p. iii. Tremellius is mentioned only in passing, and there seems little to be gained by defending his orthodoxy or fabricating his will. Nevertheless, in the absence of the actual will, Cappel's evidence should still be treated with some caution.

[53] It was thanks to his third patron, Peter Martyr, that he gained employment in Strasburg.

In addition, conversion entailed considerable sacrifice. He was obliged to break contact with his family and home community; his second conversion, moreover, forced him to leave his native country. More generally, he must have appreciated that there was a strong likelihood that he would encounter hostility from both Jews and Christians as a result of what he had done. As we saw earlier, both during the course of his lifetime and following his death, there were some (although in his case fortunately few) instances where he encountered suspicion as a direct result of being a convert.

Thus, while Tremellius' conversion opened up new career opportunities for him, there were no guarantees of this, and the risks which it entailed were surely greater. The rashness and greed implied in a conversion for careerist reasons seems otherwise entirely uncharacteristic of Tremellius. It would be simpler, and more plausible, therefore to consider that this was in some measure a genuine conversion. This interpretation is in fact further endorsed, rather than undermined, by the fact that Tremellius went through two conversions. There was nothing to be gained by moving from Catholicism to Protestantism that he had not already achieved by apostatizing from Judaism; if it was purely a matter of convenience rather than faith, either Christian confession would have been acceptable. Remaining a Catholic, moreover, would have made it far easier for him to stay in Italy. The fact that he was prepared to undergo hardships in the early 1540s and flee his home country must incline us to believe that there was a genuine commitment behind these moves.

When one looks at his career in exile, it is apparent that his contemporaries saw no reason to doubt his Calvinist credentials. For instance, the places where he gained employment – Strasburg, England, Zweibrücken, Heidelberg, Sedan – were all Reformed at least at the times when he was there. Moreover, his association with Calvinism was sufficient to determine his employment and its termination. For instance, it was the conversion of the Duke of Zweibrücken from Calvinism to Lutheranism that obliged Tremellius to leave his post as rector of the Academy in Hornbach, and the succession of the Lutheran Ludwig VI as the Elector of the Palatinate after the Calvinist Frederick III ended Tremellius' time as a Professor at the University of Heidelberg. The figures with whom he corresponded, including men like Calvin and Beza, also clearly puts him in this camp, although this must at least in part be seen as a reflection of the practical requirements of his career.

Tremellius' Protestant affiliations are also indicated by his involvement in two brief diplomatic engagements at the start of the 1560s. The first mission was on behalf of the town of Metz, the birthplace of his wife. On 5 October 1559, King Francis II of France had prohibited the Huguenots from remaining in Metz.[54] Following Francis's death in December 1560, the people of Metz appealed against this prohibition to the Regent, Catherine de' Medici. In January 1561, Tremellius, along with Didier Rolin, a burgher of Metz, led a delegation to Orléans, where the French Court was assembled for an Estates General. In the event, the Edict of Orléans of that month granted greater freedoms to the Huguenots of France as a whole; nonetheless, Tremellius and Rolin successfully campaigned for a number of specific further points, including the free return of those who had already been exiled, and the release of Guillaume Palisseau who was being held in Auxerre on religious grounds. Whether Tremellius deserves as much credit for this as some of his biographers have suggested is perhaps debatable, but his readiness to involve himself in this effort is striking nonetheless.

Moreover, Tremellius' attendance at the French Court at this time brought him to the notice of two English diplomats, the Earl of Bedford and Nicholas Throckmorton. They too had arrived at Orléans in January 1561, where, according to their testimony, they found Tremellius pleading the case of the Metz Huguenots.[55] They spoke with him, and persuaded him to join them in an effort to establish an antipapal coalition. In particular, the Englishmen wanted to utilize Tremellius' existing connections and negotiating abilities to persuade the German Protestant princes to join this coalition. These princes were then to send envoys who would, in turn, attempt to persuade the French not to participate in the third session of the Council of Trent, which was about to commence.[56] In early May, Tremellius returned with messages from the German princes which he delivered personally to the kings of Navarre and France.[57] He was paid 100 crowns for his services.[58] Again, his efforts in this regard testify to his commitment to the Protestant cause; whether or not he realized the full implications of his actions, and whether he could square this sabotaging of Catholic efforts at regrouping with his irenicism, on the other hand, is less clear. As with so many events in Tremellius' career, in the absence of detailed autobiographical sources, we are left uncertain as to what he made of matters.

---

[54] On these events, see R.P. Meurisse, *Histoire de la Naissance, du Progrès et de la décadence de l'hérésie dans la ville de Metz* (Metz, 1670), pp. 147 ff.; Henri-Tribout de Morembert, *La Reforme à Metz* (3 vols, Nancy, 1971), Vol. II: *Le Calvinisme 1553–1685* pp. 24 ff.

[55] *Calendar of State Papers, Foreign Series, of the Reign of Elizabeth, 1560–61*, ed. Joseph Stevenson (London, 1865), no. 1020.

[56] Ibid., no. 1022. See also the essays in this volume by Alain Tallon and Elizabeth Tingle.

[57] *Calendar of State Papers, Foreign ... 1561–62*, nos 189, 197.

Finally, we have the evidence of Tremellius' published writings. Two, in particular, are of relevance here. We have already considered Tremellius' translation of Calvin's catechism into Hebrew in relation to the Jews, but this text also gives a clear indication of his religious alignment. Indeed, if one were wishing to 'prove' one's orthodoxy, one could hardly find a work which would have made this point any more clearly. In any case, it seems very much out of keeping with the other works for which he was responsible. No other polemical or theological works exist from his career which would endorse the genuine nature of his assumed faith. Instead, he produced a Hebrew and Syriac grammar, various translations, an edition of lectures which Martin Bucer had delivered in Cambridge on the Epistle to the Ephesians, and his biblicae editions.

In his biblical scholarship, too, Tremellius did little more than hint at his religious beliefs. Even in the copious annotative materials with which he supplemented his translations, there are virtually no traces of Calvinist exposition. For instance, he did not use his annotations on Romans, as others had, as a launching pad for a discussion of the doctrine of predestination. At best there are a handful of underlying theological principles which occasionally surface during the course of the annotations, most noticeably trinitarianism and christocentrism, when these are not necessarily immediately prompted by the text. Such principles were universal to all Christian faiths: while they may in part have been included in order to distance himself from his Jewish background, they also served the purpose of emphasizing the points of commonality between the Christian confessions. In fact, there was relatively little that would not have also appealed to a Catholic audience, let alone to the other Protestant confessions. Because of its later date we cannot be sure about Tremellius' Old Testament edition, but we do have the comments of the censors responsible for the Antwerp Index of 1571 on Tremellius' New Testament. The preface was forbidden, the author was condemned, but the censors conceded that the work could be useful, at least once about 130 annotations had been removed.[59]

V

The nature of Tremellius' Calvinism must, in some respects, have been shaped by a concern for self-preservation. With the complex religious

---

[58] *Calendar of State Papers, Foreign ... 1560–61*, no. 1030.
[59] *Index des Livres Interdites VII: Index d'Anvers de 1569, 1570 et 1571*, ed. Jesus M. DeBujanda (Geneva, 1990), pp. 552–3.

background from which he had emerged, he would have appreciated his susceptibility to allegations of insincerity or careerism. One of the most effective ways of dealing with such a situation was to avoid drawing attention to himself, by ensuring that he minimized the occasions on which he had to advocate one religious position over another. But it was more than this. Tremellius was an academic and a man of wide cultural, religious and intellectual experiences, the combination of which inclined him towards an irenic outlook. His biblical exegesis emphasized, above all, doctrines that were acceptable to virtually all Christian confessions; he could not have taken quite such an open-minded approach towards Judaism without encountering accusations of heresy, but even there he continued to emphasize, throughout his career, the value of Hebraic and rabbinic sources for furthering Christian understanding.

These attitudes, moreover, had their origins in the Italian phase of Tremellius' career. For the first 20 years or so of his life, he had lived in Ferrara, under the protection of the Este; this was followed by a time spent studying at Padua University. Both were unusually tolerant of Jews at this time. The relative lack of antagonism between Christians and Jews in these two environments was certainly untypical, but such sentiments can only have been enhanced when Tremellius underwent his two conversions. As we have seen, he made his transition from Judaism to Reformed Protestantism in the company of a number of the leading figures of the *spirituali* in the late 1530s and very early 1540s. That environment was characterized by, among other things, individualism, intellectual freedom, the absence of dogmatism and a readiness to identify helpful ideas in a range of conflicting viewpoints. It was an outlook which could not be publicly maintained as the 1540s progressed, as Tremellius himself appreciated: his journey into exile was the product of the hardening of confessional lines that originated at that point.

Nonetheless, these attitudes, acquired at the time of his two conversions, remained with Tremellius for the rest of his career. He was sensitive to the changing political and religious world around him, and adapted accordingly. The underlying attitudes remained the same, but he appreciated that different times required them to be expressed in different ways. For him, 'lukewarm Calvinism' provided that alternative. Adherence to one of the principal confessions was virtually the only means of survival in the second half of the sixteenth century, but Tremellius understood that there was a spectrum of positions which could be occupied within each. As his attitudes to the Jews and Judaism, Calvinism and Christianity as a whole indicate, he preferred to place himself at the moderate end of that spectrum. Paradoxically, it was more dangerous for him to take this position than to have become a staunch Calvinist. Especially for someone of Tremellius' background, moderation was not the easy option. It was fraught with dangers, which could only be avoided through very careful handling. That he managed to do so for four decades is a testament to Tremellius' skills and the strength of his beliefs.

CHAPTER FIVE

Cooperation and Confessional Identity in Mid-Tudor England: Three Berkshire Courtiers

Michael Riordan

A study of the religious polemic of mid-sixteenth century England can give the impression that the period was one of unremitting religious conflict. Writers such as John Foxe and John Bale portrayed this conflict as one between the true and the false churches; they saw the world divided between the followers of Christ and the Antichrist, locked in conflict.[1] But strife is at the heart of polemic, and so the polemical authors were fighting a battle which left little room for compromise. They professed to think it impossible that someone could be anything other than a zealous worker for one side or the other.

This polemic has encouraged historians to regard the Reformation as a simple battle between Protestants and Catholics, judging each side according to their successes and failures. For centuries the history of the Reformation in England was considered to be the story of the conversion of England to Protestantism.[2] A more recent generation of historians has challenged this, suggesting that the Reformation was not a popular movement, but one forced on a reluctant people by the government from above.[3] This has led other scholars to consider why, if this is true, the population of England accepted the reforms. Robert Whiting has argued that the doctrines of duty and obedience to the regime were stronger than opposition to the reform, while Christopher Marsh has suggested that there was a sufficient degree of continuity between traditional and Reformed religious practices to stifle opposition.[4]

---

[1] See Richard Bauckham, *Tudor Apocalypse: Sixteenth Century Apocalypticism, Millenarianism and the English Reformation* (Oxford, 1978).

[2] Most recently in A.G. Dickens, *The English Reformation* (London, 1964).

[3] The most prominent works, though with differering emphases, have been Eamon Duffy, *The Stripping of the Altars* (New Haven and London, 1992); Christopher Haigh, *English Reformations* (Oxford, 1993); Jack J. Scarisbrick, *The Reformation and the English People* (Oxford, 1984).

[4] Robert Whiting, *The Blind Devotion of the People* (Cambridge, 1989); Christopher Marsh, *Popular Religion in Sixteenth-Century England* (Basingstoke, 1998).

But all these studies are based on the assumption, inherited from the religious polemicists of the sixteenth century, that conservatives and reformers must always act in opposition to each other, and that there could be no middle ground. Therefore when people did act without confessional motivation they are frequently dismissed as *politiques*.[5] Ethan Shagan has recently suggested that these models are too constrictive. He has argued that the Reformation in England was a result of political negotiation between government and subjects, and that the English people adopted or rejected government policy in order to promote their own political, social and religious interests.[6] The middle ground was in fact well populated.

Shagan admits that his argument might overemphasize conflict in mid-Tudor society,[7] and this essay agrees, suggesting that cooperation and concord could be strong factors in sixteenth-century England. However, this reinforces Shagan's central argument that the story of the English Reformation is too complex to be told merely in terms of antipathy between conservatives and reformers. It was possible for them to live together in peace, and this essay shows how three men, conservative, reformer and *politique*, could do just that.

John Norris, Richard Ward and Thomas Weldon were all members of the royal Household in the mid-sixteenth century. Ward and Weldon both worked in the service departments of the Household, though both were to obtain the post of Cofferer, the highest office attainable to those 'below stairs' in the Household. Although Norris had a post in the Chamber, amongst the courtiers, it was not an honorific post, but one that required constant menial service; it was neither a sinecure nor a post for a politician.

Thomas Weldon claimed descent from a Northumberland family who had represented Newcastle-upon-Tyne in the House of Commons during the fifteenth century. The family built on this position by placing men in royal service. It has been suggested that in the sixteenth century 'no family better illustrates the potential for monopoly of household officers than the Weldons', a success that was achieved over three generations.[8] Hugh Weldon, the first of these, was a Sewer of the Chamber to both Henry VII and Henry VIII, and when the latter came to the throne in 1509 Hugh was able to obtain the post of Cofferer's Clerk for his son Edward.[9]

---

[5]   See the introduction to this volume, pp. 9–10, for a discussion of this term.
[6]   Ethan Shagan, *Popular Politics and the English Reformation* (Cambridge, 2003).
[7]   Ibid., p. 22, n. 54.
[8]   R.C. Braddock, 'The Royal Household, 1540–1560' (unpublished PhD thesis, Northwestern University, 1971), 133.
[9]   *LP*, vol. 1, no. 82; vol. 2, no. 3446; vol. 4, p. 867; *Original Documents … from the Private Archives of … the Duke of Rutland*, ed. William Jerden, *CS* n.s. 21 (1842), p. 102. Explanations of the various Court posts are given in David Loades, *The Tudor Court*, 2nd edn (Bangor, 1992).

When Edward vacated this post in 1518 he was succeeded by his younger brother, Thomas. The younger Weldon can have spent only a few years in this post, for by 1522 he had a post in the Ewery, the sub-department of the Spicery responsible for sugar and spices. In 1533 Thomas was sufficiently senior to serve at Anne Boleyn's table at her coronation feast, and by 1535 he had obtained a clerkship in the Kitchen, the largest and most important of the Household departments.[10] It is not clear whether he had been promoted through the lesser departments, or whether he had passed over them with the help of his brother, now sitting on the Board of the Green Cloth, the chief accounting body in the Household. By 1537 Thomas was Chief Clerk of the Kitchen, the highest clerkship in the Household departments, from which promotion to the Counting House was the natural step.[11]

The Counting House was responsible not only for the expenditure of the Household, but for all aspects of its organization and operation. By the mid-sixteenth century the daily work of the Counting House was supervised by the Cofferer, assisted by the Clerks of the Green Cloth. In 1540 it was re-organized, and four posts called the Masters of the Household were created. The exact role of these officers is obscure, but they were senior to the Clerks of the Green Cloth, and seem to have acted as the Cofferer's deputies.[12] On their creation, Edward Weldon was appointed to be Third Master, the head of the Queen's side, but his younger brother Thomas was promoted over his head from the Kitchen to be First Master of the Household, head of the King's side, and to all intents and purposes the deputy to the Cofferer. Thomas had to wait for over a decade to be promoted further, but in 1552 he was successful in reaching the pinnacle of any Court servant's ambition by obtaining the Coffererership. However, his success was short-lived, for at the accession of Queen Mary he was removed and it was not until her death that he was restored, thereafter retaining the post until his own death in 1567.[13]

Weldon was succeeded as Cofferer by Richard Ward. His father, Thomas Ward, had served both Henry VII and Henry VIII amongst the King's Harbingers.[14] From this theoretically lowly position Thomas had amassed great wealth, which he had used to educate his son. Richard was enrolled first at Eton College, just a few miles north of the family

---

[10] LP, vol. 2, no. 722, Appendix 58 (10); vol. 6, no. 562; vol. 10, no. 392 (14); The House of Commons, 1509–1558, ed. Stanley T. Bindoff (3 vols, London, 1982), vol. 3, p. 571; Documents of the Duke of Rutland, p. 58; Braddock, 'The Royal Household', p. 88.
[11] LP, vol. 13, no. 190 (32).
[12] Loades, Tudor Court, pp. 60–61.
[13] LP, vol. 16, no. 394 (5); Acts of the Privy Council of England, ed. John R. Dasent (46 vols, London, 1890–1964), vol. 4, p. 173.
[14] LP, vol. 1, nos 18, 40.

residence at Winkfield, then at King's College, Cambridge, where he may have taken a BA, and finally the Inner Temple where he was Reader in 1534 and Treasurer in 1537.[15] During 1537 he entered the royal Household, and with his education, which made him unique amongst the Clerks of the mid-Tudor Household, and perhaps with the assistance of Edward and Thomas Weldon, he was able to enter the Household as Clerk to the Poultry. It was usually necessary to serve in at least one of the Pastry, Larder, Scullery, Woodyard and Bakehouse, but Ward was able to pass them all over.[16] During the war with France in the mid-1540s Ward proved his usefulness as a victualler for the army, and by 1547 he had been rewarded with promotion to the Second Clerkship of the Spicery, an accounting department that supervised the sub-departments of the Wafery, Chaundry, Confectionary, Ewery and Laundry. By 1553 he was Chief Clerk there. Promotion to the Counting House seemed likely, and by the end of Mary's reign he had not only achieved this, but sat at its head as Cofferer.[17]

Each Tudor monarch had removed their predecessor's Cofferer, and Elizabeth was no exception, replacing Ward with Thomas Weldon. At first the two men served together, but this was a temporary expedient, and by 1565 Ward had been demoted to be the senior Clerk of the Green Cloth, a post which, the Masters of the Household having been abolished by Queen Mary, was once again junior only to the Cofferer.[18] Ward's demotion was not a comment on his own abilities, but represented Elizabeth's wish to favour Weldon, and so consequently, on Weldon's death in 1567, Ward was restored to his former post, which he retained until his own death in 1578.[19]

Unlike Weldon and Ward, John Norris followed not his father but a more distant kinsman into the Household. Henry Norris shared an early fifteenth-century ancestor with John, and Henry's branch of the family had served at Court for several generations. He himself was a Gentleman of the Privy Chamber and it was no doubt through his influence as a courtier that John was able to obtain a place in the Chamber in contrast to Weldon and Ward in the service departments.

Norris had probably been at Court for some time before his first recorded attendance in 1536, shortly before his kinsman Henry's

---

[15] Thomas Harwood, *Alumni Etonenses* (Birmingham, 1797), p. 143; John Venn and John A. Venn, *Alumni Cantabrigsienses* (10 vols, Cambridge, 1922–54), part 2, vol. 4, p. 333.

[16] *LP*, vol. 12, no. 1150 (26); Braddock, 'The Royal Household', pp. 112, 134–5, 137.

[17] *LP*, vol. 19, no. 675; NA LC 2/3/1 p. 76, LC 2/4/2 fol. 20^r.

[18] *Calendar of the Patent Rolls Preserved in the Public Record Office: Elizabeth*, ed. Margaret J. Post and Ann Morton (9 vols, London, 1939–), vol. 4, p. 1237.

[19] Ibid., vol. 5, p. 194.

execution for adultery with Anne Boleyn.[20] His fall seems not to have affected John, who continued to serve as a Gentleman Usher of the Chamber, a post requiring varied duties. These included guarding the door of the Privy Chamber during the day, and riding ahead of the Court to prepare royal residences for its arrival. The Gentlemen Ushers also represented the monarch at a range of official and unofficial functions. For example, in 1547 Norris attended St Paul's for the obsequies for Francis I, and represented the King at the christening of Lord Paget's child.[21]

On the accession of Queen Mary Norris attracted her favour, and apparently obtained promotion to the office of Chief Usher of the Privy Chamber.[22] No record survives of this appointment, but the fact that a 'Mr Norris' is amongst the Gentlemen of the Privy Chamber and not with the Gentlemen Ushers in the list of the Court drawn up at the time of Mary's funeral suggests that it might be true. Records do exist of his appointments in 1554 as Gentleman Usher to King Philip and as Usher of the Black Rod of the Order of the Garter, a post he retained until his death in 1577, when he was succeeded by his son William.[23] Under Mary, Norris was 'a man to be reckoned with in Court circles', but the influence did not continue under her sister.[24] In November 1558 he was summoned to Hatfield by the first meeting of Elizabeth's Privy Council, who described him as the 'late Gentleman Usher of the Privy Chamber to the late Queen'.[25] It has been suggested that the summons was issued in order that the new Queen might discuss the staffing of her Court with Norris, and this may be true, but if so Elizabeth could find no place for him in her Privy Chamber, and by the time of her coronation he was serving as a Gentleman Usher again. His prominence as one of the leading courtiers was limited to the reign of Queen Mary.

It might be presumed that Weldon, who suffered removal from the Coffererership under Mary, was sympathetic to religious reform, while Norris who found greater influence in that reign was a conservative, and there is certainly some evidence to confirm this. However, evidence of religious belief is difficult to construct. None of the three men left any writings apart from wills, and there is scant reference to them by others.

---

[20] *LP,* vol. 10, no. 392 (11).

[21] Braddock, 'The Royal Household', p. 40; *LP,* vol. 11, no. 643; *'Trevelyan Papers Prior to AD 1558,* ed. J.P. Collier, *CS* o.s. 63 (1857), pp. 194, 199.

[22] The evidence for this title is the account of William Underhill in *Tudor Tracts 1532–1588,* ed. Albert F. Pollard (London, 1903), p. 187.

[23] *Calendar of the Patent Rolls Preserved in the Public Record Office: Philip and Mary,* ed. Montague Giuseppi (4 vols, London, 1936–9), vol. 1, p. 120.

[24] Braddock, 'The Royal Household', p. 152.

[25] *Acts of the Privy Council,* vol. 7, p. 4.

The use of wills as evidence of belief has been called into doubt,[26] but there is some value to them, particularly for men like Norris, Ward and Weldon. They were literate members of the elite, and it is therefore less likely that they would have allowed the use of a formula based on the scribe's own beliefs to influence the preamble used, and more likely that they would wish to make their own beliefs clear. The funerary arrangements made in their wills can be used to confirm the validity of these preambles. Using these sources, with the few others that are available, it is possible to find some indications of the beliefs of these three men.

The evidence is strongest in relation to Weldon. In the seventeenth century his great-grandson set up a tablet in Cookham parish church to celebrate his family history. Thomas Weldon received particularly strong praise from his descendant, largely because 'not without danger to his life, he preserved his religion, that is Reformed, with a constant spirit'.[27] This surely refers to Weldon's brief imprisonment in 1543 for aiding and maintaining Anthony Persons, a priest who was one of three men burnt later that year at Windsor under the Act of Six Articles. Weldon was imprisoned with several other members of the Household, all similarly charged, including Sir Philip Hoby, another Berkshire landowner whose stepdaughter Weldon was later to marry. The imprisonment lasted for little more than a week, and all of the courtiers were released and pardoned by Henry VIII, who objected to proceedings against his own servants, whatever their beliefs.[28] There were greater men than Weldon involved, so his reformist views must have been sufficiently strong for him to have been noticed and included with them. He must have been aware how dangerous it was to hold these views; only the mercy of the highly capricious King saved him.

---

[26] James D. Alsop, 'Religious Preambles in Early Modern English Wills as Formulae', *JEH* 40 (1989), 19–27; Christine Litzenberger, *The English Reformation and the Laity* (Cambridge, 1997), pp. 168–78; Christopher Marsh, 'In the Name of God? Will-Making and Faith in Early Modern England', in Geoffrey H. Martin and Peter Spufford (eds), *The Records of the Nation* (Woodbridge, 1990), 215–49; Margaret Spufford, 'The Scribes of Villagers' Wills in the Sixteenth and Seventeenth Centuries and Their Influence', *Local Population Studies* 7 (1971), 28–43; Michael L. Zell, 'The Use of Religious Preambles as a Measure of Religious Belief in the Sixteenth Century', *Bulletin of the Institute of Historical Research* 50 (1977), 246–9.

[27] '*Qui non sine vitae periculo Religionem suam i.e. Reformatani Constantis Animo retenuit.*' Stephen Darby, *Chapters in the History of Cookham, Berkshire* (privately printed, 1909), pp. 178–9. I am grateful to Robin Darwall-Smith for discussing this with me.

[28] *Acts of the Privy Council*, vol. 1, pp. 97–8; *LP*, vol. 18, no. 241 (6); John Foxe, *Actes and monuments of matters most speciall in the church* (London, 1583), p. 1221; 'The Letters of Richard Scudamore to Sir Philip Hoby, September 1549–March 1555', ed. Susan Brigden, in *Camden Miscellany* 30 (CS, 4th series 39, 1990), 67–148, p. 119.

Exactly what Weldon believed in 1543 is not recorded, but when he wrote his will in 1567 he bequeathed his soul to the Holy Trinity:

> havinge a perfect truste and belieffe that my savior and redeemer Jhesus Chrsyte thoroughe the shedinge of his moste precious bloude hathe paied the full Rawnesom for my sinnes And for the sinnes of all those that stedfastely truste and beleve in hym And that I shall ryse again and be a partaker of the eaverlastinge lyffe provided for his ellecte.

He further directed that his burial be carried out 'with out any pompe or excesse at all', although he wished that 'myne executors shall procure a precher well learned in godes true and hoolie worde to preache a Sermonde at the tyme of my burialle'.[29] Given this reformist attitude, it is not surprising that three years earlier Bishop Jewel of Salisbury, when submitting his views on the Berkshire JPs to the Privy Council, had declared Weldon to be 'a furtherer' of the Gospel.[30]

No comment by Bishop Jewel exists for Norris, though the fiercely evangelical Edward Underhill stated that he considered Norris to have been 'always a rank papist'.[31] Underhill was prone to exaggeration, so it is unlikely that Norris was a papist in a strict sense outside of Mary's reign, but it is probable that he was always a religious conservative. Not only did he find favour at the hands of Queen Mary, but also from her Lord Chancellor, the arch-conservative Bishop of Winchester, Stephen Gardiner. Between 1553 and 1558 Norris sat in Parliament for Downton, Taunton and Bodmin, all seats in the episcopal patronage of Gardiner, whose funeral Norris was to attend as a mourner. It seems likely that this patronage was brokered by James Bassett, a devoted servant to Gardiner and Norris's colleague in Mary and Philip's Privy Chambers, as well as his friend.[32]

At first sight this story – a reformist Weldon promoted by Edward and Elizabeth and removed by Mary in contrast to a conservative Norris finding high influence under Mary – seems to lend support to the traditional models of Tudor government and society functioning along confessional lines. Yet it is not quite so simple. Although Norris was especially favoured by Mary, he had served as Gentleman Usher to her brother and continued to do so under her sister. This was an important post for the security of the Court, and one that placed him close to the

---

[29] NA PROB 11/50 fol. 30ᵛ.
[30] 'A Collection of Original Letters from the bishops to the Privy Council, 1564', ed. Mary Bateson, in *Camden Miscellany 9* (CS n.s. 53, 1895), p. 38.
[31] *Tudor Tracts*, p. 187.
[32] *House of Commons*, vol. 3, p. 20. Norris referred to Basset in correspondence with Basset's mother, Lady Lisle, *The Lisle Letters*, ed. Muriel Byrne (6 vols, Chicago, 1981), vol. 6, p. 19.

monarch daily. It is particularly noteworthy that no concerns were raised about this conservative at the heart of the Court by the Dukes of Somerset or Northumberland, both so conscious about security after it had been breached by Thomas Seymour; and that Elizabeth, far from dismissing him, seems to have valued his advice. Not only did he retain his post in the Chamber, but also his prestigious post of Usher of the Black Rod to the Order of the Garter.

Norris not only continued to be employed at Court by Edward and Elizabeth, but also remained a government agent in Berkshire. He had first been appointed a Justice of the Peace in 1538 and he continued to serve on this and other commissions throughout the reigns of Henry VIII and Edward VI. He was one of the commissioners to collect the third part of the Relief in Berkshire and for the town of New Windsor in 1550, and for furnishing the Berkshire markets with victuals in 1551. Norris also sat on the commission to assess church plate for the county and for New Windsor in 1553, an activity which we might expect him to have found distasteful.[33] Yet, not only was Norris prepared to serve his government in this way, but the increasingly reformist Edwardian regime found this conservative too useful an agent to discard from local government.

The same is true of Thomas Weldon. Under Edward VI he had found his career blossoming in central and local government. His presence on an occasion when one William Wycherley used a crystal to invoke a spirit 'at the commaundement of my lord protector' suggests that he was close to the Duke of Somerset,[34] yet the Earl of Warwick still considered him sufficiently trustworthy to organize the guard at Windsor Castle in the year following Somerset's fall, and to be a commissioner for the sequestration of Paget's property after his arrest in 1552.[35] Although Weldon found himself out of favour and out of the Household after Mary's accession, like Norris he was too useful a local agent for the government to lose. Not only did he continue to serve as a Justice of the Peace, but he did so on the panel of senior JPs known as the Quorum – unlike the favoured Norris. He also sat on the commission of Oyer and Terminer summoned in 1554, and in the same year the Privy Council entrusted him with the punishment of one Richard Bigges, who had spoken seditious words against the Queen. He may also have been the Mr Weldon who was appointed to wait on the Marques de les Navas at

[33] *LP*, vol. 13, no. 1115 (69); *Calendar of the Patent Rolls Preserved in the Public Record Office: Edward VI*, ed. Robert H. Brodie (6 vols, London, 1924–29), vol. 4, p. 142; vol. 5, pp. 351, 362, 413, 416.
[34] *Narrative of the Days of the Reformation*, ed. J. Nichols (CS o.s. 77, 1859), p. 333.
[35] *Acts of the Privy Council*, vol. 3, p. 137; vol. 4, p. 28.

Southampton in May 1554.[36] It has been suggested that the Marian regime continued to entrust such business to him in order to test his loyalty, which is possible; but if so, he passed the tests, and the government continued to make use of his loyal service.[37]

The careers of John Norris and Thomas Weldon demonstrate that although the Tudor monarchs did place religious sympathizers around themselves, they were not prepared to exclude talented, loyal and useful men from government. Thus Mary removed Weldon, a man who had come close to the stake in 1543, from the important post of Cofferer of the Household, but she still found a use for him in local government. Edward VI did not purge the Court in the same way, and although it was gradually packed with reformers it was rare for conservatives to be removed.[38] But Norris and Weldon were by no means exceptional in being used by unsympathetic regimes. Edward Underhill's quarrel with Norris came about when Underhill, a fervent gospeller, fulfilled his duties as a Gentleman Pensioner by protecting the Queen during Wyatt's rebellion. Conversely, the conservative Sir Anthony Browne remained one of Edward VI's most influential Gentlemen of the Privy Chamber until his death in 1548. Despite being so closely involved with Northumberland's regime, even William Cecil, like Weldon, continued to be used as a government agent by Mary.[39] Though religious sympathizers were favoured in government, there was still room for talented and useful men who held opposing doctrines. The history of mid-Tudor government cannot be written entirely along confessional lines.

Richard Ward's religious position is more ambiguous than that of Norris or Weldon. His will, written in 1577, a year before his death, contained no specifically traditional funeral arrangements, though he did distribute black gowns to his friends, and money to the poor of the parishes in which he held land. He bequeathed his soul 'unto Almighty god and to his holye company in heaven there to remaine in joye and blisse for ever and ever Amen', a preamble which contains hints, though no more than hints, of traditional religion.[40] In 1564 Bishop Jewel of Salisbury had considered that Ward was 'supposed no hinderer' to the

---

[36] CPR, Philip and Mary, vol. 1, pp. 17, 28; Acts of the Privy Council, vol. 5, pp. 28, 33.
[37] House of Commons, vol. 3, p. 571.
[38] Michael Riordan, 'The Court and the Promotion of Religious Change under Edward VI' (unpublished MSt thesis, Oxford, 1999).
[39] Conyers Read, Mr Secretary Cecil and Queen Elizabeth (London, 1955), pp. 102–16; M. Riordan, 'The Court and the Promotion of Religious Change', 15–16; Tudor Tracts, pp. 187–88.
[40] NA PROB 11/60 fol. 145ʳ. See Litzenberger, The English Reformation and the Laity, pp. 168–78 for a discussion of the classification of will preambles.

Gospel.[41] Yet this ambiguity need not be evidence that he was insincere in his religious beliefs. His funerary monument states: 'His pedigree was distinguished, and he truly feared Christ,/Moreover, his chief concern was to please God./For this reason he was loved by Christ, and Christ cherished him.'[42] Clearly this is not an objective assessment, but it suggests that his descendants did not regard his lack of confessional partisanship as a reason to doubt his piety. Ward is no different to much of the laity across England in the mid-sixteenth century. They had seen the foundations of traditional religion swept away, but had not become devotees of Reformed doctrines. Ward was not, apparently, yearning for a return to traditional religion, nor was he seeking further reform; there is no evidence for his having overtly adopted any dogmatic position.

Historians have found it difficult to fit men like Ward into their models. Neither the traditional picture of an enthusiastic Protestant Reformation, nor the revisionist model of a reluctant people accepting the reforms of an eager government can easily accommodate them. Faced with this difficulty many historians have described those who subjected religious motives to other considerations, particularly those amongst the elite, as *politiques*. The term *politique* originated in France in the 1560s, as a term of abuse by militant Catholics to describe those Catholics who preferred a degree of religious toleration and coexistence with the Huguenots to war.[43] In English historiography it has also been used as a derogatory term. Its starting point, the subjection of religious beliefs to political considerations, remains the same, but it has been used in such a way as to suggest that these men were prepared to adopt any confessional stance in order to gain or retain political power or even that they had no religious beliefs at all.

This conception of motives and behaviour is too simplistic. The leading courtier William Paulet, for example, has been described as one always careful to 'trim his sails to the prevailing wind' and 'who avoided the complications of politics'. This is based on his possibly apocryphal claim to be 'made of the plyable Willow, not of the stubborn Oak';[44] but this was probably meant to express his willingness to follow the policies of his monarchs rather than an attack on conscience as it can sound to

---

[41] 'Original Letters from the bishops', ed. Bateson, p. 38.
[42] 'Stemmate clarus erat, vere Christumque timebat,/Atque placere Deo maxima cura fuit./Hinc Christo dilectus erat, Christusque favebat.' Elias Ashmole, *The Antiquities of Berkshire* (3 vols, London, 1719), vol. 2, pp. 401–2.
[43] I am grateful to Luc Racaut for discussing this with me.
[44] *Dictionary of National Biography*, ed. Leslie Stephen and Sidney Lee (66 vols, London, 1885–1901), vol. 44, p. 93; Geoffrey Elton, *England under the Tudors* (London, 1974), p. 209. Paulet's claim, reported by an unnamed 'intimate friend', was recorded in *c*.1630; Robert Naunton, *Fragmenta Regalia*, ed. Edward Arber (Birmingham, 1870), p. 25.

modern ears. William Paget has been described as 'a natural *politique*' who acted on 'the simplest grounds of expediency' and whose 'attachment to the reformist cause was never more than tactical'. Yet it is possible to piece together what his biographer calls 'a mildly Protestant position', despite his vital service to Mary's papist regime.[45] But Paget, Paulet and Ward were not alone in subjecting religion to politics, for there was a little of the *politique* in everyone. Norris served Edward VI, and Weldon served Mary. Even Underhill, who held strong evangelical beliefs, took up arms to protect Mary from Wyatt's rebellion.[46] The fact that Norris and Weldon were allowed to serve unsympathetic regimes suggests that the governments, as well as their subjects, could subject religious motivations to political considerations. In sixteenth-century England it was impossible to separate politics and religion, for obedience to God and obedience to the monarch were both matters of conscience. Therefore, when it was necessary to serve a regime with a disagreeable religious policy, as most English people did at some stage in the mid-sixteenth century, it was not easy to balance religious beliefs with loyalty to the Crown.

If men of different confessional stances found themselves retained together by different mid-Tudor regimes then it was necessary for these men to work alongside each other. This is particularly true for Thomas Weldon and Richard Ward. From Weldon's appointment as First Master of the Household in 1540 until his exclusion from the Court in 1553, he and Ward were brought into regular contact by their duties. The role of the Masterships is obscure, but they seem to be a grander form of the Clerks of the Green Cloth, described in Elizabeth's reign as 'auditors of the Household'.[47] Weldon was therefore one of the financial officers to whom Ward was responsible. Their working relationship became closer when Weldon returned to the Court in 1558 as Cofferer, the chief executive financial officer of the Household. Ward, stepping down from the post, became the senior Clerk of the Green Cloth, in effect Weldon's deputy. They were also appointed together to various Household commissions, such as that to hear all pleas and offences committed within the verge of the Court in 1564 and that of Oyer and Terminer in 1566.[48] It is inconceivable that they were not working together on a daily basis.

---

[45] Samuel Gammon, *Statesman and Schemer: William, First Lord Paget* (Newton Abbot, 1973), pp. 118–20; Haigh, *English Reformations*, p. 169; David Starkey, *The Reign of Henry VIII* (London, 1985), p. 154.
[46] *Tudor Tracts*, pp. 186–91.
[47] Loades, *Tudor Court*, p. 61.
[48] *CPR, Elizabeth*, vol. 3, pp. 931, 2711.

Norris, an officer of the Chamber, would have had less contact with Weldon and Ward. As a Gentleman Usher he was responsible for guarding the door to the Privy Chamber and preparing residences for the arrival of the Court. He would therefore have had little business in the Counting House, but its officers would occasionally have had business with him. It is likely that the Masterships of the Household were created in order to give their holders greater standing when dealing with defaulting members of the Chamber,[49] and if this is correct then Norris must on occasion have needed to deal with Weldon, who was Head of the King's Side for 12 years. There were other occasions when their duties brought them together. On 24 December 1537 six Gentlemen Ushers, including Norris, and the Chief Clerk of the Kitchen, Thomas Weldon, received material from the Wardrobe, probably as part of the preparations for Christmas.[50] On such occasions it was necessary for the conservatives and the reformers to cooperate and work together to fulfil their duties.

This is true not only at Court, but also in Berkshire where the three men served together amongst the more important officials of local government. In February 1543 Ward and Weldon (shortly before his imprisonment) joined Norris as Justices of the Peace for Berkshire, and all three men were appointed collectors of the third part of the Relief for the county and New Windsor in 1550. They also sat on the Berkshire commission for assessing church plate in 1553, though Ward was left off the parallel commission for New Windsor. Weldon and Norris served on the commission of Oyer and Terminer issued for Berkshire in 1554, and Norris was commanded with Ward to attend the fair in Reading in July 1555 to ensure order and good behaviour. Both were Justices of the Peace in Berkshire in 1555 as well as sitting together as commissioners for the Loan in September 1557.[51] Weldon and Ward continued to serve together as Justices of the Peace in Berkshire throughout the 1560s.[52] In performing these duties it was necessary to cooperate with each other; there was no room for confessional conflict. This is particularly apparent in 1545 when Weldon and Norris were commanded to conduct 40 men from Berkshire to Dover, to join the army against France. It would have been a difficult journey had there been tension between the two men.[53]

---

[49] Loades, *Tudor Court*, p. 61.
[50] *LP*, vol. 13, no. 1191.
[51] *LP*, vol. 18, no. 226 (26); vol. 20, no. 622; *CPR, Edward VI*, vol. 5, pp. 351, 362, 413, 416; *CPR, Philip and Mary*, vol. 1, p. 28; *Acts of the Privy Council*, vol. 5, p. 163; *Calendar of State Papers, domestic series, of the reign of Mary I, 1553–1558*, ed. C.S. Knighton (London, 1998), pp. 160, 656.
[52] *CPR, Elizabeth*, vol. 2, p. 434; vol. 3, p. 110.
[53] *LP*, vol. 21, no. 643.

The three men held other offices in which cooperation was necessary. During the 1530s they had obtained the reversions to the many offices that Richard Ward's father Thomas had acquired in Windsor Castle. On Thomas's death in 1538, his offices of Keeper of the Outer Gate of the Castle and Keeper of the Armoury, Ordnance and Harness passed to Richard. Thomas Weldon was appointed Keeper of the Keys for the Upper Bailey and Keeper of the Butts, while John Norris, already Keeper of Folyjohn Park since 1536, gained the prestigious post of Comptroller of Works in the Castle.[54] In 1540 Richard Ward was appointed Bailiff of the Lordship of Bray and Cookham, a Crown manor, and in the following year Weldon was appointed steward, a post traditionally associated with the Norris family. It returned to that family on Weldon's death in 1567, when it was granted to William Norris, whose father John had been appointed woodward and warrener of the Lordship in 1545.[55]

These appointments were made because the three men were all landowners in Berkshire. All had acquired land in Cookham: Norris had inherited land in the manor in 1536, while Ward and Weldon, who already leased land there from the Crown, both bought land in the manor under Edward VI. Weldon also acquired the advowson to the parish church.[56] The three men held other lands in the vicinity. Norris had inherited the manor of Fifield, as Ward had Winkfield. Ward also owned Waltham St Lawrence, which is adjacent to White Waltham, where all three men owned land.[57] In 1530 Ward was granted land in Hurst, where Norris also held land, and he acquired more in 1540 after the dissolution of Abingdon Abbey. Like his colleagues, Thomas Weldon also continued to acquire land in Berkshire. He leased land formerly of Bisham Abbey from Sir Philip Hoby whose stepdaughter he had married, and in 1563 he bought the manor of Pangbourne.[58] These lands are all enclosed together in a small triangle based on the three points of Cookham, Reading and Windsor, making Ward, Weldon and Norris very close neighbours.

At times, like most sixteenth-century landowners, they were in dispute with their neighbours, but never with each other. In fact, there are

---

[54] *LP*, vol. 10, no. 1256 (30); vol. 12, no. 1150 (26); vol. 13, nos 190 (32), 453, 1280; vol. 15, no. 831 (31).

[55] *LP*, vol. 16, nos 305 (75), 1308 (3); vol. 20, no. 465 (30).

[56] *Victoria County History of Berkshire*, ed. William Page and Peter Ditchfield (4 vols, London, 1906–24), vol. 3, p. 128; *LP*, vol. 16, no. 503 (28); vol. 17, no. 1154 (12); *CPR, Edward VI*, vol. 1, pp. 404–5, vol. 2, pp. 423–5.

[57] *CPR, Elizabeth*, vol. 4, p. 2327; *LP*, vol. 13, no. 491 (17); *CPR Edward VI*, vol. 3, p. 424; *CPR, Philip and Mary*, vol. 3, p. 381.

[58] *Victoria County History of Berkshire*, vol. 3, pp. 248, 251–2; *LP*, vol. 21, no. 648 (10); *CPR, Edward VI*, vol. 5, p. 192; *CPR, Elizabeth*, vol. 2, p. 614.

indications that they were friends, or at least on friendly terms with one another. When Thomas Ward, Richard's father, made his will in 1538 he provided black gowns for Thomas and Edward Weldon to wear at his funeral, and made John Norris the supervisor of his executors.[59] Norris continued to be friendly towards Richard Ward, and they leased land in Gloucestershire together in 1552.[60]

There is not enough extant evidence to be sure of the exact relationships between John Norris, Richard Ward and Thomas Weldon, or to be certain of their attitudes to each other, but there is enough to suggest that it is too simplistic to assume that conservatives and reformers must necessarily always be in conflict, or that both should always have disapproved of the *politiques* whose religious beliefs were not so clearly defined. These three men were certainly not exceptional, and were on occasion drawn into conflict along confessional lines. It was differences in belief that prompted Underhill's quarrel with Norris; and Weldon had enemies amongst the conservatives at Court who used his evangelical beliefs as a means of imprisoning him in 1543. But their religious beliefs were only part of their motivations, and there were also political and social considerations underlying their negotiations with each other and with the government. Norris, Ward and Weldon cooperated at Court and in Berkshire, demonstrating that it was possible for the reformer, the conservative and the *politique* to live in peace and concord during the mid-sixteenth century.

This essay echoes Ethan Shagan's complaint against those historians who assume that 'the confessional lens is the only lens that matters',[61] and who therefore dismiss the *politiques* as time-servers and as insincere. In fact the *politiques* seem to be not the exception, but the rule. Cooperation, concord and perhaps even friendship could cut across confessional lines, and the adoption of a confessional identity did not necessarily exclude non-religious motivations. Political, social and cultural considerations could be equally important for the men and women of mid-Tudor England.

---

[59] NA PROB 11/27 fol. 169[r-v].
[60] CPR, *Philip and Mary*, vol. 3, p. 404.
[61] Shagan, *Popular Politics*, p. 6.

CHAPTER SIX

National Church, State Church and Universal Church: The Gallican Dilemma in Sixteenth-century France

Alain Tallon, trans. Luc Racaut

In the midst of the religious turmoil of the sixteenth century, the Gallican Church may seem to have played a pacifying role, even to have served as an intermediary between the conflicting confessions. While being hostile to Roman absolutism it remained faithful to the old religion, and could as a result have offered a thorough reform of the Church without the same theological and liturgical rifts that Lutheranism and above all Calvinism provoked. 'Gallicanism' – a word that was coined in the nineteenth century and is applied retrospectively to the realities of the *ancien régime*, not without some problems of definition[1] – would therefore have borne within it a vision of the Church that could have provided a meeting ground for the warring brothers of the sixteenth-century religious reforms. This vision of the Church is summarized in two central pronouncements made by the lawyer Pierre Pithou at the end of the sixteenth century:

> The first is that the Popes cannot command or ordain, either in general or in particular, anything that concerns temporal things in countries and lands under the obedience and sovereignty of the Most Christian King; and if they command or rule anything, only the clerics of the King's subjects are held to obedience by virtue of their status alone. The second is that if the Pope is recognized as sovereign in spiritual things, his absolute and infinite power has no currency within France, but it is bound and checked by the canons and the rules of the ancient councils of the Church recognized in this kingdom.[2]

The narrow legal character of this definition of the Gallican Liberties seems to place Gallicanism on a different planet from that of the bloody

---

[1] Alain Tallon, *Conscience nationale et sentiment religieux en France au XVIe siècle: Essai sur la vision gallicane du monde* (Paris, 2002).
[2] Pierre Pithou, *Les Libertez de l'Église Gallicane* (Paris, 1594), in *Traictez des droits et libertez de l'Église gallicane*, ed. Jacques Gillot (Paris, 1609), p. 251.

religious conflicts of the sixteenth century. This limited conception of pontifical power, as simple ministerial and not absolute power, does not seem enough to serve as a platform for reconciling Christians divided at least as much by the questions of justification and the Eucharist as by the question of the Roman primacy. But if the irenic character of Gallicanism is far from being obvious, one cannot deny the ability to dialogue with the Protestant world that the most rigorous defenders of the Liberties of the Gallican Church maintained throughout the century, from the Cardinal Jean Du Bellay to the historian Jacques-Auguste de Thou. This ability has mostly been highlighted by historians working on the beginning of the seventeenth century who sought to compare the various challenges to Roman absolutism with the Gallican movement.[3] The great conflict of 1606, which saw Paul V place an interdict on the Republic of Venice for having sought to limit ecclesiastical privileges, paved the way for the temporary unification of all opponents of Rome, Catholic and Protestant, throughout Europe. Venice and its champion Paolo Sarpi stirred the enthusiasm of the Gallican intellectuals. At the same time, these selfsame Gallicans were approving James I of England's defence of the divine right of kings and were not indifferent to his projects of religious reconciliation.[4] At that juncture the French Gallican movement seemed to unite all expressions of 'doctrinal antiromanism'[5] that transcended the confessional divisions against a common enemy: a pontifical absolutism that had failed to stay within the limits of the primacy set by the Gallicans for the Roman Church, but had turned into a *totatus* – to use the neologism coined by Paolo Sarpi in a letter to a Gallican correspondent.[6] It offered a precedent for going back to an old

---

[3]   It is not insignificant that these historians are all English-speaking and therefore more sensitive to a potential parallel between Gallicanism and Anglicanism – a term just as anachronistic as 'Gallicanism' but used by earlier historians to denote the Church of England from the reign of Elizabeth. William J. Bouwsma, 'Gallicanism and the Nature of Christendom', *Renaissance Studies in Honor of Hans Baron*, ed. Anthony Molho and John Tedeschi (Dekalb, IL, 1971), 809–30; Jonathan Powis, 'Gallican Liberties and the Politics of later Sixteenth-century France', *HJ* 26 (1983), 515–30; John H.M. Salmon, 'Gallicanism and Anglicanism in the Age of the Counter-Reformation', in his *Renaissance and Revolt: Essays in the Intellectual and Social History of Early Modern France* (Cambridge, 1987), 155–88.
[4]   William B. Patterson, *King James VI and I and the Reunion of Christendom* (Cambridge, 1987), esp. pp. 1–3.
[5]   The phrase is that of Silvio-Herman de Franceschi: 'Antiromanisme doctrinal, pouvoir pastoral et raison du prince: le prisme français (1606–1611)' (unpublished thesis, École des Chartes, 1999), pp. 191–204.
[6]   'Apostolicae sedis primatum, imo et principatum, nemo gnarus antiquitatis et historiae negavit. Hic, quem modo affectant, non est *primatus*, sed *totatus*, si liceat vocabulum effingere ex eo quod abrogato omni ordine totum omnino uni tribuit.' Paolo Sarpi, *Lettere ai Gallicani*, ed. Boris Ulianich (Wiesbaden, 1961), p. 134.

order that had been jeopardized by the pontifical pretensions, and where the independence of each national Church was the best guarantee of their unity and peaceful coexistence within the bosom of the universal Church.

This moment of confluence between quite different religious currents often serves as a field of observation for describing the irenic or simply moderating role that Gallicanism would have played at the time of the confessional rift. As such it appears as a kind of Catholic Anglicanism, focusing on national specificity, the role of the King in the Church and the conformity of its ecclesiological ideas with the early Church, when Rome exercised only a purely spiritual primacy.[7] This kinship with Anglicanism became even more pronounced for those amongst the Gallicans who did not hide their sympathy for a theology of justification by faith. Such was Arnaud Du Ferrier, a well thought of *parlementaire*, close to Michel de L'Hôpital, future ambassador to the Council of Trent and to Venice, and trusted advisor to Catherine de' Medici and later to Henri III. At the beginning of 1562 he wrote a *Mémoire* to Catherine de' Medici where he admitted that he shared 'this religion that is said to be new, although I myself think it is old and Apostolic, in that it teaches the free and whole justification through the death and passion of Jesus Christ alone'.[8] But this confession did not lead Du Ferrier officially to break with the Gallican Church to adhere to Calvinism. He evaded such a confessional clarification all his life. Even Pierre de L'Estoile could let himself be seduced by the English liturgy that he preferred to that of the French Reformed Church of Charenton, and by the doctrinal soundness of the preaching that he heard when he went to a sermon at the English embassy on 3 August 1609.[9] Coming from such a fierce Gallican, this avowed sympathy for some aspects of the Church of England came no doubt from their affinity with the reform of which he dreamt for the Gallican Church, which needed to purge itself of all sorts of abuses and superstitions without following the Calvinist model. Of course, Du Ferrier's adherence to justification by faith or de L'Estoile's sympathy for the English liturgy does not make them 'Anglican'. But they prove that, at the heart of the Gallican Church, there were spiritual movements close to what has been termed the Elizabethan compromise: a Calvinistic theology, the maintaining of traditional structures and ecclesiastical

---

[7] Bouwsma, 'Gallicanism and the Nature of Christendom'; Salmon, 'Gallicanism and Anglicanism'.

[8] BNF, Fr. 4.766, fol. 28ᵛ. On Du Ferrier, see A. Tallon, 'Diplomate et "politique", Arnaud Du Ferrier', in Thierry Wanegffelen (ed.), *De Michel de L'Hôpital à l'édit de Nantes: Politique et religion face aux Églises* (Clermont-Ferrand, 2002), 305–33.

[9] Pierre de L'Estoile, *Mémoires-journaux*, ed. Gustave Brunet et al. (12 vols, Paris, 1875–96), vol. 9, pp. 111–12.

hierarchy and liturgy. The royal government, if it had wanted to pursue a Gallican reform along these lines, would not have lacked support from the French elite, notably in the *parlement*.

Could this Gallican reform have been a *via media* between the two Reformations? It is necessary to distinguish between two kinds of possible intervention for appeasing the religious debate: the mediation between adversaries in order to set up the conditions necessary for a dialogue, without intervening directly, or the proposition of a precise programme on which the reconciliation could be based. In the first half of the sixteenth century, the French monarchy, driven by the political need to form a united front against Charles V, from the Pope to the Protestant German princes via the King of England, attempted to reconcile religious adversaries in order to resolve, or at least moderate, the differences that jeopardized the creation of such a coalition. This accounts for the invitation that was issued in 1534–35 to Melanchthon to come to Paris to talk to the doctors of the Faculty of Theology.[10] The strong reservations that this raised amongst the theologians show that the royal wish for mediation was not shared by the majority of the Gallican Church. The latter was divided between partisans of intransigence and advocates of moderation, without one or the other side renouncing for all that their common allegiance to Gallican exceptionalism. This is an important point because it proves that, as early as the 1530s, the Gallican defiance of Rome did not necessarily lead to sympathy for those who had seceded from the old religion nor, conversely, that concern for the repression of religious dissent automatically led the more intransigent Catholics to endorse the thesis of pontifical absolutism.

It is therefore improper to identify Gallicanism strictly with religious moderation, because both sides, intransigent and moderate, fell back on Gallican principles in the face of the new religious climate. The royal project of 1534–35 was characteristically Gallican in its religious appeasement: at the cost of recognizing a kind of primacy for the papacy that could even be limited to being nominal, each national Church would have had greater autonomy in terms of ecclesiastical organization, liturgy, even certain questions of theology for the boldest. Similarly, partisans of intransigence conceived of repression along purely national lines: it fell to the Faculty of Theology of Paris, the bishops and the *parlements* to pursue and chastise heresy. The dogmatic definition of this heresy could well have been left in theory to the general council that all

---

[10] On this, see Karl J. Seidel, *Frankreich und die deutschen Protestanten: Die Bemühungen um eine religiöse Konkordie und die französische Bündnispolitik in den Jahren 1534/35* (Münster, 1970).

claimed to wait for, but in fact the characterization and punishment of religious dissent fell to national jurisdiction, either ecclesiastical or lay. In this respect it is significant that French opponents of heresy were completely indifferent towards the new Roman Inquisition, reorganized in 1542. Even in 1557 when Henri II considered reforming the inquisitorial procedures in the kingdom, he set up a Gallican Inquisition, independent from the Roman congregation, the King and the Pope. This organization remained notwithstanding a dead letter.[11]

In keeping with the Gallican ecclesiology of communion between largely autonomous churches – reminiscent of the Greek Church – advocates of dialogue and its adversaries alike always restricted their projects to the national arena. This allowed for some, and above all the monarchy, to reconcile repression within the kingdom with toleration of foreign Protestants in the name of the autonomy of each Church. This national preference, however, was not altogether bereft of any ambitions for the rest of Christendom. For many subjects of Francis I and Henri II, it was obvious that France and its King would resolve the religious conflict by giving the example of a true reform of the Church that broke with Roman corruption without threatening the communion of national Churches. This feeling derived mainly from the analysis that the Gallican movement, for the most part, made of the religious crisis and its causes. According to this reading, the monstrous development of pontifical power and the moral corruption of the ecclesiastical order that followed were the true causes of the split. The Gallican Church, with its Liberties intact (that were not privileges but rights), offered more than any other Church the prospect of a return to the purity of ancient ways. This discourse re-emerged with every tense moment in the relationship between Rome and France. When the conflict between Henri II and Julius III put the kingdom on the verge of a break from Rome in 1551, Jean Du Tillet, the royal councillor most hostile to pontifical pretensions, asserted that:

> There cannot be a better outcome and more favourable to God and men than for our sovereign the King to be the instigator of a good Reformation of the ecclesiastical estate of his kingdom. Because there will follow a Reformation of the other estates that will assuage the wrath of the Maker, provoked by the sins of the irreligious, and the return to the fold of those who have taken pretext of the errors and scandals of the ministers of the Church mainly of Rome and been led astray, and lead the way for other monarchs and princes to imitate the said King in this part, which will lead to universal peace between Christians.[12]

---

11 A. Tallon, 'Inquisition romaine et monarchie française au XVIᵉ siècle', in Gabriel Audisio (ed.), *Inquisition et pouvoir* (Aix-en-Provence, 2002), 311–23.
12 BNF, Fr. 473, fol. 10.

Indeed, this arrogant confidence in the pacifying role of the French King was also nourished by the illusion that 'only Gaul is free of monsters', to reproduce the famous quote by Saint Jerome that was cited at leisure by the French. Convinced that the kingdom was always and would always remain devoid of heresy, the French elite underestimated the strength of religious dissidence within France itself or was convinced that repression would easily stem its flow.

From the mid-1550s onwards, such short-sightedness was no longer in order and the kingdom seemed to be the European country worst hit by heresy. Nevertheless, confidence in the defence of the Gallican Liberties as the best hope for reconciliation remained intact. As late as the 1580s, with Venice and Spain resisting the trespassing of lay jurisdiction by Rome, Arnaud Du Ferrier, Henri III's ambassador to the Republic, could write back to his master:

> the credit and authority of the Roman courtiers diminishes, so much so that if the ancient rights and freedoms of your Gallican Church were to be passed on to the other countries of Christendom, things could well go back to their first state and be governed according to the old councils of the Catholic Church and decrees of the Roman Church.[13]

A few months later, he added, again on the same subject of lay resistance: 'if we continue to keep good this course the rights and freedoms of your Church will be common to all Christendom and in this, sire, we can hope for the whole pacification of your kingdom'.[14] Even against the background of the religious split within France itself, some Gallicans continued to think that only problems of jurisdiction were involved: the restoration of the authority of the magistrates in the face of Rome and the respect of the old Liberties of the Church was a universal panacea.

This confidence was not always expressed with as much clarity; in part because, after the Conspiracy of Amboise in March 1560, the French elite attempted a policy of conciliation that encompassed not only specifically devotional and liturgical but also theological questions, even if they were careful to speak officially of mere modifications of ecclesiastical discipline. Different programmes were thought up in diverse, sometimes rival, circles but they shared characteristics with the French plans that were submitted to the Council of Trent in its third and final session.[15] In the elaboration of this programme of concord, the

---

[13] BNF, 500 Colbert 368, p. 164.

[14] Ibid., p. 194.

[15] A. Tallon, *La France et le concile de Trente (1518–1563)* (Rome, 1997), pp. 283 ff., 827 ff.

Cardinal of Lorraine always seems to have played a crucial role. It is unclear when Charles of Lorraine rallied to such a solution based on negotiation rather than the policy of pure and simple repression that marked the end of the reign of Henri II and that he pursued as the first minister of Francis II. The Conspiracy of Amboise, the Assembly of Fontainebleau, the death of the young King and the withdrawal of the Cardinal from the Court were milestones in the journey that led Lorraine to propose the confession of Augsburg as a possible meeting ground – not, it seems, as a permanent settlement – to the Reformed ministers during the Colloquy of Poissy in September 1561.[16] His failure led him to meet with Duke Christopher of Württemberg, old brother in arms of the Duke of Guise, and his Court theologian Johannes Brenz at Savern between 15 and 18 February 1562. During these talks, Lorraine made multiple concessions, which some have interpreted as being a mere red herring and others have seen as evidence of a clear adherence to Lutheranism, an attachment that would have been dissimulated for obvious reasons of political expediency.[17] Both hypotheses are to be rejected, however. Lorraine wanted above all to establish a dialogue, in the hope of convincing the Lutherans to come to the general council which was opening for the third time at Trent. Catherine de' Medici pressed Elizabeth to send English bishops to the council for the same reason: Lorraine did not want the French to be isolated in front of the curial party and he hoped that a Protestant presence would force the assembly towards reconciliation rather than condemnation. He gladly saw himself in the role of mediator that he already virtually occupied in being capable of talking to the Protestant theologians as well as to papal ambassadors.

But along which *via media* did Lorraine, in complete agreement with Catherine de' Medici, want to lead Christendom?[18] The various plans that were offered, from the Estates General of Orléans to the first Tridentine

---

[16] On the difficult question of Lorraine's real intentions, see Stuart Caroll, 'The Compromise of Charles Cardinal de Lorraine: New Evidence', *JEH* 54 (2003), 469–83; A. Tallon, 'Les Guise pionniers de l'œcuménisme?', in various (eds), *Homo religiosus: Autour de Jean Delumeau* (Paris, 1997), 361–7; Tallon, *La France et le concile de Trente*, pp. 308–15; Mario Turchetti, 'Une question mal posée: La *Confession d'Augsbourg*, le Cardinal de Lorraine et les moyenneurs au colloque de Poissy en 1561', *Zwingliana* 20 (1993), 53–101.

[17] The view that Lorraine was simply dissembling reproduces doubts that had been expressed by the Genevans, notably Theodore Beza. Jules Michelet, *Renaissance et Réforme* (Paris, 1982), pp. 532 ff. On the view that Lorraine actually adhered to the confession of Augsburg, which also has its origins in the sixteenth century, see Caroll, 'The Compromise of Charles Cardinal de Lorraine', p. 477 ff.

[18] On Lorraine and Catherine's agreement, see Tallon, *La France et le concile de Trente*, pp. 291, 349 ff.

debates in which the French took part from autumn 1562, shared many components:[19] a stern reform of the ecclesiastical abuses, massive introduction of the vernacular in the liturgy (notably in the singing of psalms in French), communion in both kinds, the struggle against 'superstition' in the cult of saints and in the veneration of images and relics. Doctrinal coyness can be explained no doubt by the embarrassing failure of Poissy, where the elaboration of a compromise on Christ's presence in the Eucharist proved impossible. The project's silence on theological aspects proper of the conflict also stemmed from its Erasmian[20] inspiration, which shied away from any clear theological pronouncements on the points in conflict. Lastly, for many, it was essential to re-establish communion, even at the cost of postponing the question of a lasting basis on which to maintain it. Autonomy of the Churches, dear to the Gallicans, should have eased the difficulties that remained.

The civil wars in France that erupted at the beginning of 1562 did not put an end to these projects but on the contrary rejuvenated them. Catherine de' Medici even cultivated for a time the hopes of constituting a European front to promote the Reformation of points of discipline, such as she conceived them, like communion in both kinds or liturgy in the vernacular, and to thus put an end to the confessional rift. Her best ally in this was the Emperor Ferdinand, who sought to obtain the same concessions from the Council of Trent and from the Pope with some success,[21] even if the reactions of the Protestant powers were more disappointing: Queen Elizabeth preferred to help the Prince of Condé in exchange for Le Havre, while the German princes remained deaf to the proposals of a French government that was warring with its Protestant subjects.[22] The closing session of the Council of Trent seemed to have

---

[19] See, for example, the project proposed by Lorraine to the German Lutherans in June 1561: Henry O. Evennett, *The Cardinal of Lorraine and the Council of Trent* (Cambridge, 1930), p. 485; the advice given to the Queen Mother in early 1562 by the moderate *parlementaires* Christophe de Harlay, Paul de Foix and Arnaud Du Ferrier: BNF, Fr. 4.766; Lorraine's propositions to the *conseil privé* in August 1562: Caroll, 'The Compromise of Charles Cardinal de Lorraine', pp. 473–4; the instruction given to Lanssac and to Lorraine when they left for Trent and the articles brought forward by the French to the legates in December 1562: Tallon, *La France et le concile de Trente*, pp. 827 ff, 842 ff.

[20] I am fully aware that this adjective's definition is elastic to the point of meaninglessness. But I do not believe that there is an alterative that can do justice to the partisans of a 'philosophy of Christ', devoid of 'superstition' but also free of the concern for a rational and strict definition of dogma that characterizes medieval scholasticism.

[21] Gustave Constant, *Concession à l'Allemagne de la communion sous les deux espèces: Étude sur les débuts de la Réforme catholique en Allemagne (1548–1621)* (Paris, 1923).

[22] For example, see Andreas Wirsching, 'Konfessionalisierung der Aussenpolitik: Die Kurpfalz und der Beginn der französischen Religionskrieg (1559–1562)', *Historisches Jahrbuch* 106 (1986), 333–60.

put a final stop to any potential openings. The moderate Gallicans missed the historic opportunity to reunite all Christians around a formula of compromise. The dogmatic intransigence of the institutional Churches, that the supposed rallying of the Cardinal of Lorraine to the Roman theses at Trent encouraged, was the main reason for this failure. The French monarchy's refusal to receive the canons of the council left some room to manoeuvre within the Gallican Church, but the irenic efforts to transcend the confessional rift could no longer hope to go beyond the confines of the national, even the local context by relying on the royal policy of pacification. Only the old Gallican religion was left standing, the last to conform to the Apostolic tradition according to its most zealous defenders, but it was caught in a vice between two new confessional inflexibilities. Such was the lesson that Etienne Pasquier drew from the failure of the Colloquy of Poissy:

> the assembly breaks; after its end, we had presently three different religions in this France: one that would swear by nothing but the name of Christ in its sermons; the other by the name of Jesus in its synagogues, and the third, us old Catholics who do not recognize anything else in our churches and base our faith on nothing but the name of Jesus Christ.[23]

Loyola and Calvin, and their heirs Lainez and Beza, the two adversaries that were face to face at Poissy, had succeeded in making the split irrevocable. In Pasquier's eyes, each side mutilated in its own way the true Christian religion, but the latter was jealously kept in the Gallican enclave, and always remained untamed.

This dichotomy, posited by Pasquier in a polemical attempt to equate Gallican conformity with true Christianity, has been reproduced in recent scholarship, even if in a different formulation.[24] It is not difficult indeed to see here a form of inverted apologetics against the old confessional historiography: the 'heroes' are the adogmatic Christians, whereas the 'villains' are both Rome and Geneva, united in imposing a confessional straitjacket on their followers and in preventing a return to unity. However laudable the ecumenical inspiration that underpins this vision of the confessional conflicts of the sixteenth century, it is nonetheless marked by the sin of anachronism. If the failure of the irenic plans of the Gallicans of the 1560s was due to confessional intransigence, it is necessary to understand the motivations that led the

---

[23] Etienne Pasquier, *Le catéchisme des jésuites*, ed. Claude Sutto (Sherbrooke, 1982), pp. 144–5.
[24] In, for example, T. Wanegffelen, *Une difficile fidélité: Catholiques malgré le concile en France XVIe–XVIIe siècles* (Paris, 1999), marked by a polemic against falling in line with Trent that is in fact quite naive.

former defenders of this *via media* to rally to such intransigence; to try to measure the continuities that may have existed between attitudes of religious moderation and confessional mobilization; and finally to avoid reducing the diversity of Tridentine Catholicism to a unanimity that only existed in the polemic of the Protestant adversary.

The Cardinal of Lorraine, the very same whose 'U-turn' at Trent is supposed to have provoked the failure of the moderates, did not betray the programme that he had set himself: many of the Tridentine decrees on the training of the clergy, on the re-establishment of episcopal power (notably against chapters and regulars), on preaching and catechism, on decency of worship, on struggle against superstition, met the demands formulated in the various Gallican programmes between 1560 and 1562. Regarding the disciplinary concessions, such as communion in both kinds or the introduction of the vernacular in the liturgy, the council refused to make a pronouncement; this disappointed the French and the Imperials but left these options open. In any case, the Pope's concession allowing German Catholics to take communion in both kinds showed very quickly that it had no pacifying influence. This point was even conceded by the Gallicans who remained faithful to the boldest forms of irenicism at the beginning of the 1560s, like Arnaud Du Ferrier. As early as 1565, he wrote to Charles IX: 'Sire, the troubles that arose in Istria because of religion that I reported in my last letters have become worse, despite the fact that communion in both kinds and the marriage of priests were conceded to them.'[25] Even if Trent failed to satisfy all the aspirations of the Gallican reformers, the conciliar decrees were not only an expression of curial intransigence – something to be nuanced considering that it was Cardinal Morone, former prisoner of the Inquisition under Paul IV, who was closing the council – but were also the result of a compromise that took into account the French hopes.

If we relinquish the stark dichotomy between Gallican tradition and the spirit of Trent, the failure of the projects of reconciliation of the early 1560s takes on a whole new meaning. It is no longer the lacklustre victory of confessional fanaticism over the softness of the 'third way', but the internal elucidation of tensions inherent in the Gallican Church. And it did not take place independently from the political and religious evolutions that marked the whole of Europe, from the hardening of confessional identities to the domination of Philip II's new monarchy. But if this European backdrop played a considerable role, the specificity of the Gallican Church was without doubt even more important. The tensions that ran through it in the first half of the sixteenth century,

---

[25] BNF, Fr. 10.735, fol. 63.

largely underestimated by the monarchy, and recently by historians, interfered with the confessional debate and ended up determining it to a large extent. These tensions stemmed from the increasing influence of royal power over the Church of France: the Church resented this as keenly as pontifical absolutism but could not complain about it with the same force. The Concordat of 1516 did call up a violent opposition that was brutally repressed by Francis I. The strong monarchy of the knight King and his son prevented unrest from being voiced, but as soon as royal power was weakened by the death of Henri II, denunciations of the Concordat and its main disposition – the nomination of major benefices by the King – picked up again. The clergy were not the only ones to make the connection between the religious troubles and the violation of the Liberties of the Church by the temporal powers. Pierre de Ronsard, a Court poet who would not lightly criticize his masters, dared nonetheless, in the *Discours des misères de ce temps*, to lament the civil wars and the progress of heresy:

> You, princes and kings, the fault that you have committed
> For which all the Church now suffers,
> Although in your time you did not know
> Or feel the misfortune that has befallen us.
> The ease with which you sold the offices
> That gave to the great the vacant benefices,
> Who filled the Church of God with the unlearned,
> Who filled the courts with private knaves,
> Is the cause of this evil.[26]

The parallel between the venality of the offices and the royal nomination to the major benefices was common, because it tarred the enforcement of the Concordat with the brush of simony. So the monarchy was not only an accomplice of the clerics' worst abuses, but also responsible for them, using them to its advantage instead of reforming them. So the debate around the Reformation of the Church takes on a new meaning. Those who wished for an even stricter royal wardenship of the clergy in order to restore its dignity readily argued that since at least 1516, the monarchy had had all the means to fulfil these wishes but that it had chosen instead to deepen the moral crisis of the first estate of the kingdom. It is arguable that the King of France, even after 1516, did not have full power over the Church and that the Protestant princes or Henry VIII could take measures that were unthinkable in the context of the French Concordat.[27] But not all contemporaries saw things in this way: in their estimation, the Concordat

---

[26] Pierre de Ronsard, *Œuvres complètes* (2 vols, Paris, 1994), vol. 2, pp. 1028–9.
[27] Robert J. Knecht, 'The Concordat of 1516: A Re-assessment', *University of Birmimgham Historical Journal* 9 (1963), 16–32; also in Henry J. Cohn (ed.), *Government in Reformation Europe 1520–1560* (London, 1971), 91–112.

had gone too far and conferred excessive powers on the King, placing him above a Church of which he was only a member. At the Colloquy of Poissy, although he was fully committed to the policy of concord which he perhaps even initiated himself, the Cardinal of Lorraine nonetheless reminded the King of the limitation of his power to intervene in religious matters. In his speech of 16 September 1561, he asserted the obedience of the clergy to the King whose power was subordinate to God, but he added: 'Nevertheless you should remember, Sire, that you are not only minister of God and our Lord Jesus Christ, but also of his Church, which you nourish and keep; you are her son and not her lord, member and not chief.'[28] Each royal intervention evoked amongst the French clergy, even its most moderate members, unease at seeing the King become the judge of properly religious questions. This misgiving went from strength to strength until the time of the League and remained strong until the beginning of the seventeenth century, nourished by the quarrel surrounding the place of the Church in the state, or the state in the Church.

Gallican resentment towards the monarchy, nourished first by the perceived abuse of power that royal nominations represented, turned into real concern, especially when the Protestants did not hide their intentions to use the Crown's attempts at conciliation to rally the Gallican Church to their cause. The Gallican third way was in their eyes more of a stepping stone or short cut to the truth of the Gospel. These hopes survived the disappointments of the 1560s and when, after the third religious war, the government seemed to be more favourable to the Reformed, they once more dreamt of a massive conversion of the Gallican Church. When the question of the marriage between Queen Elizabeth and the Duke of Anjou arose, the *vidame* of Chartres wrote to the marshal Francis de Montmorency, figurehead of the moderate party, to outline the future. He foresaw an alliance with England; help given to the Prince of Orange and to the Swiss and German Protestants; and an alliance with the Turk that would allow France to take Flanders and place the Duke of Anjou at its head, and to recapture Milan and Naples in order to give them to the Duke of Alençon. Victory against Spain would also be the victory of the Gallican Reformation:

> Then the Gallican Church will be free from the errors of the Roman Church, as it has been numerous times in the past; a general council could then be called and the errors that were introduced by the ambition and avarice of the Roman Church will no longer be favoured and confirmed by practice and corruption; and an order and policy of religion and unity of doctrine will be introduced within

---

[28] *Collection des procès-verbaux des assemblées générales du Clergé de France, depuis l'année 1560 jusqu'à présent*, ed. Antoine Duranthon (8 vols, Paris, 1767), vol. 1, part 2, p. 16.

France, Germany and England, that all the other provinces of Christendom will be forced to embrace and the quarrels between subjects and their prince, that are used by Satan to destroy Christendom, and to favour the Turk while the Christian princes are distracted by the defence of the papal superstitions and maintain his [the Pope] power, will end.[29]

If the St Bartholomew's day massacre crushed for many years the hopes of a conversion of the French monarchy, Henri IV's accession gave them new currency. Many expected the Protestant King of a Catholic kingdom to be the architect of a reconciliation in favour of the Reformed camp. In the *Advis sur la nécessité du concile et sur la forme de le rendre légitime et libre pour l'union chrestienne*, published in 1591, Pierre de La Primaudaye asked for the calling of a national council, presided over by the King. If the council re-established religious unity within France, its example would be followed in all Christendom.[30] There was little consensus amongst the Reformed over the hypothetical third way or Gallican *via media*: many saw it as a subterfuge intended to lead them back to Catholicism via tortuous paths; others thought on the contrary that it would clear the way for the Reformation; but all agreed to deny it any future as a lasting solution to the religious conflict.

The prospect of a victory for the Reformation thanks to the royal attempts at concord cleverly borrowed familiar themes from the royal mystique: the King of France, temporal vicar of the Prince of Peace, would punish the vices of his clergy and take leadership of Christendom in order to free Constantinople and the Holy Land, where he would surrender his power to Christ.[31] The Protestant interpretation of these prophecies, that had become a commonplace of monarchical ideology, had been in circulation at least since Francis I, but became more widespread at the beginning of the 1560s, contemporary with the royal policy of concord. It also skilfully played on the old Gallican precept of the authority of the King in matters of ecclesiastical polity, extending it to cover the restoration of the purity of faith. Charles Du Moulin encouraged the King to follow 'the examples of the good kings of Judea Hezekiah and Josiah, who restored religion under the Word of God, toppling and banishing the idols and their idolaters, because there are no other ways to avoid the wrath of God that is imminent (Ps. II). And to say that this does not befit the kings and princes is to deny that their

---

[29] Catherine de' Medici, *Lettres de Catherine de Médicis*, ed. Hector de La Ferrière (10 vols, Paris, 1891), vol. 4, pp. 8–9.

[30] A. Tallon, 'La Fin d'un instrument de paix: Le concile œcuménique' in Paul Mironneau and Isabelle Pébay-Clottes (eds), *Paix des armes, paix des âmes* (Paris, 2000), p. 25.

[31] Alexander Y. Haran, *Le Lys et le globe: Messianisme dynastique et rêve impérial en France aux XVIe et XVIIe siècles* (Paris, 2000), esp. chs 3–4.

authority and power devolves from God, and it is a crime of *lèse-majesté* royal and divine; moreover such calumny is principally offensive against God'.[32]

These calls for the intervention of the Sovereign increased in turn the Gallican suspicion towards the projects of royal mediation. Because if the Catholic partisans of a policy of concord, like the Cardinal of Lorraine, were willing to consider a Reformation of abuses, they were not prepared to allow it to go as far as Protestantism and a break from Rome. This point of view was more widely shared than is commonly thought, even if some historians have highlighted the unshakable loyalty of the *politiques* to Rome during the great debates at the end of the century.[33] The Gallican *parlementaires* condemned papal interference in the internal affairs of the kingdom, but they were equally unwilling to tolerate a schism. They upheld the right and even the duty of the King to re-establish purity of conduct, even faith, within the Gallican Church, but on the condition that he always recognized himself as an obedient son of this Church. At the beginning of 1562, Paul de Foix offered his advice on religious matters to Catherine de' Medici along these terms. He subordinated the political to the religious order, with Machiavelli implicitly in his sights when he spoke of the ancient Romans 'who only held religion as means to advance their policy. And we on the contrary think that the republic should serve religion instead'.[34] The very duty of the King to serve the religious order and to keep his subjects in the true faith forced him to intervene in the crisis that hit the Church. Paul de Foix approved the calling of a Colloquy of theologians under the presidency of the Sovereign, even if such a meeting seemed to have become impossible. In order to keep the kingdom from the worst evil – atheism – the King even had to envisage tolerating the right of dissidents to assemble. If Paul de Foix was very bold in his propositions, he nonetheless always subordinated royal intervention to the duty to preserve an intangible patrimony, which escaped the control of the Sovereign. He implicitly admitted the existence of a limit to royal

---

[32] Charles Du Moulin, *Traicte de l'origine, progres et excellence du royaume et monarchie des François, et coronne de Fran[c]e, oeuvre monstrant que toutes monarchies, empires, royaumes et seigneuries sont periz et ruinez par l'idolatrie* (Paris, 1561), fols 30^v–31.

[33] Powis, 'Gallican Liberties'. Much less convincingly, Nancy L. Roelker argues that the *parlement* gave priority to the struggle against heresy until the early 1560s, and then, frightened by the Roman offensive after Trent, attempted to confine the forces favourable to pontifical absolutism: *One King, One Faith: The Parlement of Paris and the Religious Reformation of the Sixteenth Century* (Berkeley, CA, 1996). For a more nuanced rendering of parliamentary Gallicanism, see Jotham Parsons, 'Church and Magistrate in Early Modern France: Politics, Ideology and the Gallican Liberties, 1550–1615' (unpublished PhD thesis, Johns Hopkins, 1997).

[34] BNF, Fr. 4766, fols 29–33.

action, even if he pushed its limits much further than other moderate Gallicans, notably within the clergy.

Although in reality Reformed theology also limited magisterial intervention in the Church's affairs, even the most moderate French Catholics were convinced that Protestantism gave all powers, including dogmatic, to the Sovereign alone, so transforming the Church to a simple organ of the state and making faith a question of politics. They derived this conviction from an English example they totally rejected, with a few exceptions that have attracted an inordinate amount of attention from the historiography. Indeed, the evolution of the English Church represented a bad example for the whole moderate fringe of Gallicanism. This rejection can be explained partly by an Anglophobia that remained very strong, even stronger perhaps than the Hispanophobia that developed in the second half of the century. A throwback from the Hundred Years War, the vision of the English as cruel and power-mad was revived by the eccentricities of Henry VIII. This monarch was the object of a veritable black legend throughout Catholic Europe,[35] and if Francis I officially tried to humour this indispensable ally against Charles V, France was not the last to denounce the Henrician Reformation. The horror that Henry VIII's policy evoked mainly derived from the perception in the eyes of the French that it turned a national Church into a state Church. Charles de Marillac, ambassador in England, painted such a picture of the situation in England to the constable de Montmorency; 'Evil has reached such a height here that all examples of misfortune now strike England'; Henry VIII's bishops submitted themselves willingly to his every whim:

> In order to be found loyal and good ministers, when they write about true obedience, they allow their King to interpret divine law, to add, subtract and do more than the Apostles or their vicars and successors ever dared to undertake; so much so that through their good arguments, everything that he says should be held as a dictate from God or oracle of his prophets, and they want to render to him not only the obedience that is due to a King, obedience and service that bind them on earth, but make him into a true idol to be worshipped.

As a tyrant, Henry pillaged the goods of the Church and lived in perpetual defiance of all and sundry. 'Every day new bloody edicts are issued so that one man even taking a thousand precautions cannot be safe; and at the slightest occasion may be lost.'[36]

---

[35] See for the Spanish case, Peter Marshall, 'The Other Black Legend: The Henrician Reformation and the Spanish People', *EHR* 116 (2001), 31–49.

[36] *Correspondance politique de MM. de Castillon et de Marillac, ambassadeurs de France en Angleterre 1537–1542*, ed. Jean Kaulek (Paris, 1885), pp. 211–13.

What is striking in the development of the black legend of Henry VIII is that it not only concerned the intransigent circles. Marillac was a diplomat who wished above all to constitute a great alliance against the Emperor and he had no qualms of conscience when faced with the prospect of an alliance with the Protestants or the Turks. Rewarded for his services with the bishopric of Vannes, and then the archbishopric of Vienne, he was one of the stouter defenders of the policy of concord during the Assembly of Fontainebleau. In a celebrated speech given there, he called for the Reformation of the ecclesiastical abuses and a national council. His pessimistic vision of the English Church did not stem from doctrinal intransigence, but from a rejection of tyranny, and the refusal to endorse the total usurpation of ecclesiastical affairs by temporal power. For the moderate Gallicans the English example was revealing of the ineluctable degeneration of a state Church into arbitrariness and chaos. This counter-example stood as a warning against the development of events in France itself. The monarchy had already violated the Liberties of the Church in obtaining from the Pope the nomination to the major benefices. It must not be allowed to go any further and usurp new powers, lest France be plunged in the same tyranny as England.

This fear was expressed during the Gallican crisis of 1551. Because of the alliance between Pope Julius III and the Emperor against Henri II's clients the Farnese, the King threatened to break all contacts with Rome and to establish a patriarchate in France. The Gallican Church had not been so close to schism since the distant time of Louis XII and Julius II. The circles that were most hostile to pontifical absolutism, however, did not seem to be pleased. Cardinal Jean Du Bellay had been the staunchest defender of the Gallican Liberties and of royal power in the face of the Pope throughout the reign of Francis I, and was one of the architects of dialogue with the German Protestants.[37] Sent to Rome at the beginning of the reign of Henri II, he showed himself to be a merciless critique of pontifical abuses, all the while rejecting all proposals of reform emanating from the Pope. One could have expected a stauncher support for Henri II in his struggle against the Pope from the caustic patron of Rabelais. On the contrary, in August 1551, at the heart of the crisis, the Cardinal moved away from the Court 'so that he cannot be witness to the events that will unfold', and all the while blaming Julius III for the conflict, he shared his concerns: 'Even if the intention of the King was not to leave the obedience of the Church, but only Julio its minister, I can see clearly what will unfold in the end. The beginning in England was slow, even less rash than what is here proposed, but the end was such

---

[37] See Alexandra Kess's essay in this volume.

that can be found today.'[38] The comparison between the English and the Gallican situation, far from encouraging a rapprochement, on the contrary inspired fear of an evolution on the English model.

This wholesale rejection of the English experience was manifested through fundamental differences between the two national churches: for the Gallicans, the monarchy had to remain within the bounds of common law and Catholic tradition. The Liberties of the Church were indeed threatened by pontifical absolutism, but it was inadmissible to fight it by surrendering blindly to royal absolutism. If opposition to the second form of absolutism was more discreet, it was nonetheless resolute. The Gallican *via media* had to take it into account: if it relied on a certain autonomy of the national Churches to put an end to the religious crisis, it was unthinkable that this autonomy should be at the cost of allowing the temporal powers to conflate Church and state. This idea shone through clearly in the defence of the jurisdiction of the great French abbeys in all Christendom that Paul de Foix, who was ambassador in Rome, submitted to Pope Gregory XIII. The Pope, like the King of Spain, wished to create independent congregations in Italy and in the Iberian Peninsula. For Paul de Foix, Gregory XIII ran the risk of creating a dangerous precedent: the princes would 'put an end at last to the spiritual state which limits their temporal state and bring about a situation where there will be as many spiritual leaders as there are temporal kingdoms'. The Pope had to remind 'the princes and people that if they were distinct and separate in the temporal sphere, they were conjoined united and common in the spiritual sphere, namely in Jesus Christ, and in the bosom of our mother the Holy Church, and in the Christian and Catholic Faith, in their obedience to the Holy Apostolic See'. Even in times of temporal conflicts, this spiritual union remained.[39] Beyond the usual arguments, Paul de Foix gave a clear example of a Gallican conception that was at the opposite of the 'anti-universalism' that is usually attributed to him.[40] It was necessary to preserve the 'amiable concert of the Church', according to the quaint formula of a convinced Gallican *parlementaire*, Louis Servin.[41] Each national Church played its instrument and read from its own songsheet, but it had to keep time with the orchestra. This harmony would be broken if the national Churches, transformed into state Churches, introduced drastic political differences in the spiritual domain.

---

[38] Jean Du Bellay, letter of 18 August 1551, *Revue de la Renaissance* 4 (1903), pp. 176–7.
[39] BNF, Fr. 16.044, fol. 45.
[40] See the vision of Gallicanism in Donald R. Kelley, *History, Law and the Human Sciences: Medieval and Renaissance Perspectives* (London, 1984), esp. pp. 135, 270–72.
[41] Cited in Jacques-Auguste de Thou, *Histoire universelle* (16 vols, London, 1734), vol. 14, p. 122.

But for the Gallicans the unity of the Church was guaranteed by Rome; even if the ambitions of pontifical power had to be contained because they were at the origin of the crisis. In 1594, Antoine Hotman had this paradoxical idea: the more freedom a Church managed to keep, the more Rome was assured of its obedience:

> A regulated submission is the more secure, and the firmer the limits and guards of the superior power are, the less likely they are to be shaken. France is a prime example, as it always remained firm in its reverence towards the holy see of Rome, when many other nations, who had subjected themselves to a blind obedience, as if ashamed of their abject condition, have turned rebellious and have shaken off the yoke of obedience through a servile treachery. It is always better to deal with those who are honest, free and in possession of their rights than with serfs and slaves, who only do they duty as long as strength and fear constrain them.[42]

The Gallican Liberty was for Hotman a precious gift for the whole of Christendom, since it provided an opportunity for the Churches that had been duped through a 'servile treachery' to take once more an honourable place in the bosom of the universal Church.

The various Gallican projects of concord offered a great diversity, from an agreement with the Protestants on essential points of dogma to simple measures of disciplinary reforms for the clergy. These projects emanated from competing institutions: the monarchy, certain *parlementaires*, members of the clergy and so on. All, however, were secure in the knowledge that the ancient order of the Church, the only guarantor of concord, resided in the respect of the Liberties of the national Churches, by the Pope as well as by temporal power, and in the continuation of a communion between these national Churches through the recognition of the spiritual primacy of the Pontiff. This conviction anchored Gallicanism firmly within a forward-looking Catholic Church, representing one of its incarnations and mirroring in its own way its great developments, at once preventing it from evolving towards the Reformation, but also from transforming itself into a possible *via media*, despite the hopes of the partisans of concord. The discourse of the latter should not be transformed anachronistically into an ecumenical project; nor did it constitute a form of ecclesiological Nicodemism, masking a de facto adherence to the Reformation; lastly it was not the mark of a critical Catholicism that refused all forms of dogmatic strait-jacketing. It should be interpreted as nothing more than what it pretended to be: a discourse of loyalty to tradition, which had its rightful place in the Roman Church, and even, over the years, in the Tridentine Church.

---

[42] Antoine Hotman, *Traicté des droicts Ecclesiastiques, privilèges et Libertez de l'Église Gallicane*, in *Traictez des droits et libertez*, ed. Gillot, p. 307.

CHAPTER SEVEN

The Battle for Indifference in Elizabethan England

Ethan H. Shagan

No other Church in the Reformation was quite so successful at claiming the mantle of 'moderation' as the Church of England. The assertion of a *via media* by English theologians and politicians took many forms in the sixteenth century; in the 1560s, for instance, the Church of England claimed a predestinarian middle way between Catholic and Anabaptist free-willers, while in the 1590s it claimed a legal middle way between the Spanish Inquisition and the Genevan consistory.[1] Yet there was one claim to moderation that shaped the Church of England's identity from the break with Rome all the way through the seventeenth century: the requirement of conformity and obedience to the magistrate in so-called 'things indifferent'. The Protestant rejection of Catholic traditions had left ambiguous a whole category of religious practices, 'things indifferent' or *adiaphora* in Greek, that were neither positively commanded nor absolutely forbidden by Scripture. In these matters, most notably Church ceremonies, the Church of England maintained a strict Erastian position: if something was neither commanded nor forbidden by God, it was left to the discretion of properly constituted civil authorities according to the laws of the realm. Hence if parliament and the monarch demanded conformity to the ceremonies of the *Book of Common Prayer*, then English subjects were morally and legally bound to obey, regardless of their own beliefs. This position has long been seen as a genuinely moderating influence in the Reformation, despite its emphasis on 'obedience', because it forced religion to conform to the law rather than the reverse. Or, to put it slightly differently, the Church of England's emphasis on law rather than dogma allowed for the possibility of civil order without spiritual unanimity in the aftermath of a particularly messy Reformation.[2]

---

[1] See my forthcoming monograph on the varied polemical uses of the trope of moderation and the *via media* in English history.

[2] Historians who see adiaphorism as a genuinely moderate force in the Church of England include G.W. Bernard, 'The Church of England, *c.*1529–1642', *History* 75 (1990), 183–206; T.F. Mayer, *Thomas Starkey and the Commonweal* (Cambridge, 1989); Bernard J. Verkamp, *The Indifferent Mean: Adiaphorism in the English Reformation to 1554* (Athens, OH, 1977); Peter White, *Predestination, Policy and Polemic: Conflict and*

In the centuries since Queen Elizabeth I's reign it has been virtually unquestioned that the Church of England's official view of *adiaphora* was an essentially moderate and judicious response to the basic Protestant dilemma of reconciling the spiritual authority of the Word with the institutional authority of the Church. This essay is intended to challenge this assurance, not by arguing that there was anything intrinsically immoderate about the Church of England's position, but rather by arguing that 'moderation' very much depended upon one's point of view. Traditionally, historians divided Elizabethan Protestants into 'Anglicans' who accepted the requirement of obedience in *adiaphora*, and 'puritans' who rejected it. More recently, Peter Lake has shown that puritans were themselves divided on this subject, with 'moderate puritans' arguing that obedience was indeed due to the government on ceremonial issues, even if the government should be pushed to reform its ceremonies along more godly lines. In this essay, then, I want to push further along the lines suggested by Lake, examining a broad range of manuscripts which accepted the category of 'things indifferent' as a crucial one but interpreted that category and its requirements in very different ways. In the process, I hope to show that there was in fact a much wider debate than historians have recognized over what exactly indifference was and what effects it should have on the ecclesiastical polity.[3]

This essay will suggest that many Elizabethans, both puritan and non-puritan, believed that things indifferent should *not* be left to the magistrate but rather, in various ways and with various provisos, should be left to the discretion of individual Christians, allowing a remarkable degree of latitude for conscientious belief and practice. In some sense, of course, these arguments for variation and autonomy within the Church were quite 'radical', calling to mind Anabaptist arguments for toleration and questioning the whole premise of 'uniformity' on which the confessional Churches of the later Reformation were built. Yet on the other hand, they were also remarkably 'moderate' in their insistence that the

---

Consensus in the English Church from the Reformation to the Civil War (Cambridge, 1992). Among divinity scholars, and especially the vast literature on Richard Hooker, this view is ubiquitous; for a recent, extreme version, see I.M. MacKenzie, *God's Order and Natural Law* (Aldershot, 2002). Among literature scholars, see Daniel Doerksen, *Conforming to the Word: Herbert, Donne, and the English Church before Laud* (Lewisburg, PA, 1997); Christopher Hodgkins, *Authority, Church, and Society in George Herbert* (Columbia, MO, 1993). On the European context, see Gary Remer, *Humanism and the Rhetoric of Toleration* (University Park, PA, 1996).

[3] This analysis is of course not exhaustive. I have focused on the 1580s and 1590s because they appear to be particularly fertile decades for adiaphorist thought, and on manuscript evidence because it is relatively unknown. But there is also much still to be learned about the battles for indifference in the 1560s and 1570s.

Church could be comprehensive without losing its coherence. By taking these broader opinions into account, I want to suggest that our normative vision of 'moderation' in the Reformation has unwittingly accepted an 'Anglican' ideal that was in fact intended to suppress other, equally valid versions of the *via media* that were available in Elizabethan England.

I

I want to begin by discussing two well-known views of *adiaphora* that were described by their proponents (and have been seen by historians) as partaking of 'moderation'. The first of these views, traditionally understood as the default 'Anglican' position but now more cautiously described as ideological 'conformity', is perhaps most classically distilled in the writings of John Whitgift.[4] Despite the arguments of puritans against human invention in Christian ceremonies, Whitgift believed unequivocally that in 'things indifferent' change over time was not only acceptable but positively beneficial as the outward circumstances of the Church evolved. He utterly rejected the idea that 'nothing is to be tolerated in the Church of Christ, touching either doctrine, order, ceremonies, discipline, or government, except it be expressed in the Word of God'. This constituted illogical reasoning from lack of evidence, not unlike the Anabaptists' claim that because there was no mention of infant baptism in the Scriptures it was necessarily forbidden. On the other side, moreover, Whitgift argued that when analysing the Bible's requirements one must interpret the text very narrowly. The mere fact that Christ and the Apostles did things a certain way did not constitute a perpetual obligation for the Church, since what suited the Church as a persecuted community might not suit it as a settled ecclesiastical polity. As Whitgift put it, there was a world of difference between things 'commanded in the Word of God' and things merely 'expressed in the Word of God'. Christ fasted 40 days, for instance, but only papists believed that this required human beings to do so.[5]

---

[4]   The term 'conformity' in this sense refers not merely to bare attendance at the Church of England but to the emergent intellectual tradition which saw such attendance as the core of religious identity and political loyalty: see Lori Ann Ferrell, *Government by Polemic: James I, the King's Preachers, and the Rhetorics of Conformity, 1603–1625* (Stanford, 1998); Peter Lake, *Anglicans and Puritans?* (London, 1988); Anthony Milton, *Catholic and Reformed: The Roman and Protestant Churches in English Protestant Thought, 1600–1640* (Cambridge, 1995); Nicholas Tyacke, *Anti-Calvinists: The Rise of English Arminianism, c.1590–1640* (Oxford, 1987).
[5]   *The Works of John Whitgift*, ed. John Ayre (3 vols, Parker Society, Cambridge, 1851–3), vol. 1, pp. 175–80.

Indeed, Whitgift argued that the external, ceremonial actions of Christians were quite specifically and intentionally *not* specified by Scripture; that was the essence of Christian liberty. To accept that anything not specifically endorsed by Scripture was forbidden would be 'a great servitude and bondage to the conscience' and would 'utterly overthrow that part of Christian liberty which consisteth in the free use of indifferent things, neither commanded nor forbidden in the Word of God'.[6] Whitgift's ideal of Christian liberty, however, did not extend to anarchy within the Church, and his notion of 'free use of indifferent things' was carefully circumscribed. When St Paul wrote that ceremonies should be framed so as not to give offence to weaker brethren, for instance, that did not mean that 'the Church should so depend upon one or two men's liking or misliking that she should be compelled to alter the same so oft as any should therewith be offended'. If this were the case, then there could never be a settled Church on earth, since there would always be disagreement and imperfection in the visible Church. Rather, Whitgift argued that the judgement whether particular 'things indifferent' were appropriate at any given time was left to the 'government of the Church' as a whole rather than to each individual Christian.[7] Most important for this argument was St Paul's blanket injunction that 'things indifferent' should always be 'done decently and in order'; for Whitgift, this meant that 'the Church hath authority in external things to make orders and appoint laws', since there could be no decency or order if each Christian invented his or her own ceremonies.[8] From a starting point of Christian liberty, then, Whitgift deduced that the only safe way for the Church to function was if its people obeyed strict laws.[9]

What made these arguments seem reasonable to English Protestants, moreover, was that despite Whitgift's conservatism they could hardly be derided as crypto-popish; they were in large part presented as a gloss on Calvin's *Institutes*. As Whitgift noted, Calvin himself had admitted that God had left 'ceremonies and external discipline ... to his Church, to make or abrogate, to alter or continue, to add or take away, as shall be thought from time to time most convenient'. Furthermore, Calvin had written that 'it is the duty of a Christian man, without superstition

---

6 Ibid., vol. 1, p. 194.
7 Ibid., pp. 196–7.
8 Ibid., p. 212.
9 Here I am indebted to J.S. Coolidge, *The Pauline Renaissance in England* (Oxford, 1970), who pointed out that Christian liberty was the 'basic principle of Elizabethan Erastianism, since it amounts to saying that matters which were once prescribed as religious duties by the Word of God can now be regulated for civil purposes by the magistrate', p. 26.

willingly to obey such constitutions, not to condemn them, not to neglect them, much less stubbornly and arrogantly to break them'. It was only the Anabaptists and other radicals – with whom Whitgift gleefully equated Presbyterians – who interpreted Christian liberty so licentiously that it might excuse individual Christians from obeying the law on matters that were not positively determined in Scripture.[10]

In the English context, of course, as opposed to Calvin's Geneva, the prerogative of the Church to settle 'things indifferent' implied an Erastian Church in the hands of civil governors; authority rested with the bishops, parliament and finally the Queen. For Whitgift, this was not a necessary evil but a positive byproduct of England's ancient constitution and divinely-sanctioned monarchy. Whitgift wrote that 'the external government of the Church under a Christian magistrate must be according to the kind and form of government used in the commonwealth'; hence if the English state was ruled by a Queen in parliament, so must the English Church, or else steal from the Queen 'one half of her jurisdiction and authority'.[11] In his polemical context, this allowed Whitgift to argue that Presbyterianism was a fundamental threat not merely to the Church but to the monarchy. In a broader sense, it also enabled him to argue that puritan claims of 'conscience' in things indifferent were tantamount to lèse-majesté. The Queen, after all, had adopted rules for outward worship with the consent of the bishops, lords and commons representing the whole realm. In this context, Whitgift wrote, 'it is no tyranny to restrain the people from that liberty that is hurtful to themselves and must of necessity engender contentions, tumults, and confusion'.[12]

This understanding of *adiaphora*, with some variation around the edges, was so often repeated that it has come to represent in our historical imagination very much what it was intended to: a moderate *via media* between the alleged legalism of Catholic works theology and the alleged anarchy of puritan enthusiasm. Indeed, this view of *adiaphora* has become so ingrained that we are in danger of accepting its assumptions and categories as self-evidently true. A useful corrective to this tendency, however, can be found in another position that has recently been analysed: the so-called 'moderate puritan' perspective so eloquently and persuasively described by Peter Lake and perhaps best exemplified by Laurence Chaderton, master of Emmanuel College, Cambridge.[13] It is important from the outset to understand what Lake

---

[10] *Works of Whitgift*, vol. 1, p. 247.
[11] *Works of Whitgift*, vol. 2, pp. 263–4.
[12] Ibid., vol. 1, p. 408; vol. 2, pp. 239–40.
[13] Peter Lake, *Moderate Puritans and the Elizabethan Church* (Cambridge, 1982).

meant by 'moderate puritanism', since it has often been misunderstood. Certainly the idea of a 'moderate puritan' was never meant to describe someone who was intrinsically or temperamentally anodyne. As William Hunt has noted, the idea of a puritan who minds his own business is a contradiction in terms.[14] Rather, Lake insisted that 'moderate' must be used as an adjective rather than a noun: there is no such thing as 'a moderate', only a moderate *something*. A moderate *puritan*, then, was no less puritan than his colleagues but pursued further Reformation in more subtle, politic or expedient ways.

The moderate puritan view of *adiaphora*, then, was moderate exactly because it shared Whitgift's rejection of 'negative scripturalism' in which only those forms of worship specifically mandated by the Bible were licit. Writers like Laurence Chaderton joined Whitgift in arguing that Christians were 'set at liberty' in external forms of worship, freed from the ceremonial law and hence not 'burdened still with negative traditions'. On the use of the surplice, for instance, Chaderton separated himself from his more radical brethren with a simple syllogism upholding the principle of *adiaphora*: 'If it be not lawful, it is in the Scriptures forbidden either expressly or by necessary deduction. But it is not forbidden in the Scriptures either expressly or by necessary deduction. Ergo, the surplice is lawful.'[15] Yet if Chaderton accepted the idea of 'things indifferent', he nonetheless defined its importance quite differently from Whitgift. Whereas the Archbishop had emphasized that 'things indifferent' were left to the discretion of magistrates to preserve order in the Church, Chaderton emphasized that they were 'left in man's liberty and choice, to use or refuse as occasion shall serve'. Thus for Chaderton, while there was no sin in the *mere* use or non-use of 'things indifferent', there could still be sin in *particular instances* of their use 'which God hath forbidden in his word'.[16]

The key question, then, was how could it be determined if particular uses of ceremonies were 'abuses' or not, and who had the authority to decide? Chaderton provided a long list of complex and sometimes contradictory answers to this question. So, for instance, he admitted that authorities could require certain ceremonies, but it was imperative that 'in using those ceremonies and such like we do not judge them to be any parts or parcels of God's worship or service'; in other words, things indifferent required by the magistrate should be adopted for the sake of obedience, but only as long as it was acknowledged that they were in no

---

[14] Cited in C. Durston and J. Eales, 'Introduction', in their *The Culture of English Puritanism*, 1560–1700 (Basingstoke, 1996), p. 26.

[15] LPL, MS 2550, fol. 40[r].

[16] Ibid., fol. 43[v].

way pleasing to God. Chaderton also displayed the politic aspect of his 'moderate puritanism' by suggesting that required ceremonies should be used by the godly in order to protect their positions in the Church and avoid deprivation: 'We may and ought to use them to purchase and procure liberty to win souls by preaching the gospel, yea though they were forbidden by men, much more when they are required by them.' In other words, if puritan ministers conformed to 'the customary manner of the Church' and showed that they would not disturb the peace over mere 'things indifferent', that would leave them free to perform their real business, the preaching of the Word.[17] Indeed, in general Chaderton was willing to toe the government's line that lawful magistrates could compel obedience on things indifferent. He wrote, for instance, that in all *adiaphora* 'we must use them lest we give offence to our superior governors', just as Christ himself accepted the jurisdiction of Caesar. The word 'must' here is significant; in his other answers, Chaderton had simply said that Christians 'may' use ceremonies or 'may and ought' to use them under particular conditions, but here he required their use, a step away from the more usual puritan understanding of Christian liberty.[18] Chaderton's overall view, then, was very much in accord with Whitgift's: subjects should indeed obey the magistrate in things indifferent as long as they understood that they were required to do so for the sake of obedience rather than the things themselves.

This basic agreement on the requirement of individual Christians to conform to the positive laws of the Church, however, disguised a fundamental disagreement on how magistrates should enforce those laws. Chaderton accepted that, in particular circumstances, it might be necessary for magistrates to require strict conformity for purely worldly reasons. To require conformity in externals *always and as a matter of course*, however, implied that those externals were in some sense essential, which was exactly the definition of 'abuse' and hence negated any requirement that they be followed! Thus while Chaderton admitted the need for puritans to obey the law, the principle behind this obedience imposed an equal and opposite obligation upon magistrates *not to enforce the law* upon Christian consciences except when worldly circumstances made it absolutely necessary. In particular, the magistrate had an overwhelming duty not to enforce conformity when doing so would give offence to tender consciences or the weak of faith; if they did so, they rendered the ceremonies in question sinful, and hence undermined their own claim that those ceremonies were indifferent. Only when both Church authorities and individual Christians accepted

---

[17] Ibid., fols 58ʳ–59ʳ.
[18] Ibid., fol. 58ᵛ.

the dual, reciprocal nature of these obligations according to the 'law of love' could a godly commonwealth function.[19]

To conclude these brief summaries of Whitgift and Chaderton on *adiaphora*, then, one could choose to stress either their similarities or their differences. Certainly the two men were enemies, and it would be imprudent to ignore their monumental clash in the 1580s over the lawfulness of enforced subscription to the *Book of Common Prayer*. Yet on the other hand, they were both genuine defenders of the royal supremacy who accepted the need to 'tarry for the magistrate' in reforming the Church. Unlike Presbyterians and other radical puritans, they agreed that scriptural commandments and prohibitions had to be read narrowly, leaving a great deal of room for the post-Apostolic Church to alter the externals of worship. They were also, not insignificantly, both unequivocal Calvinists who steadfastly opposed any changes to the Church of England that threatened to undermine the doctrinal victories of the Reformation. Their major disagreement over *adiaphora*, then, concerned not the duty of Christian subjects but the duty of Christian magistrates: Whitgift saw nonconformity as the thin end of a heretical wedge and thus had no problem outlawing it, while Chaderton saw laws outlawing nonconformity as the thin end of a popish wedge and thus had no problem disobeying them.

II

So far, we have considered two views of *adiaphora* that had more in common than we might have suspected, and differed primarily in their understanding of compulsion rather than their understanding of obedience. Yet if we look deeper in the doctrinal manuscripts of the era, we quickly find other positions which were not so sanguine about the idea that 'conformity' was a true *via media* in the Reformation.[20] Let us consider next, then, another puritan perspective that was likewise 'moderate' in its acceptance of 'things indifferent' but went well beyond Chaderton in its understanding of individual freedom of conscience. This view belonged to Robert Beale, an MP and clerk of the Privy Council

---

[19] Ibid.

[20] Perhaps the quintessential expression of this scepticism in the European Reformation was Jean Calvin's 1549 dismissal of Philip Melanchthon's adiaphorism as a form of extremism, because it reduced true religion to a merely internal affair: '*Cuius dementiae est, sic ad extremum tueri omnia, ut totius evangelii summa negligatur?*' Timothy Wengert, '"We Will Feast Together in Heaven": The Epistolary Friendship of Jean Calvin and Philip Melanchthon', in Karin Maag (ed.), *Melanchthon in Europe* (Grand Rapids, MI, 1999), p. 36.

whose political power gave him the clout to oppose Whitgift and whose status as a layman protected him from the threat of deprivation that was usually the Archbishop's last resort. Early in 1584, in the context of the subscription controversy, Beale wrote directly to Whitgift a treatise and a series of letters which described a view of *adiaphora* that he hoped might allow for individual nonconformity while protecting the integrity of the state Church.

It is important to note that Beale was every bit as concerned with order and decency in the Church as Whitgift, and he was determined to conduct policy debates through private channels rather than through public opinion. He wrote near the beginning of his tract, perhaps with less than full sincerity but certainly with a clear message of his own political temperance:

> [It is not] my meaning hereby to declare anything to the derogation, disproving, or despising of the *Book of Common Prayer*, which according to the right rules of Christian freedom I have used and so do still. For this my writing and art shall not be open but addressed to your Lordship only, and so circumspect have I been from offending in this point that I have neither made any other person acquainted with my doing who might help me therein, nor so much as seen what hath been written by others in these matters, your Lordship's great book only excepted.[21]

Here, then, Beale made it clear that he himself was happily but *voluntarily* conformable, and he would never put his views into print in ways that might encourage others to break the law.[22]

Moreover, Beale stressed the common ground that he and Whitgift shared. He noted that when Whitgift had been Bishop of Worcester he 'did charitably bear with such as behaved themselves honestly, although they were not altogether of the same opinion with your Lordship in matters of rites and ceremonies'.[23] Thus when Whitgift had become Archbishop, Beale had appealed to him:

> To deal mildly and charitably with such good and learned ministers as (albeit were not in matters of rites and ceremonies of the same opinion that your Lordship was, nor could perhaps be induced to allow of all things that your Lordship did) yet might be profitable instruments in teaching faith and bringing men to the true knowledge of Christ Jesus and suppressing of Antichrist, who at this time had many teachers, favorers, and followers. Wherefore the very

---

21 BL Additional MS 48039, fol. 3ʳ.
22 In 1592, Beale made a similar point in a letter to Burghley, appalled at the slanderers who had suggested that he was Martin Marprelate or had written other seditious books: BL Lansdowne MS 73, fol. 6ʳ.
23 BL Additional MS 48039, fol. 2ʳ.

necessity of the preservation both of the estate [i.e. state] and Church
required such a charitable moderation to be used by your Lordship
... bearing one with another to join together to uphold and defend
the common cause against the common enemy.[24]

This attempt to appropriate the ideal of moderation was predicated on
the belief that Beale, Whitgift and the nonconforming ministers were all
on the same side against *real* radicalism, which Beale defined as
treasonous disobedience of a Catholic or Anabaptist flavour. The Queen
had been informed that nonconforming ministers attended 'conventicles
of such kind of people as though the bearing with them would be
dangerous to her person and estate'.[25] In fact, nothing could be further
from the truth, and true Protestant ministers 'are not such persons as
ought to be coupled in yoke with papists, Anabaptists, and rebels'.[26]

Within this rhetorical positioning, however, Beale also had very real
differences with Whitgift over the nature of things indifferent. He argued
that there are three types of laws commanded by magistrates: 'good of
themselves, or bad, or indifferent and neuter'. Those which are good
'ought to be obeyed for conscience'. Those which are bad must not be
obeyed, in accordance with St Paul's admonition to obey God before
man. So far this was all unimpeachable. Indifferent laws, however, Beale
defined as those which 'may be used both to good ends and bad ends'.
Here we can begin to see an understanding of the 'abuse' of things
indifferent that was somewhat more open-ended and promiscuous than
Chaderton's. For Beale, it was not the case that things indifferent were
neither good nor bad and hence were left to the discretion of magistrates
unless they abused their authority. Rather, things indifferent *were* good
or bad; what made them indifferent was that they could be *either* good
or bad depending upon the circumstances, rather than being either
always good (like laws against murder) or always bad (like laws against
vernacular Bibles).[27] It was wrong, then, to believe that 'things
indifferent lose their nature [i.e. cease to be indifferent] when they be
commanded'. In scorn of Whitgift, Beale called it 'a very strange peace
of divinity, that it consisteth in the prince's authority to make an
indifferent thing absolutely good or bad'.[28]

Instead, Beale argued, what made 'things indifferent' either good or
bad was faith: 'whatsoever we do in these indifferent things must
proceed from faith, and be done to the Lord'. That meant that the

---

[24] Ibid., fol. 1[r].
[25] Ibid., fol. 1[v].
[26] Ibid., fol. 2[v].
[27] Ibid., fol. 10[r].
[28] Ibid., fol.10[v].

performance of an indifferent ceremony, even when required by the King, could be good for one person but bad for another depending upon their inward conscience. As Beale put it: 'If faith be of the gift of God and not of man, so must the true knowledge of indifferent things be also, *ipse stabiliet*, when he shall think good. For although we have one faith and one lord Jesus, yet *non est eadem scientia in omnibus*.' To compel Christians through 'princes' laws and decrees of magistrates, that all their prescriptions in indifferent things ought to rule men's consciences ... I hold for no Christian but doctrine fit for Antichrist, who must in such sort sit in *templo dei*.'[29] Here, then, was a rationale for nonconformity that did not oppose the concept of things indifferent but rather was based on it. Beale thus presented the Elizabethan regime with a very considerable challenge, given the government's oft-repeated claims that despite the requirement of outward uniformity 'consciences are not to be forced, but to be won and reduced by the force of truth and the aid of time'.[30]

The theological underpinning of Beale's arguments was a distinctly Lutheran (and indeed an *early* Lutheran) emphasis on Christian liberty. Beale noted Whitgift's claim that obedience to the magistrate in *adiaphora* was 'not to bring us again into the bondage of the law and deprive us of our Christian liberty' because such obedience was not 'a matter of justification, but of order'. Yet Beale rejected this logic on the grounds that the concept of Christian liberty must *always* refer to outward order rather than salvation, and that no good Christian would ever have suggested 'that justification, the principle most assured and irremovable foundation of our salvation, was reputed among things indifferent'. For Whitgift to argue that true Christian liberty referred only to inward beliefs rather than outward order threatened the whole Protestant cornerstone of salvation through faith alone, since it was ceremonies rather than faith that were abrogated by Christ.[31] Of course Beale did not believe that Christian liberty was the same as free licence, nor did he believe that his views contradicted the moral requirement of obedience to magistrates. He simply defined true obedience in a very different sense, arguing that 'he that enforceth things indifferent against conscience seeketh for no true obedience'.[32] Or, as he put it in a slightly later tract, 'the Apostle teacheth us that all obedience ought to be grounded upon conscience, and otherwise it is no true obedience'.[33] This, then, was a far bolder version

---

[29] Ibid.
[30] BL Harleian MS 859, fol. 40[r] (an anonymous, late Elizabethan anti-Catholic tract entitled 'Of the Proceedings Against the Pretended Catholics').
[31] BL Additional MS 48039, fol. 13[r–v].
[32] Ibid., fol. 19[r].
[33] BL Additional MS 48116, fol. 199[r].

of Laurence Chaderton's argument that magistrates were not to enforce ceremonial laws even if the laws themselves were valid. In Beale's view, this position reflected back upon the subject and changed the nature of obedience itself. 'Decency and order' now were seen to depend upon conscientious behaviour, and *real* disobedience and disorder were now defined as the coercion of tender consciences – in other words, the practices of Whitgift and his bishops.

This did not mean that for Beale Catholics or heretics enjoyed the same liberty in things indifferent that true Christians did; their inward beliefs were not conscience but the prescriptions of the sinful world. And certainly it was dangerous for priests to practise traditional ceremonies in England, even if those ceremonies were technically indifferent, because they represented the yoke of the law which ought not to be laid upon Protestant subjects. Beale was therefore not in favour of 'toleration' in a broader sense. Yet despite these limitations, Beale accepted that the logical consequences of his arguments did allow a certain latitude for ignorance. In the 'first Reformation of the Church', he wrote, 'I do not deny but some toleration might have been used with popish ceremonies, being not contrary to the Word of God', and he cited on behalf of this opinion 'the godly martyrs Cranmer, Ridley, and others'. So here, buried within Beale's highly puritan demands for toleration of Protestant nonconformity, was a distinctly non-puritan acceptance that the superstitions of the first Edwardian Prayer Book had been a necessary and lawful expediency.[34] Moreover, Beale also accepted that the logical consequences of his views of conscience made individuals rather than magistrates the final arbiters of their own actions on issues of *adiaphora*. In a remarkable passage that is almost shocking coming from a clerk of the Privy Council, Beale argued that if Elizabeth and her bishops were serious about not making 'windows into men's souls', they would have to abandon their attempts to enforce the Act of Uniformity:

> A magistrate's office extendeth so far as God hath appointed it ... and is not to be drawn farther. But the Lord hath reserved the conscience of man to be settled by himself in his good time, as he thinketh meet in these indifferent things of days and meats, as the Apostle teacheth. And therefore the magistrate ought not to intermeddle with that case which the Lord hath reserved unto himself. And as the Lord hath not left the judgment of Christian doctrine unto the commandment of every magistrate whatsoever, either spiritual or temporal, but unto the particular conscience of every one of his sheep which *vocem eius audiunt et alienum non recipient*.[35]

---

[34] BL Additional MS 48039, fol. 14^r.
[35] Ibid., fol. 18^r; cf. John 10:4–5.

III

The approach to *adiaphora* advocated by Beale was not exactly opposed to Laurence Chaderton; their different visions could be more-or-less compatible if people chose not to interrogate the concept of 'indifference' too closely. Yet in practice, Beale's arguments might be seen to constitute an alternate pole of moderate puritanism that stressed ceremonial latitude rather than the reform of ceremonies from within the Church. And in particular contexts, Beale's vision of a comprehensive rather than narrow national Church could exercise considerable influence.

Let us begin with an anonymous, undated position paper entitled 'A Supplication Humbly Desiring an Indifferent Toleration of Indifferent Ceremonies'. It is clear that the writer accepted the legitimacy of significant latitude in Church practices, and indeed he explicitly claimed that historically 'uniformity in ceremony was seldom seen in the Church, yet was there still held the unity of faith'. Moreover, while many puritans like Chaderton claimed to be 'moderate' because they sought to alter the Church through lawful parliamentary process, this writer turned such arguments on their heads, arguing that pushing for fundamental change was far more risky than his own acceptance of diversity: 'The thing desired is no alteration but a toleration, and therefore of the less dangerous event.' Here, then, we seem to have a view of *adiaphora* that is similar to Robert Beale's. Yet far more than Beale, this author defended the established Church and lambasted puritans who turned their own inward consciences into agendas for the Church as a whole. While he wanted toleration for ministers who silently omitted controversial ceremonies, he insisted that anyone who openly condemned those ceremonies as ungodly or taunted ministers who used them should be 'punished according to the laws and canons in that behalf provided'. More importantly, he also suggested that the whole point of toleration in things indifferent was that it would help to heal the Church's wounds: 'It will be a good means of love and unity between inferior ministers and the bishops, and so of the peaceable continuance of the established Church government so much heretofore oppugned.' This, then, was not exactly puritan by traditional ways of measuring; this author opposed alteration in Church government and condemned any suggestion that the ceremonies of the *Book of Common Prayer* were ungodly. Yet at the same time he was no 'conformist'. The whole point of his brief tract was that indifference was *really* indifference: the mere inclusion or exclusion of a ritual should not be considered offensive unless the minister in question upset the unity of the Church by arguing about its legality.[36]

---

[36]   BL Additional MS 38492, fols 51ʳ–52ʳ.

More common than these arguments for latitude were arguments that productively combined aspects of Beale's perspective with other, more traditional puritan arguments. We can see this productive co-mingling, for instance, in the puritan lawyer James Morice, who wrote a series of tracts against the so-called '*ex officio* oaths' in ecclesiastical courts that required deponents to incriminate themselves. Part of what made these oaths so controversial was that the government took oaths themselves to be ceremonies, 'a kind of religious act, whereby we give worship to God'. As such, they were spiritually indifferent and could be demanded by magistrates.[37] To many radical puritans, on the other hand, the fact that oaths were religious acts was precisely what made them *not* indifferent but rather admissible only when they had specific scriptural warrant. So, for instance, one tract against *ex officio* oaths claimed that 'considering that an oath is a principal worship of God, it is clear that the direction thereof must be taken from the Word of God'.[38] Being a moderate puritan, James Morice accepted that since oaths were ceremonial, 'magistrates may impose an oath upon such as are subject to their jurisdiction'.[39] Yet this was not the end of the matter. He argued in a 1594 manuscript that if a person swore the oath and then was asked a question that violated his conscience, that would make the imposition of the oath itself sinful. Like Beale, in other words, Morice accepted that the 'ceremony' in question was not inherently unlawful, but if it were performed against a godly conscience it would become *provisionally* unlawful. So what was the solution to this dilemma? One possible answer was that, if a deponent were asked a question under oath that violated his conscience, he could simply refuse to answer it. Morice rejected this argument, however, suggesting that if it were put into the hands of each individual to choose when to obey the law, the result would be anarchy: 'may and ought the Anabaptist and any fanatic to be a judge for himself?'[40] Here he begins to sound more like Chaderton and less like Beale. Morice's own solution, however, was *not* that the ecclesiastical courts should refrain from imposing oaths upon tender consciences, which would presumably have been Chaderton's view. Instead, he argued that *ex officio* oaths should be banned altogether because their undue 'rigour' – a code word for legalism over Christian

[37] Richard Cosin, *An apologie for Svndrie proceedings by iurisdiction ecclesiasticall, of late times by some chalenged, and also diversly by them impugned* (London, 1593), part III, sigs C1r, F1r. On *ex officio* oaths, see Ethan H. Shagan, 'The English Inquisition: Constitutional Conflict and Ecclesiastical Law in the 1590s', *HJ* 47 (3) (September 2004), 541–65.
[38] LPL, MS 445, p. 438.
[39] BL Harleian MS 1694, fol. 65r.
[40] Ibid., fol. 107r-v.

liberty – would *inevitably* lead to violations of conscience.[41] Thus when faced with the oath, Christians should not pick and choose which questions to answer but refuse to take the oath entirely: 'In godly wisdom, silence and secrecy may be used.'[42]

Other puritans also found themselves torn between Beale's version of moderate puritanism and Chaderton's. So, for instance, around 1584 a group of laymen who called themselves 'the gentlemen of Suffolk' petitioned the Privy Council on behalf of puritan ministers. These gentlemen freely admitted that, like the government, they desired 'one uniformity in all the duties of the Church, the same being agreeable to the proportion of faith'. These were elite magistrates, after all, and they insisted that 'we reverence both the law and the lawmaker. Law speaketh, and we keep silence. Law commandeth, and we obey. Without law we know that no man can possess his own in peace.' Furthermore, they accepted that wholly legitimate laws for uniformity had been made in the early years of the Elizabethan Settlement in order to 'bridle the enemy', in other words to force Catholic priests to conform or else face deprivation. Yet these laws, they argued, had never been intended for use against conscientious Protestants and should not be enforced against them. So far we seem to have a reproduction of Laurence Chaderton's arguments. In a remarkable passage, however, the 'gentlemen' then suggested that 'weak ceremonies and their like' were 'so indifferent as their use or not use may be left to the discretion of the minister', and they thus suggested that it was 'very hard to have them go under so hard handling, to the utter discredit of the whole ministry and profession of truth'. This was an attempt to square the circle: the laws of uniformity were indeed valid and binding, but their enforcement was left not to the magistrate but to the discretion of each godly clergyman according to his own conscience.[43] Ministers, after all, were also magistrates in the ecclesiastical polity.

Another manuscript tract suggested, like Beale, that 'that which the Word of God maketh conditional, human law cannot make absolutely necessary'. But more interestingly, it also expanded this argument to suggest that in deciding whether to use indifferent ceremonies, the Christian subject had to consider 'the ends for which they were ordained'. Things indifferent were never ordained simply for themselves, but rather for some larger purpose; ideally they were created out of a desire for 'order, decency, and edification'. Thus, the author argued, 'the indifferent things of the Church commanded by the Christian

---

[41] See, for example, LPL, MS 234, fol. 30ᵛ, and Louise Campbell's chapter in this volume.
[42] BL Harleian MS 1694, fol. 70ᵛ.
[43] BL Lansdowne MS 109, fols 27ʳ–28ʳ.

magistrate ... do not simply bind the conscience as if they were absolutely necessary, but may with godly wisdom be omitted when the strict observation of them frustrateth the ends for which they were ordained, and when the omission of them, without any contempt of authority or scandal given, attaineth the ends proposed'. This seems to be an elaboration of Robert Beale's notion that indifference allowed for latitude in Church practice. Yet the author used this rationale not only to argue that the Church of England's ceremonies could lawfully be omitted, but also to argue, like more radical and separatist puritans, that those ceremonies could not lawfully be used! After all, many of the Church of England's ceremonies were popish survivals and 'monuments of idolatry', and thus by definition they were not ordained to promote 'order, decency, and edification'. This author, then, did not deny that Christian ceremonial was indifferent, but he argued that any positive ordinance of the Church created under Roman jurisdiction was intrinsically sinful as a result of its corrupt and anti-Christian purposes.[44]

The point of this survey of puritan or quasi-puritan arguments for *adiaphora* has been to widen the lens with which we examine moderation. After all, by what standard can we judge any or all of these positions to be 'moderate'? Is latitude in ceremonies more or less 'moderate' than enforcement of the law? Is 'moderation' to be found more in respect for the will of the individual or the will of community? Could England better achieve a *via media* in the Reformation by distancing itself from Catholic views of the authority of the Church or from Anabaptist views of individual conscience? In practice, because a wide variety of positions challenged the Church of England's normative characterization of the 'middle way', we must recognize that moderation itself functioned as a polemical category more than an irenic one.

IV

If we turn now to the non- or anti-puritan side of the spectrum, it is all the more surprising that we again find a series of opinions being canvassed which stress individual conscience and Christian liberty rather than the authority of magistrates. This evidence not only shows that there was a much wider spectrum of belief about *adiaphora* than we might expect, but also suggests that our easy equation of support for the Church of England with 'conformity' may be a product of good public relations rather than an accurate assessment of reality.

---

[44] BL Additional MS 38492, fols 44^r–45^r.

One argument often made by non-puritans was that the whole debate over *adiaphora* was itself in some sense indifferent and hence was no more than a storm in a teacup. We can see this argument, for instance, in the work of Francis Bacon, especially his 'Advertisement Touching the Controversies of the Church of England' written (but not published) in 1589 in response to the Martin Marprelate controversy.[45] It suggested in no uncertain terms that both the puritans and the bishops ought to leave the Church of England well enough alone and that the disputes disrupting it were not worth bothering with. Bacon claimed to be unwilling to discuss the merits of the cases put forward by either side, since 'the disease requireth rather rest than any other care'. The real problem, in other words, was that there was no real problem: 'Thus much we all know and confess, that they [the disputes in the Church] be not of the highest nature, for they are not touching the high mysteries of faith such as detained the Churches after their first peace ... We contend about ceremonies and things indifferent, about the extern policy and government of the Church.' For Bacon, then, while 'indifference' still maintained its theological sense of something neither required nor forbidden by Scripture, it also had something close to its modern connotations of irrelevance. He expressed the same notion in Aristotelian terms, lamenting that 'accidents' rather than 'things themselves' had caused dissention in the Church. He even claimed to be an advocate of the old saying that 'diversities of ceremonies doth set forth the unity of doctrine' – although we may suspect that he invented this 'old saying' himself.[46]

His ostensible reason for writing, then, was to lambaste both sides for the impolitic and uncharitable nature of their arguments rather than to concern himself with the content of the debate. On the puritan side, for instance, he called for an end to 'this immodest and deformed manner of writing lately entertained, whereby matter of religion is handled in the style of the stage'. This was a common sentiment in the months after Martin Marprelate scandalized the capital, and even many puritans expressed similar ideals as they tried to distance themselves from the radicals. Yet Bacon was no puritan, and he attacked those who 'think it the true touchstone to try what is good and evil by measuring what is more or less opposite to the institutions of the Church of Rome, be it ceremony, be it policy, or government'. He considered it ridiculous that so many English divines wanted to imitate the supposed perfection of foreign Churches, when in fact they should seek '*non quod optimum*,

---

[45] BL Harleian MS 1893, fols 5^r–17^r. This tract was apparently first printed in 1641, under the suggestive name *A Wise and Moderate Discourse, Concerning Church-Affaires*.
[46] BL Harleian MS 1893, fols 5^r–6^r.

sed e bonis quid proximum, not that which is best, but of good things which is best and readiest to be had'.[47] He complained of the magnifying of preaching to the exclusion of 'liturgy and forms of divine service'. All in all, the puritans had forgotten 'that there are sins on the right hand as well as on the left'.[48]

On the bishops' side, he had just as many criticisms, but again he worked hard to criticize their lack of charity rather than their positions per se. They had treated the puritans as if they 'had denied tribute to Caesar' and had unfairly tried to associate them with the Family of Love. They had been 'swift of credit to every accusation against them' and then dealt with those accusations unreasonably strictly. They had been 'bold in open preaching to use dishonorable and derogatory speech and censure of the Churches abroad' and referred to the puritans themselves as a 'sect'. In general, they had become stagnant and unreasonably stiff in denying their own faults, forgetting that 'to take away many abuses supplanteth not good orders but establisheth them'.[49]

In sum, Bacon wanted a middle way that would be big enough to encompass both puritans and conformist bishops. In his view, three things were necessary for this dream to become a reality. First, men would have to admit that their opinions were only opinions rather than glimpses of absolute truth; they would have to stop claiming that their ideas were '*non ego, sed dominus*'. Second, they would have to stop debating religion in front of the common people, which he described as a 'point of great inconvenience and peril'. Third, they would have to change 'their manner of handling the Scriptures', seeking biblical backing for every tiny point of difference and making points through 'forced allusions'.[50] These, of course, were all commonplace conformist complaints against the puritans, so we might suspect that in some ways Bacon was not as neutral as he claimed to be. Yet on the other hand, this middle way that put the peace of the Church over details of worship – an irenicism that makes modern latitudinarian Anglicans proud – was written *explicitly against* the drive for conformity that was at the heart of the Church of England's official view of *adiaphora*.

Another, more daring position was also available on *adiaphora*, which we would be tempted to call 'religious toleration'. This position was clearly a minority view, but it can be found fully formed in an anonymous manuscript entitled 'Whether a Protestant Prince May Tolerate Mass'.[51] The author began by noting that according to St Paul

---

[47] Ibid., fols 7ᵛ, 10ʳ⁻ᵛ.

[48] Ibid., fols 15ʳ–16ʳ.

[49] Ibid., fols 12ʳ–13ʳ.

[50] Ibid., fols 5ʳ, 6ʳ, 15ᵛ–16ʳ.

[51] BL Lansdowne MS 97, fols 41ʳ–42ᵛ.

'the meat dedicated by the infidels unto idols might be used and suffered of the Christian Corinthians with a safe conscience'. This was a classic proof text for Christian liberty, used by many puritan authors including Robert Beale. In this author's view, however, Paul's precedent also implied that '*ergo* the papistical Mass may now be used and suffered of the right Christians with a safe conscience'. This was a particularly compelling argument because for Protestants the Mass was precisely an example of eating food that had been falsely offered up as a physical sacrifice despite the abrogation of the law. The author of this treatise, then, argued that 'that which is offered to idols is not unlawful by itself, but in that it is offered up to the devil and not unto God'. Even this 'abominable abuse and idolatry mar not the liberty and indifference of the meat so ungodly abused, but that it may always be eaten lawfully where no offense is given to the weak'. He therefore concluded that 'the wicked abuse of the Mass taketh not away the free and indifferent using of the same without the abuse'. Here, then, was not only an argument for toleration of the Mass, but an argument that Protestants could *participate* in the Mass as long as they did so without idolatry in their hearts. This argument, then, presumed that the Mass itself was indifferent, just like any other outward ceremony; whether it was good or bad depended upon the beliefs of the participant.

The upshot of all this was a more general argument for tolerance of wrongheaded opinions, just as St Paul commanded that 'none should condemn the Jews which for conscience and religion durst not eat the meat that was forbidden by the abolished law of Moses'. If the papists 'judge it necessary for salvation' that they should receive Mass, then just as 'the superstitious users of the abolished law of Moses were borne withal, so ought we to bear with the superstitious users of the Mass'. At the heart of this argument, then, was a recognition that for papists to violate conscience was no less sinful than for Protestants. Likewise, the author was convinced that 'we may use the company of papists' in everyday life, because unless those papists were given the benefit of good Protestant company, how else could Protestants 'win them' from their superstition. In theory, of course, this argument was not surprising, and it was shared by many early modern proponents of religious toleration like the Levellers of the 1640s.[52] Yet in practice, the consequence of 'using the company' of Catholics in Queen Elizabeth's reign would have been extraordinary, effectively separating the community of the Church from the community of the commonwealth.

---

[52] *The English Levellers*, ed. Andrew Sharp (Cambridge, 1998), especially the texts of William Walwyn.

The last version of 'indifference' that I want to consider is a Roman Catholic position. The inclusion of this perspective may seem odd, both because Catholic views on the authority of Rome might seem to render the issue moot, and because modern scholars rarely imagine that Catholics participated in wider English debates.[53] But in fact, many Catholics opposed the requirement of absolute recusancy demanded by Rome and the Jesuits, and these men and women had to find theoretical reasons why Catholics might in some cases attend Church of England services if that attendance was required by law. Their solution was often an argument from *adiaphora* that tracks remarkably closely with English Protestant debates over 'moderation' but reached very different conclusions.

Let us look at one of the most important texts against recusancy written by an Elizabethan Catholic: Alban Langdale's 'treatise to prove that attendance at the Protestant Church was in itself no sin', which survives in a single, incomplete manuscript in the State Papers.[54] Langdale's first goal was to prove that 'the bare being and accompanying' with Protestants 'in their churches at the times of their prayers is not *per se peccatum mortale* so as no circumstance can make it tolerable'.[55] To make this argument, Langdale described a series of scriptural figures who, for various reasons, legitimately attended the ceremonies of the heathen despite their devotion to the Judaeo-Christian God. Namaan the Syrian, for instance, was servant to 'his King, an idolater' yet was permitted to give this King 'external service' in the heathen temple.[56] Gamaliel, a 'disciple of Christ and a companion with the Apostles', did not 'forbear the fellowship of the Pharisees, but to the end he might pacify their fury, he remained among them even in their consultation as well touching the law of God as touching their civil policy'. Likewise, Joseph of Arimathea was present with the Jews 'in their synagogue and consultations'. Even the Apostles themselves 'were mixed among the wicked Jews in the temple, and there prayed amongst them, though not with them'.[57] The point of these examples was not to delineate the precise terms in which attendance was lawful, but merely to show that such conditions existed. As such, Langdale argued that

---

[53] For proposed antidotes to this tendency, see the essays in Ethan H. Shagan (ed.), *Catholics and the 'Protestant Nation': Religious Politics and Identity in Early Modern England* (Manchester, forthcoming 2005).

[54] On Langdale, see Peter Holmes, *Resistance and Compromise: The Political Thought of the Elizabethan Catholics* (Cambridge, 1982), ch. 7; Alexandra Walsham, *Church Papists* (Woodbridge, Suffolk, 1993), ch. 3.

[55] NA SP 12/144/69, fol. 138[v].

[56] Ibid., fol. 137[r].

[57] Ibid., fol. 138[r–v].

attendance at ungodly services could not be, in and of itself, forbidden by divine law. Moreover, against the particular objection that Namaan's actions were only lawful because he had asked for and received a special dispensation to go to the heathen temple, Langdale responded that this in essence proved his point: if it had been against divine law, no earthly power could have dispensed it.[58] It was no coincidence that this was exactly the logic that Henry VIII had used against Rome in his divorce case half a century before; Langdale was not only arguing that Catholics could conscientiously conform in some circumstances, but was also making a larger point that Catholics could be loyal English subjects.

This was a version of indifference to which neither Archbishop Whitgift nor most puritans would have objected: bare attendance at a sinful church service was not a sin. Yet when we look more closely at Langdale's arguments, we find that his views of what made particular forms of attendance either lawful or unlawful diverged dramatically from both the regime and the puritans. To begin with Langdale's divergence from theological 'conformity', while the regime demanded conformity up to and including actual receipt of the sacrament, for Langdale this was utterly forbidden: refusing communion and other forms of positive participation was the *signa distinctiva* that insured that mere attendance at unlawful services would not encourage weakness of faith.[59] Moreover, if other Catholics were aware of an act of casuistic conformity and might be disheartened by it, the conforming Catholic was to make a 'profession of his faith, and such a declaration as may give sufficient occasion to the weakest to take no example of evil thereby, but rather example of good'. This, of course, was not what Whitgift had in mind when he demanded conformity to the Act of Uniformity; it was closer to the puritan idea of godly services within the hollow shell of the Church of England: 'Note many parishes in E[ngland] there be where neither the curate nor parishioners are open professors of P [Protestantism? *Peccata?*] nor known P but dissembling Catholics.'[60] Most importantly, Langdale argued (like Beale) that the interior condition and conscience of the practitioner was crucial in determining whether the performance of an indifferent thing was actually licit; as he put it, 'it is much material with what mind a man doeth a thing'. When the Bible says to 'come out from among them and separate yourselves' from the heathen, it means separation from 'corruption of vice and sin, and not of corporal separation'.[61]

---

[58] Ibid., fol. 137[v].
[59] Ibid., fol. 141[r].
[60] Ibid., fol. 140[v].
[61] Ibid., fols 139[v], 140[v].

Yet Langdale also diverged sharply from puritan views of *adiaphora*. Those who attended Church of England services without accepting the legitimacy of those services – a position that might equally be applied to reluctantly conforming Catholics and Protestants – Langdale equated with the New Testament figures who 'using the liberty of the gospel' ate meats dedicated to idols. Those who condemned this conformity – in other words both Jesuits and puritans – he described as 'the ignorant' whom St Paul rebuked: 'What art thou that condemnest another man's servant, as much to say as why doth thou think sinisterly of thy brother's fact when thou knowest not for what intent, upon what occasion, or in what respect thy brother doth it?' If that ignorant Christian is scandalized by the conformity, the conforming party must explain his reasons and make a testimony of his faith to remove the scandal; if the ignorant Christian is not thus satisfied, 'he is to be blamed'.[62]

Here, then, was a position on things indifferent explicitly defined as a *via media* in the Reformation: neither Jesuit/puritan insistence on nonconformity in ceremonial matters, nor 'Anglican' insistence on bare legalism over inward conscience. As Langdale put it, 'for a matter which might be made indifferent, to stir trouble is not the best course to quietness', yet for conscience's sake a Christian must remain 'utterly abhorring of all consent' to the sinful Church. Yet this *via media*, based no less than the Church of England on the concept of things indifferent, was expressed by a Roman Catholic who saw the Church of England's alleged moderation as nothing but 'the wrath of the persecutor'.[63]

V

By highlighting these alternative arguments, I hope to alter our received views in several ways. First, I want to suggest that ideas of religious latitude and toleration were not so unthinkable in Elizabethan England as is often assumed. Besides their ubiquity among persecuted Catholics, versions of tolerationism were found on all parts of the Protestant spectrum. These ideas were of course not comparable to modern notions of toleration in either their breadth or depth, but their emphasis on individual conscience – as opposed to the Anabaptist emphasis on the separation of the True Church through the voluntary association of the godly – suggests that the Church of England's demands for uniformity were not by every standard as 'moderate' as they purported to be.

---

[62]   Ibid., fols 141^v–142^r.
[63]   Ibid., fol. 140^v.

Second, I want to suggest that puritanism was a considerably more dynamic intellectual movement than it has been made out to be – although of course the small number of texts discussed here can only begin to make this point. Puritanism used to be associated with religious radicalism, an assumption which the work of Patrick Collinson and Peter Lake has done much to dispel. Yet our new and more sophisticated understanding that most puritans were in some sense 'moderate' has had the unfortunate side effect of restricting our analysis of both puritanism and moderation. If to be 'moderate' was to respect the institutions of Church and state, then certainly most puritans fit the definition, but that does not mean they agreed about what that meant or how it should be practised. Debates over *adiaphora* suggest that even the most conformable puritans were engaged in negotiations over the conditions of their own loyalty that were every bit as fraught as the negotiations of those who chose separation and exile; their 'moderate' conclusions should not blind us to the potential instabilities that underlay their positions.[64]

Third, and most importantly, this essay has been intended to challenge the whole notion of 'moderation' as a useful analytical category in understanding the Reformation. That is not to say that I want to adopt a philosophically relativist position; certainly historians need to create and utilize categories, and reasonable people can provisionally agree that, for instance, executing one's enemies is less 'moderate' than imprisoning them. The danger, however, lies in how quickly we move from these provisional or utilitarian categories to normative ones which presume what we are trying to prove. When we look for moderation in the Reformation, we inevitably find it, and then we announce that this movement or that theologian was *really and truly* more moderate than another. Yet through this process we have not proved that one position deserves to be placed at the centre of the spectrum, but rather we have defined the spectrum in a particular way – often a way that maps suspiciously closely onto the topologies proposed by one or more early modern partisans. In conclusion, then, when we study a world where 'moderation' and 'indifference' were themselves the subjects of intense and sometimes deadly conflicts, our goal must be to analyse those conflicts rather than arbitrate them.

---

[64]   Cf. Patrick Collinson, *The Religion of Protestants* (Oxford, 1982).

CHAPTER EIGHT

'Wolves and Weathervanes': Confessional Moderation at the Habsburg Court of Vienna

Elaine Fulton

In 1573, the high-ranking Catholic counsellor Dr Georg Eder described the confessional moderation of the Habsburg Court where he worked in deeply unflattering terms.[1] His favourite word for its members was *Hofchristen*, or 'Court Christians', and these he characterized as weathervanes, who moved whichever way the wind blew.[2] According to Eder, such figures were neither Catholic nor Lutheran, but placed the highest value on the maintenance of peace and, with it, the outward appearance of confessional neutrality.[3] As a result, complained Eder, the unity of the Catholic Church had been turned into a 'Babylonian

---

[1] Georg Eder was one of Vienna's most significant figures from his arrival in the city in 1550 until his death in 1587. The holder of doctorates in canon and civil law, Eder acted as *Reichshofrat* from 1563 to 1583, a post in which he served directly under the Emperor to facilitate the administration of imperial justice. Eder was also elected rector of Vienna University an unprecedented 11 times from 1557 to 1584 and, as a personal lifelong friend of Peter Canisius, worked closely with the Jesuits in Vienna. Eder gained notoriety, however, for his outspoken criticism of the policy of moderation pursued at the Habsburg Court. Of particular note is his 1573 publication, *Evangelische Inquisition wahrer und falscher religion wider das gemain unchristliche claggeschray, das schier niemand mehr wissen künde, wie oder was er glauben solle: in forma aines christlichen rathschlags, wie ein jeder christen mensch seines glaubens halben ganzlich vergwißt und gesichert sein moge: dermassen, daß er leichtlich nit künde betrogen noch verfurt werden* (Dillingen, 1573). So damning was its critique of the Court of Maximilian II that the work was fiercely condemned by the Emperor and all copies confiscated. On the *Evangelische Inquisition* crisis, see Howard Louthan, *The Quest for Compromise: Peacemakers in Counter-Reformation Vienna* (Cambridge, 1997), pp. 127–9. On Eder's career, see also my 'Catholic Belief and Survival in Late Sixteenth-Century Vienna: The Case of Georg Eder (1523–87)' (unpublished PhD thesis, St Andrews, 2002); and my forthcoming book on the subject, to be published by Ashgate in 2006.

[2] Eder, *Evangelische Inquisition*, p. 166. This is an image Eder employs elsewhere in the same work, describing as weathervanes those who are 'blown to and fro in the wind', p. 8.

[3] Ibid., p. 166.

confusion', in which no one could distinguish any longer between black and white, or right and wrong.[4]

Eder also had a second target for censure. In equally vivid terms, he made reference to another confessional breed that emanated from the same Court: wolves in sheep's clothing. These too Eder described as religious dissemblers, but with an even more dangerous agenda: the spread of heresy and false doctrine. According to Eder, such persons were not truly Christian, but were false teachers who hid their sharp teeth with sweet words, and their rough wolves' hair with sheep's skin.[5] Elsewhere, Eder described how the Church had been left at the mercy of such dangerous forces, saying that the shepherds had run away and left their flock to the wolves.[6]

Such comments offer a fresh perspective on a Court well known for its confessional moderation throughout much of the 1550s, 1560s and 1570s. The religious policies of the successive heads of the Austrian branch of the Habsburg dynasty caused deep frustration in Catholic Europe, particularly in the highly active Tridentine bases of Rome, Spain and Bavaria. Ferdinand I, Holy Roman Emperor between 1556 and 1564, had overseen the formulation and maintenance of the Peace of Augsburg in 1555, while his eldest son and successor as Emperor between 1564 and 1576, Maximilian II, not only upheld the Peace, but was a keen advocate of confessional moderation in all aspects of his rule.

Georg Eder's voice did more, however, than merely echo the chorus of Catholic Europe that denounced the Court of Vienna. As an important Court functionary, sometime rector of Vienna University and active Catholic layman, Eder also saw these Habsburg emperors in action on their home territory, where they ruled their patrimony as archdukes.[7]

---

[4] Ibid., p. 168.
[5] Ibid., p. 13.
[6] Eder to Duke Wilhelm of Bavaria, 29 April 1580, in Victor Bibl (ed.), 'Die Berichte des Reichshofrates Dr Georg Eder an die Herzoge Albrecht und Wilhelm von Bayern über die Religionskrise in Niederösterreich (1579–1587)', *Jahrbuch für Landeskunde von Niederösterreich*, Neue Folge 8 (1909), 108–11. This may well have been a common image in the circles within which Eder moved. As well as having a biblical origin, the phrase had also been used by Ignatius of Loyola who had opined that it was better for the flock to have no shepherd than to have a wolf for a shepherd. Cited in John Patrick Donnelly, 'Some Jesuit Counter-Reformation Strategies in East-Central Europe, 1550–1585', in M.R. Thorp and A.J. Slavin (eds), *Politics, Religion and Diplomacy in Early Modern Europe* (Kirksville, MO, 1994), p. 84.
[7] For much of the period to be examined in this essay, the Austrian lands were divided into smaller territories, most notably Lower, Upper, Inner and Outer Austria. Lower Austria and Upper Austria, with their respective centres in Vienna and Linz, were controlled by the Emperor himself. Inner Austria was controlled from Graz, and Outer Austria, or the Tyrol, was controlled from Innsbruck, by the Emperor's brothers in their capacity as archdukes. The subject of Habsburg rule in their own patrimony in the

Ferdinand I had acted as his elder brother Charles V's eastern representative since 1522, and as such had been based predominantly in Vienna. Maximilian II also centred his Court in the city, and even after his son, Rudolf II, moved the imperial Court to Prague after 1576, he left a representative in Vienna in the form of his younger brother, Archduke Ernst. The Austrian Habsburgs' moderate religious policies in the city were, however, no more acceptable to Catholics than those they pursued in the Empire.

Popular Protestantism had been preached on the streets of Vienna since the 1520s and, despite regular efforts by Ferdinand I, was never successfully suppressed.[8] It was under the rule of Maxmilian II, however, that this movement received sufficient official leeway for Protestantism to further establish itself in Vienna and its environs. By 1568, the Lower Austrian *Herrenstand* was overwhelmingly dominated by nobles describing themselves as Protestant.[9] By then, too, Maximilian II was struggling desperately to contain the Turkish threat that continually seemed on the verge of enveloping Vienna. The year 1566 had seen humiliation for the Habsburg forces in Hungary, which had only increased the prospect of a further Ottoman attack from the East. Attempts were made to negotiate terms between ruler and estates, but with a state debt standing at 2.5 million *gulden* the result was inevitable.[10] In return for the financial and military aid of the Lower Austrian estates, Maximilian II was forced not only to grant the Lower Austrian *Religions-Konzession* in 1568, but to confirm the same three years later with the so-called *Religions-Assekuration* of 1571. Maximilian had, on his own doorstep, permitted the seemingly unthinkable. Although Lutheran worship was not formally

---

sixteenth century has received relatively little attention until quite recently: see R.J.W. Evans, *The Making of the Habsburg Monarchy 1550–1700* (Oxford, 1979); Rona Johnston, 'The Bishopric of Passau and the Counter-Reformation in Lower Austria, 1580–1636' (unpublished DPhil thesis, Oxford, 1996); Rona Johnston, 'Patronage and Parish: The Nobility and the Recatholicization of Lower Austria', in Karin Maag (ed.), *The Reformation in Eastern and Central Europe*, (Aldershot, 1997), 211–27; Grete Mecenseffy, 'Wien im Zeitalter der Reformation des 16. Jahrhunderts', *Wiener Geschichtsblätter* 29 (1974), 228–39; Regina Pörtner, *The Counter-Reformation in Central Europe: Styria 1580–1630* (Oxford, 2001).

8 As early as 1523, Ferdinand had issued a mandate against the spread and possession of Lutheran books. Similar decrees followed, such as that of 1551 against Lutheran schoolmasters and the publication of Lutheran works, and that of 1554 which forbade the partaking of communion in both kinds.

9 According to Gustav Reingrabner, by the 1580s approximately 90 per cent of the Lower Austrian nobles claimed allegiance to Lutheranism: *Adel und Reformation: Beiträge zur Geschichte des Protestantischen Adels im Lande Unter Der Enns Während des 16. und 17. Jahrhunderts* (Vienna, 1976), p. 79.

10 Paula Sutter Fichtner, *Emperor Maximilian II* (New Haven and London, 2001), p. 148.

permitted in Vienna, both *Konzession* and *Assekuration* granted members of the noble estates the right to worship according to the Confession of Augsburg 'in all their castles, houses and possessions'. In the countryside, this also included the provision of churches for their Lutheran subjects.[11]

Maximilian II's provision, however, contained a loophole that made regular worship according to Lutheran rites just as possible for those living within Vienna's walls as for those living without. Lower Austrian nobles installed Lutheran *Schloßprediger*, or castle preachers, at their own properties, as permitted under the terms of the *Konzession*: a Lutheran visitation of Lower Austria in 1580 uncovered a total of 138 such preachers in what is a relatively small area.[12] What Maximilian had perhaps not anticipated was that, such was the Viennese hunger for Lutheranism, every Sunday several thousand people would flock from Vienna, theoretically excluded from the terms of the *Konzession*, to hear the Protestant preachers on the nobles' own land. Eder himself observed in 1585, almost two decades after the issue of the *Konzession*, that as many as 3000 out of Vienna's total population of 25–30 000 inhabitants were still leaving Vienna Sunday after Sunday to hear a Lutheran preacher at just one such location, Inzersdorff.[13] In a fruitless bid to stop such embarrassing infringements of Habsburg authority, Maximilian bowed even further to Protestant demands and granted a room for worship in the Viennese *Landhaus*, right in the heart of the city, and close to the *Hofburg* itself. With their own preachers, and soon a school and even a bookshop, all under noble protection, Habsburg religious policy had done nothing less than permit the exercise of Protestantism in Vienna as well as Lower Austria.[14]

Such was the incongruity of this situation, generations of historians have sought to explain how it was that members of the famously Catholic dynasty came to sponsor such a degree of religious moderation on their own doorstep at the very peak of confessional warfare in Reformation Europe. Whilst taking on board the fact that the sheer

[11] Quotation from the *Religions-Assekuration* of 11 January 1571, cited in Johnston, 'Patronage and Parish', p. 214.
[12] Reingrabner, *Adel und Reformation*, p. 85.
[13] Eder to Duke Wilhelm of Bavaria, 19 March 1585, in Bibl, 'Die Berichte des Reichshofrates Dr Georg Eder', pp. 144–6. John Spielmann suggests that the total population of Vienna remained at 50 000 until the end of the sixteenth century. He adds, however, that the 'inner' part of the city probably totalled 25–30 000 inhabitants, and it seems it is from here that the significance of the so-called *Auslaufen* should be calculated. Spielmann, *The City and the Crown: Vienna and the Imperial Court 1600–1740* (West Lafayette, IN, 1993), pp. 12, 30.
[14] Between 1576 and 1578 the Lutheran school flourished, with five members of teaching staff. Mecenseffy, 'Wien im Zeitalter der Reformation des 16. Jahrhunderts', p. 236.

proximity of the Ottoman threat left the Austrian Habsburgs little room for manoeuvre with the nobility, existing studies have tended to focus on two factors: the composition of the Court and the personality of the ruler himself.

Contemporaries and historians alike have been particularly intrigued by Emperor Maximilian II.[15] Famously dubbed 'der rätselhafte Kaiser' – 'the mysterious Emperor' – in a 1929 biography, many have struggled to make sense of his confessional position.[16] As a young man, Maximilian clashed fiercely with his own family over the very issues of moderation and toleration. His reactions to key events were completely at odds, for example, with those of his Spanish cousin Philip II. While the King of Spain described news of the St Bartholomew's day massacre as the happiest of his life, his cousin in Vienna not only condemned the massacre, but went on to object to the harshness of the Inquisition in the Netherlands.[17]

Maximilian's clashes with his own father, Ferdinand, were no less severe, and were sparked by the younger man's apparent openness to heterodoxy. One of the key members of Maximilian's household in Vienna between 1554 and 1560 was his preacher, Sebastian Pfauser. Pfauser's own confessional allegiance is also difficult to pin down; he described himself as neither evangelical nor Catholic, and claimed to be searching for a middle way based solely on Scripture. He was also, however, rumoured to have referred to Catholics as 'miserable leaders of the blind and hangmen of souls', causing great alarm to Ferdinand and his Jesuit advisor, Peter Canisius. By 1557, the Emperor was demanding that his son remove Pfauser's damaging influence from his household.[18] That Ferdinand eventually got his way in 1560 is less significant than his son Maximilian arguing the point for three years, and even considering

---

[15] Ferdinand I's personal credentials as an orthodox Catholic have rarely been doubted, despite his role at Augsburg in 1555. On Ferdinand I, see Paula Sutter Fichtner, 'The Disobedience of the Obedient: Ferdinand I and the Papacy, 1555–1564', *SCJ* 11 (1980), 25–34; also her *Ferdinand of Austria: The Politics of Dynasticism in the Age of the Reformation* (New York, 1982). On Rudolf II, see R.J.W. Evans, *Rudolf II and his World: A Study in Intellectual History 1576–1612* (Oxford, 1973). The only exclusive study of Archduke Ernst is now more than a century old: Victor Bibl, 'Erzherzog Ernst und die Gegenreformation in Niederösterreich (1576–1590)', in *Mitteilungen des Instituts für Österreichische Geschichtsforschung, VI Ergänzungsband* (1901), 575–96.

[16] Victor Bibl, *Maximilian II. Der rätselhafte Kaiser: Ein Zeitbild* (Hellerau, 1929). Bibl had already investigated this earlier, in *Zur Frage der religiösen Haltung K. Maximilians II. Sonderabdruck aus dem Archiv für österreichische Geschichte* 106 (1917). Later works, such as Sutter Fichtner's, *Emperor Maximilian II* and Louthan's *Quest for Compromise*, continue to examine this question.

[17] Sutter Fichtner, *Emperor Maximilian II*, pp. 185–6.

[18] Ibid.; Louthan, *Quest for Compromise*, pp. 85–6.

taking refuge with a German Protestant prince rather than submit to his father's demand. Maximilian's personal support for the work of the evangelically inclined also extended further than Pfauser. He granted the Lutheran Matthias Flacius Illyricus indirect access to the imperial library, with the result that Maximilian was one of those to whom the finished work was dedicated. That this work was none other than the so-called *Magdeburg Centuries*, a history of the Christian Church that portrayed evangelical reform as its grand climax, speaks volumes for how Maximilian was perceived by contemporary Protestants.[19]

Maximilian II remains, however, a confessionally elusive figure. On 7 February 1562, the same Maximilian who had acted as a determined patron for Protestants, vowed before his concerned father, brothers and his father's Privy Councillors that he would never leave the Church of Rome. The following year, an equally anxious Pope Pius IV received a written guarantee from Maximilian that he would remain loyal to the faith of his dynasty. This was, however, far from being straightforward Catholicism. In October 1561, Pius had been forced to grant a dispensation permitting Maximilian to receive the Lutheran communion in both kinds.[20] Even in death, Maximilian gave nothing away; on his deathbed in 1576, he refused to accept the last sacrament in any form at all.[21]

No doubt frustrated by such seeming inconsistencies, historians have been drawn rather to analysing the composition of the colourful Habsburg Court in sixteenth-century Vienna.[22] Ferdinand I and in particular Maximilian II were keen to surround themselves with scholarly men of talent, both for their own edification and as an economical way of re-stocking the staff of the beleaguered Vienna University. The so-called *Hofakademie* boasted many leading scholars of the day, including physician and historian Wolfgang Lazius; keeper of the imperial library, Hugo Blotius; historian and philologist Johannes Sambucus; and the botanists Johannes Crato, Augerius Busbequius and

[19] Sutter Fichtner, *Emperor Maximilian II*, p. 39.
[20] Ibid., p. 44.
[21] Louthan suggests that for Maximilian to have received communion in both kinds would have offended his family, while to have taken only the bread would have offended his own conscience: *Quest for Compromise*, p. 87.
[22] See in particular Kurt Mühlberger, 'Bildung und Wissenschaft: Kaiser Maximilian II. und die Universität Wien', in Friedrich Edelmayer and Alfred Kohler (eds), *Kaiser Maximilian II: Kultur und Politik im 16. Jahrhundert* (Wiener Beiträge zur Geschichte der Neuzeit 17, 1992), 203–31. Evans and Louthan also deal with this subject, while Joseph Ritter von Aschbach, *Geschichte der Wiener Universität: Die Wiener Universität und Ihre Gelehrten, 1520 bis 1565* (Vienna, 1888), provides a valuable source of biographical information.

Carolus Clusius. Of these, every one except Lazius was a Protestant of various hue; indeed, Blotius was a Calvinist. Not only was the Viennese Court of the 1550s, 1560s and 1570s apparently a safe home for all manner of confessional unorthodoxy, but the same policy of moderation spread to the university.[23] Shortly after his coronation as Emperor, Maximilian permitted a change in the university oath to facilitate the promotion of Lutheran doctors and professors. Instead of swearing to *romanae fidei*, they merely had to express belief in *christianae fidei*. In April 1569 Vienna University had its first Protestant rector in the shape of Kornelius Grünwald.

Just as significant is the fact that the administrative branches of the Vienna Court of the latter half of the sixteenth century also housed a significant number of Protestants or at least non-Catholics in high places.[24] Top of the hierarchy in this regard was Johann Baptist Weber, *Reichsvizekanzler* or imperial Vice-Chancellor between November 1563 and April 1577. In spite of Maximilian II's personal dislike for Weber, he did espouse the political virtues of religious tolerance and confessional moderation that were the Austrian Habsburgs' political watchwords in these years. Even the *Reichshofrat* in which Eder served had been infiltrated by Protestant jurists. Gabriel Strein, *Reichshofrat* 1564–78, was a member of a long-established, well-connected Lower Austrian noble family, while Joachim von Sinzendorf, *Reichshofrat* 1576–77, also served the imperial dynasty in various functions in Vienna and Constantinople throughout the 1570s and 1580s.

Little wonder that a devout Catholic such as Eder was disenchanted with the Court in which he worked during this apparent Golden Age for the advocates of confessional moderation. Indeed, Eder himself concluded bitterly that the *Hofchristen* had done more damage to Catholicism than the heretics themselves.[25] But is this fair? Was the Viennese Court in the third quarter of the sixteenth century full of confessional 'weathervanes' who twisted and turned in response to the

---

[23] Vienna University had long had a reputation for the nourishment and protection of Protestantism in various forms. In 1520, for example, the university rector refused to publish the papal bull against Luther. Nearly four decades later, in 1559, Vienna University was still being criticized by Rome for possessing Lutheran works and harbouring Lutheran professors.

[24] Another more practical reason for the Habsburgs' willingness to employ and promote representatives of a spectrum of religious positions lay in the desperate need for competent civil servants. Owing to the dramatic expansion of central European territories under his command from the 1520s, Ferdinand I had greatly expanded the number of Habsburg administrative bodies based at his Court in Vienna.

[25] Eder to Duke Wilhelm of Bavaria, 6 October 1582, in Bibl, 'Die Berichte des Reichshofrates Dr Georg Eder', p. 130.

political climate? And did their policies result in the release of 'wolves', whose damage to the Catholic Church was fierce and irreparable? The remainder of this essay will re-examine the nature and impact of confessional moderation at the Habsburg Court in Vienna in the second half of the sixteenth century. In so doing, it will demonstrate that this variety of moderation was much more than a panicked response to difficult circumstances, the haphazard twistings of directionless policy or the whim of personality. Rather, it was the result of an alternate vision of Catholicism, and one somewhat removed from that of Tridentine Rome, Spain and Jesuit-influenced critics such as Eder.

The brand of Catholicism espoused by the heads of the Austrian Habsburg Court in the second half of the sixteenth century was one propelled by the wish for enhanced dynastic control over their own affairs, and fuelled by the principles of humanism. As such, this policy of confessional moderation caused no lasting damage to Austrian Catholicism. The dynasty remained at heart Catholic, and any apparent concessions to Protestantism in their own lands were offset by a continued commitment to strengthening the Catholic Church for the future. The most apt description of this brand of Catholicism is 'aulic Catholicism', coined by R.J.W. Evans in the 1970s: a Catholicism that ran parallel to Rome in many ways, but was distinctively Habsburg in its perspectives and priorities.[26] Though this term has not since been much used as a tool with which to comprehend the nature of moderation at the Habsburg Court in sixteenth-century Vienna, it offers a concise statement of the intentions behind a policy that was Catholic in essence, but frequently in opposition to Rome and Rome's allies.

The 'aulic Catholicism' of the Austrian Habsburgs of the mid to late sixteenth century was centred on maintaining at least the appearance of legislative autonomy and freedom of decision-making for the Empire and their own lands. This can be seen most clearly in the troubled relationship between Vienna and Rome. Holy Roman Emperors had a long history of antagonism towards the claims of the papacy, and in the sixteenth century Habsburg–papal relations reached a new low, with Charles V's participation in the Sack of Rome in 1527, and Pope Paul IV's participation in an anti-Habsburg alliance with France in 1556. This tradition of animosity was the result of the respective powers' concern to protect their own authority and defend their influence over ecclesiastical appointments and law-making; the Vatican was also concerned by Habsburg military activities in the Italian peninsula. With Maximilian II,

---

[26] Evans, *Making of the Habsburg Monarchy*, pp. 59–61. Evans bases this on 'the dynastic ideology of the Habsburgs ... an aulic Catholicism revivified by the example of Counter-Reformation, especially after 1600, yet never identical with it'.

however, this sensitivity had a personal edge. His apparently evangelical proclivities as a young man meant that Pope Julius III had supported the election of Maximilian's cousin and rival Philip of Spain during the succession crisis of 1551.

Emphasis on legislative independence and freedom from outside influence also spilled into other areas, most notably Austrian Habsburg relations with Spain. The strained relationship between Maximilian II and Philip II has already been mentioned; this animosity was based, however, on much more than Maximilian's distaste for what he saw as the needless ferocity of his cousin's Catholic devotion. Maximilian, like many in the Empire, viewed Spain as being closely in league with Rome, Julius III's recent support for Philip II's claim to the imperial title being a case in point. Furthermore, the Estates of the Empire with whom Maximilian and his father Ferdinand had to deal with were hyper-sensitive to what might even appear to them as 'foreign' interference from Spain or Rome.[27] In order to enhance their image as 'German' Emperors, and emphasize their own authority within the Empire, Ferdinand I and Maximilian II were thus anxious to avoid any sign of susceptibility to outside influence, or lack of control in their own realms.[28]

It is through these political, dynastic and sometimes personal issues that much of the apparent confessional moderation of the Austrian Habsburgs can be explained. In the Empire, Ferdinand and later Maximilian both sanctioned the Peace of Augsburg; in part because they had no choice, in part because it would bring a measure of peace, but also because their seal of approval restored their position as the legitimate source of law and order in the Empire. This need for control over the Empire also explains the attitude of the ruling Austrian Habsburgs to the Heidelberg Confession. Not only did the rise of Calvinism in the Empire have the potential to damage the hard-won peace, but permitting any infringements of the 1555 legislation would also have been a sign of dynastic weakness and lack of authority.[29]

For the Austrian lands, the legislation of the second half of the sixteenth century, and into the seventeenth, seems not to have been guided by confessional issues as much as by Habsburg determination to assert their own independence from outside influence. In the Austrian Habsburg lands, neither the Inquisition nor the Index enjoyed any imperial sanction, while the decrees of the Council of Trent were not

---

[27] Sutter Fichtner, *Emperor Maximilian II*, p. 33.
[28] Ibid., p. 1. Sutter Fichtner comments that Leopold von Ranke saw virtue in the stance of Maximilian II, as his politics in the Empire furthered Lutheranism, the German 'national' religion.
[29] Ibid., p. 49.

promulgated until 1637, and even then only in part. An especially telling example of this dynastic wish to express independence from Rome can also be seen in the case of the implementation of the Gregorian calendar reform in the Austrian lands. The papal bull *Inter Gravissimas* of 24 February 1581 announced that ten days were to be 'lost' between 4 October and 15 October 1582 in order to realign the calendar.[30] While areas such as Spain and Bavaria did exactly as Rome asked, when Rome asked, the calendar reform was not introduced in the Austrian lands until 1583, in part due to local resistance but also due to a symbolic Habsburg insistence on autonomous control of its affairs.

There is, however, another factor behind the confessional moderation of the Austrian Habsburgs in the sixteenth century, a force that made their policies more than mere tinkering with legislation to dilute its more distateful elements. Their brand of moderation took inspiration in the principles of humanism, in particular an Erasmianism that manifested itself in a belief in open debate, inclusiveness where possible and compromise where necessary.

The courts of the Austrian Habsburgs, including that at Vienna, have been described as representing 'the climax of orthodox Humanism in Austria'.[31] This can be seen most clearly in the careers of the scholars appointed by Ferdinand and Maximilian to serve in Vienna. Though the likes of Blotius, Lazius, Sambucus, Crato and Clusius have already been mentioned as demonstrating the confessional variety of the Viennese Court of the 1550s–1570s, their initial appointments were all based on their expertise in all matters dear to humanism: the study of history, of language, of manuscripts and of natural science. In part, this can be put down simply to the emperors' considerable personal intellectual interests. Maximilian II in particular was well known in his own day for his deep fascination with science and the collection and study of antiquities. The author Andreas Camutius recorded how the Emperor liked to enter debates on literature and inscriptions, while the correspondence of his ambassadors in Spain contains many references to Maximilian's demands for rarities from the New World, especially exotic plants and animals.[32]

---

[30] Rona Johnston Gordon, 'Confessional Tensions in Lower Austria: The Gregorian Calendar Reform', unpublished paper presented at the 2001 Sixteenth-Century Studies Conference, Denver, CO. I am grateful to Dr Johnston Gordon for allowing me the use of this paper.
[31] Evans, *Making of the Habsburg Monarchy*, p. 20.
[32] Ibid., p. 21; Susanne Herrnleben, 'Zur Korrespondenz Kaiser Maximilians II. mit seinen Gesandten in Spanien (1564–1576)', in Edelmayer and Kohler, *Kaiser Maximilian II*, p. 105. What has received less attention is that the Emperor Ferdinand I had similar interests and was described by a Venetian ambassador as a most curious investigator of nature, of foreign countries, plants and animals. Mühlberger, 'Bildung und Wissenschaft', p. 217.

A number of historians, however, have also linked the intellectual interests of the mid-sixteenth-century Austrian Habsburgs and their Court scholars with a spirit of Erasmianism or Christian humanism, that placed high value on the virtues of religious moderation and compromise in the interests of salvaging Christian unity.[33] R.J.W. Evans points in particular to the efforts of Ferdinand I to have Rome authorize clerical marriage and the use of the lay chalice, describing these as 'not simply a gesture from weakness, but a real movement towards conciliation within the area of *adiaphora*'.[34] The behaviour of his successor suggests that Maximilian II was indeed attempting to follow his father's lead. Much as Ferdinand opposed his son's relationship with Pfauser, his very public employment at least educated Maximilian on the evangelical side of the confessional debate, while demonstrating his willingness to understand his Lutheran subjects. Also of note is Maximilian's little-known correspondence with none other than Philip Melanchthon, around the same time as Pfauser's appointment. Maximilian first approached Melanchthon in 1555 for his views on the key areas of doctrinal debate. Melanchthon's replies challenged the then-young Maximilian to work as 'God's tool for his *universal* Church', and centred his advice on re-building Christian unity.[35] Maximilian's subsequent support for the Peace of Augsburg, his openness to the employment of Protestants and his stance against extremism of any sort throughout his career, all suggest that such moderation was indeed based on the ideology as well as the politics of compromise.

To return to the fears of contemporary Catholic observers such as Georg Eder, however, could it not be argued that such policies also caused damage to Catholic reform, by permitting the release of heretical 'wolves'? As politically astute and intellectually sound as the confessional moderation of the Austrian Habsburgs may have been, they also permitted a measure of freedom for Lutheranism that did not exist in Catholic states less willing to compromise, such as Spain or, within the

---

[33] Louthan's *Quest for Compromise* is especially strong on how the careers of Blotius, Crato and Catholics Jacopo Strada and Lazarus von Schwendi all contributed to the Viennese Court ethos of confessional moderation in the reign of Maximilian II. Though Louthan refers to an 'Erasmian dynamic operative within Vienna', p. 2, he prefers use of the term 'irenicism' to describe the mood of the Viennese Court in this period. Sutter Fichtner also refers to the 'general Erasmianism' of Ferdinand I, while Evans makes mention of the 'Erasmian sympathies' of some of Ferdinand's advisors. Sutter Fichtner, *Emperor Maximilian II*, p. 38; Evans, *Making of the Habsburg Monarchy*, p. 19.

[34] Evans, *Making of the Habsburg Monarchy*, p. 19. Evans adds that on his death, Ferdinand I even won praise from the English Bishop Edmund Grindal.

[35] Louthan, *Quest for Compromise*, p. 103.

Empire, Bavaria. What is frequently overlooked in discussions of the Austrian Habsburg rulers of this period, and in particular of Maximilian II, is that the dynasty remained fundamentally and overwhelmingly Catholic, and as such never aimed to leave their faith at the mercy of the 'wolves' evoked by Eder. The weight of evidence points rather to their desire to bolster and regenerate the Catholic Church, both in the Empire and in their own lands, so long as this was in a manner consistent with their own demand for control and the preservation of dynastic authority.

It is Maximilian II's reputation as a Catholic that has suffered most from his apparent openness to evangelicalism and as such needs to be rehabilitated.[36] First, there never was a major rift between the two branches of the dynasty over religion: both sides remained loyal to the Catholic Church, though as we have seen, this was of necessity demonstrated in different ways. Despite his occasional differences with Philip II, relations between the Austrian and Spanish branches of the Habsburg dynasty remained close even under the rule of Maximilian II. Having spent four formative years in Spain himself, Maximilian sent his two eldest sons to stay with their uncle Philip for eight years, from 1563 to 1571. Maximilian's own wife, Maria, with whom he had a long and fruitful marriage, was Philip II's sister. Her devotion to Catholicism was such that she was publicly praised by Pope Pius V, although this was no doubt a Roman snub intended for her husband.[37] Maximilian conceded to his wife's wishes that their children be raised according to the Roman rites, and did not stand in the way of Maria's keen patronage of the Jesuits in Vienna.[38] Recent research has also brought the efforts of their daughter to light. As the 27-year-old widow of King Charles IX of France, the Habsburg Archduchess Elisabeth returned to Vienna in 1581, where she spent the remaining 11 years of her life working for the establishment of a house of Poor Clares in the city. It was known as the 'Queen's Cloister, Our Lady Queen of Angels'. She was assisted in her efforts by her aunt, Anna of Bavaria, while Elisabeth herself had a Court following while in Vienna.[39]

---

[36] Sutter Fichtner offers some helpful material on this subject: *Emperor Maximilian II*, pp. 32 ff.

[37] Ibid., p. 19.

[38] Evans notes: 'Thus Papal and dynastic Catholicism, notionally distinct, wove intricate patterns in these years and much of their interaction remains veiled and confused.' *Rudolf II*, p. 62.

[39] On Elisabeth, see Joseph F. Patrouch: 'Ysabell/Elisabeth/Alzbeta: Erzherzogin. Königin. Ein Forschungsgegenwurff'. *Frühneuzeit-Info* 10 (1999), 257–65; 'The Archduchess Elizabeth: Where Spain and Austria Met', in Conrad Kent et al. (eds), *The Lion and the Eagle: Interdisciplinary Essays on German–Spanish Relations over the Centuries* (New York and Oxford, 2000), 77–90.

Maximilian II's Court was thus one in which his family was largely free to act for the furtherance of the Catholic Church, even through agencies such as the Jesuits, which made the policy of confessional moderation all the more difficult. It was also a Court in which Catholic scholars and courtiers could equally thrive. Maximilian II's Protestant appointments tend to receive more attention, but he also acted as a patron for Catholic scholars, musicians and painters from Italy, Spain and the Spanish Netherlands.[40] In the administrative ranks, too, not only was the vocal Catholic Eder given a high position in the Court he was so fond of criticizing, but the *Reichshofrat* in which he served had a number of other influential Catholic members, all appointed by Maximilian II himself. The Bologna-trained Doctor of Law Johann Hegenmüller, *Reichshofrat* from 1566 until 1583, had been called from Bavaria into Habsburg service in Vienna, and he was held in such high regard that he taught law to Maximilian's younger brothers. Hegenmüller was rewarded as early as 1568 with enoblement, and later became *Hofkanzler* under Rudolf II.[41] Other Catholic *Reichshofräte* of the period were Christoph Pirckhaimer, praised after his death by none less than the Society of Jesus, and Siegmund Viehauser, who rose rapidly from the *Reichshofrat* in 1573 to the rank of imperial Vice-Chancellor in 1577.[42] Lastly, Dr Timotheus Jung, a regular member of the *Reichshofrat* from 1568 to 1569, was a Lutheran convert. His insistence on attending Catholic services even at the *Reichstag* in Augsburg in 1559, much to the disgust of the powerful Protestants all around him, did not hinder his promotion at the Viennese Court, and he continued to attend almost every *Reichstag* as a valued member of the Austrian delegation.[43]

Nor was such a Catholic presence at the Vienna Court of the second half of the sixteenth century limited to members of the *Reichshofrat*. Leonhard von Harrach, a representative of a leading Lower Austrian noble family, acted as *Obersthofmarschall* until 1567.[44] Such was Harrach's reputation as a devout Catholic that the dying Ferdinand I reputedly charged him with the defence of the faith in the Austrian

---

[40] Sutter Fichtner, *Emperor Maximilian II*, p. 33.
[41] Oswald von Gschließer, *Der Reichshofrat* (Vienna, 1942), pp. 119–21.
[42] Ibid., pp. 120, 131–2, 142. Pirckhaimer served as *Reichshofrat* from 1581 to 1591. Viehauser replaced Weber as *Reichsvizekanzler*, and remained so until his death in April 1587.
[43] Ibid., pp. 112–13.
[44] Thomas Fellner and Heinrich Kretschmayr, *Die Österreichische Zentralverwaltung I Abteilung Von Maximilian I. bis zur vereinigung der Österreichischen und Böhmischen Hofkanzlei* (1749) Aktenstücke 1491–1681 (2 vols, Vienna, 1907), vol. 2, p. 188. As *Obersthofmarschall*, Harrach held one of the four major posts at the Habsburg Court in Vienna, including jurisdiction over all other courtiers.

lands.[45] Another highly trusted Catholic at the Habsburg Court in Vienna was Adam von Dietrichstein. He was sent by Emperor Maximilian II to represent him in Madrid while his sons Rudolf and Ernst were there, and Dietrichstein's piety also impressed the royal Spanish host.[46] Philip II even made Dietrichstein and his sons knights of Calatrava, and paid him additional wages to urge his master back in Vienna to be more obedient to Rome.[47] Andreas Khevenhüller of Frankenburg and Hochosterwitz was another Austrian noble known for his Catholicism. Such was his reputation that he spent 32 years in a post similar to that held by Dietrichstein, as ambassador in Madrid between 1574 and 1606. Wolfgang Unversagt, another known Catholic from Vienna itself, is listed in the Vienna Court register list of December 1576 as having served as *Reichs-und Hofsecretarien* since 28 May 1567: that he also served in the Privy Council and briefly in the *Reichshofrat* places him at the heart of the Habsburg administration in Vienna.[48]

Just as this substantial Catholic presence at the Vienna Court has frequently been overlooked in favour of its more incongruous elements, so too have Habsburg concessions to Protestantism been highlighted at the expense of the weight of legislation which rather sought not only to aid Catholicism, but to ensure all concessions made to Protestants were kept to a minimum. In Lower Austria, for example, striking as the *Konzession* and *Assekuration* may have been, they were atypical of Habsburg reaction to Protestantism in the hereditary lands. Maximilian II's negotiations with the Lower Austrian estates over the *Konzession* of 1568 took a full two years in a period when his need for finance was urgent. Loud demands for a Lutheran Church in Vienna were met with provision of a single room. Nor did these compromises last. As early as 1578, Maximilian's successor in Lower Austria, his second son Archduke Ernst, oversaw their partial dismantling. On 6 May 1578 the closure of

---

[45] Louthan, *Quest for Compromise*, p. 132, citing F. Mencik, 'Das religiöse Testament Kaiser Ferdinands I', *Mitteilungen des Instituts für Österreichische Geschichtsforschung* 20 (1899), p. 105 ff.

[46] Dietrichstein was with Rudolf and Ernst between 1564 and 1571, and was also in the country from 1572 to 1573. On Dietrichstein see Friedrich Edelmayer, 'Ehre, Geld, Karriere: Adam von Dietrichstein im Dienst Kaiser Maximilians II', in Edelmayer and Kohler, *Kaiser Maximilian II*, 95–108 and Susanne Herrnleben, 'Zur Korrespondenz Kaiser Maximilians II. Mit Seinen Gesandten In Spanien', in ibid., 109–42.

[47] Sutter Fichtner, *Maximilian II*, p. 213.

[48] Fellner and Kretschmayr, *Die Österreichische Zentralverwaltung*, vol. 2, p. 194; Lothar Gross, *Inventare des Wiener Haus-, Hof- und Staatsarchivs Bd I Der Geschichte der deutschen Reichshofkanzlei von 1559 bis 1806* (Vienna, 1933), pp. 372 ff. The Privy Council consisted of a small group of senior Habsburg courtiers who usually met daily to advise on matters of state including foreign affairs and legal and financial matters.

the Lutheran church in Vienna was announced, along with that of the Lutheran bookshop and school. The city's foremost Lutheran preacher, Josua Opitz, was expelled from the city on 21 June, and a nervous Archduke Ernst even withstood a mass protest a year later.[49]

Such steps complemented the main thrust of legislation emanating from the Viennese Court in this period: the defence, reform and rehabilitation of Catholicism. Despite his numerous differences with the papacy, even Maximilian II applauded popes who sought internal reform. He was particularly hopeful, for example, at the election of Julius III's successor, Marcellus II, in March 1555, only to see these hopes dashed by Marcellus's sudden death just two months later. Maximilian's desire for reform even saw him offer input into the last session of the Council of Trent. When it began in 1562, the future Emperor compiled a list of cardinals who, in his view, were genuinely committed to reform of the Church.[50]

It has been the contention of this essay that this was 'aulic Catholicism', that is, an Austrian Habsburg version of that condoned by Rome, which sought to strengthen the Catholic Church, but only in ways that would enhance the strength of the dynasty and maintain the ideals of moderation and compromise in the interests of peace and unity. Two final examples, both from the rule of Maximilian II, demonstrate how all of these ends were achieved by the Court at Vienna, while at the same time establishing a base for long-term Catholic revival: Maximilian's ambivalence towards the Jesuits and his establishment of the *Klosterrat*, or monastery commission.

The attitude of Maximilian II regarding the Jesuits is, at first sight, almost wholly negative. His father, Ferdinand, had held the order in the highest regard; he had first called them to Vienna, and was described by a contemporary as loving those who came as brothers.[51] Such was Ferdinand's approval of their work in the city, that he requested Peter

---

[49] The so-called *Sturmpetition* or *Fußfall der Fünftausend* took place in Vienna on 19 July 1579, and was a protest by the evangelical nobles, knights and Bürger at the anti-Lutheran laws of the previous year. Georg Eder recorded the event in vivid terms, describing how when the young Archduke went to a window of the *Hofburg*, he was met by the sight of 6000 people falling to their knees and calling loudly for the Word of God. Eder to Duke Albrecht, 10 August 1579, 'Die Berichte des Reichshofrates Dr Georg Eder', p. 90.

[50] Sutter Fichtner, *Emperor Maximilian II*, p. 42.

[51] Friedrich Staphylus to Stanislaus Hosius, then Bishop of Ermland, 16 February 1555. Staphylus referred in particular to Ferdinand's regard for Bobadilla, Le Jay and Canisius, who all served in the early phase of the Viennese mission. Bernhard Duhr, 'Die Jesuiten an den deutschen Fürstenhöfen des 16. Jahrhunderts', in Ludwig Pastor (ed.), *Erläuterungen und Ergänzungen zu Janssens Geschichte des deutschen Volkes*, II Band 4. Heft (Freiburg im Breisgau, 1901), p. 7.

Canisius to compose what would become his highly influential Catholic catechism with an introduction by Ferdinand himself.[52] Maximilian, however, saw the Jesuits in a rather different light, and regarded them as a serious threat to the key points of his policy: the maintenance of dynastic control, independence from Roman and Spanish influence, and the pursuit of peace through moderation and compromise. On a personal level, matters were complicated by Pfauser's suggestion that certain Jesuits, distrustful of Maximilian's confessional allegiance, had persuaded his father that he should not be permitted to govern Bohemia. Such was his fury that Maximilian delayed the publication of the first edition of Canisius' catechism in 1555, instigating yet another row with his father.[53]

On closer inspection, though, it seems that Maximilian was just as aware as his father of all that the Society of Jesus could offer to the ailing Church in their own lands. Maximilian's tactic with regard to the Jesuits was thus one of publicly denying them influence, but privately facilitating their missions. A useful example comes from July 1571, when the Lower Austrian monastery commission noted that the house of St Anna remained wealthy but was inhabited by only one nun. It subsequently advised the Emperor to incorporate the house into that of St James, but the Jesuits seized their chance and asked the Emperor to use the St Anna property to boost the income of the over-stretched Jesuit college in Vienna instead. Maximilian agreed, albeit slowly, thus demonstrating his goal of furthering Catholic reform on his own terms and without risk to his public image of control, authority and moderation.[54] The same policy seems to explain the fact that it was under his authority that the Carmelite property in which the Viennese Jesuits had been based since 1554 was formally handed over to them.

The establishment of the *Klosterrat* in 1568 is in itself a further indication of the Habsburg's concern for reform, but on his own terms. Maximilian II was no doubt aware of the financial benefits to be gained from greater secular control over the monasteries in the Austrian lands; he was, however, also deeply concerned at the level of spiritual decline within religious houses. He thus established the monastery commission as a practical means of monitoring the quality of preaching, appointment of abbots and administration of sacraments as well as the economic status of every monastery within Lower Austria. This was accompanied by the predictable Habsburg–papal battles over authority. As a direct

---

[52] John O'Malley, *The First Jesuits* (Cambridge, MA, 1993), pp. 123, 207.
[53] Sutter Fichtner, *Emperor Maximilian II*, p. 37.
[54] L. Bittner, *Inventare des Wiener Haus-, Hof- und Staatsarchivs Bd. V Gesamtinventar des Wiener Haus-, Hof und Staatsarchivs* (5 vols, Vienna, 1936), vol. 5, pp. 519–21.

response to the commission's establishment in 1568, Pope Pius V ordered Cardinal Commendone to undertake a visitation of Austria as, it has been observed, 'more a staking out of claims and territory than a well-thought-out attempt to reform the monasteries visited'.[55] It was 1592 before an uneasy compromise was reached between the secular and ecclesiastical authorities over the source, direction and supervision of Catholic reform in the Austrian Habsburg lands.[56] The point is, however, that the establishment of the *Klosterrat* was yet a further manifestation of a policy that simultaneously allowed for the reform and reinforcement of Catholicism, while maintaining the appearance of dynastic control.[57]

Allowing for the inevitable process of re-education and generational change, this interpretation of Austrian Habsburg religious policy in the second half of the sixteenth century both explains the later revival of Catholicism in the Austrian lands, and says much about the nature of its spell of confessional moderation. This was no knee-jerk reaction to pressure, but consistent with humanist and dynastic principles. It allowed, furthermore, for the continued patronage of Catholic reform – at least Catholic reform under Habsburg control. What looked to one man like the random movements of a weathervane and the destructive acts of a wolf was, to its Habsburg advocates, a form of confessional moderation that allowed their dynasty to survive and their faith to reform and revive.

---

[55] Joseph F. Patrouch, 'Methods of Cultural Manipulation: The Counter-Reformation in the Habsburg Province of Upper Austria, 1570–1650' (unpublished PhD thesis, Berkeley, 1991), 117. For more on this, see also Patrouch's 'The Investiture Controversy Revisited: Religious Reform, Emperor Maximilian II, and the Klosterrat', *Austrian History Yearbook* 25 (1994), 59–77.

[56] This was via the Passau Treaty of 6 November 1592, signed in Prague by Rudolf II and Bishop Urban of Passau.

[57] Joseph F. Patrouch, 'The Investiture Controversy Revisited: Religious Reform, Emperor Maximilian II, and the Klosterrat', in *Austrian History Yearbook* 25 (1994), p. 61. It should be noted that Habsburg authority to legislate in ecclesiastical matters was not wholly without precedent. In 1446 Pope Eugenius IV had allowed Maximilian II's ancestor Frederick III the right of nomination of suitable candidates for bishoprics that lay within Habsburg holdings. The dynasty also held the *placetum regium* or the right to allow the promulgation of papal decrees in their own lands.

CHAPTER NINE

René Benoist: Scripture for the Catholic Masses

Alison Carter

The Reformation period in France has traditionally been viewed as a time of deep division which brought about a polarization that sometimes appeared to operate as a way of defining systems of belief. For instance, whereas Protestants advocated the wide availability of Scripture in the vernacular, the Parisian Faculty of Theology had banned French translations of the Bible as early as the 1520s. This antagonistic 'dialogue' between Protestant and Catholic authorities helped to define doctrine and underscore differences; when these differences led to civil war, it no doubt seemed unwise to depart from the position outlined by one's Church. Yet recent work by Thierry Wanegffelen has cast doubt on the traditional categories and language used when considering the Reformation landscape in France.[1] His research has concentrated on a number of figures who acted in a manner that can be categorized neither as entirely 'Protestant' nor entirely 'Catholic' in a restricted sense. To use Wanegffelen's terminology, they were *d'entre-deux* – somewhere between Rome and Geneva. He sees the Catholic theologian René Benoist (1521–1608) as coming into this group.[2]

On first appearance, this may seem strange; indeed, it may seem strange that Benoist should be studied in a volume discussing moderate currents, for his output includes many polemical tracts attacking Protestant doctrine and practices and his position on heterodox thought did not alter at any point in his career. Benoist's agenda, however, differed in many respects from those of his colleagues at the Faculty of Theology and, after considerable controversy following the publication of a French Bible in the 1560s, resulted in his expulsion from the

---

[1] Thierry Wanegffelen, *Ni Rome ni Genève: Des fidèles entre deux chaires en France au XVIe siècle* (Paris, 1997); see also his *Une difficile fidélité: Catholiques malgré le Concile en France, XVIe–XVIIe siècles* (Paris, 1999).

[2] Wanegffelen's work has had a mixed reception. Certain aspects have been criticized by Alain Tallon (for instance, his *Conscience nationale et sentiment religieux en France au XVIe siècle: Essai sur la vision gallicane du monde* (Paris, 2002), p. 16, n. 2); cf. Mack P. Holt's more favourable review in *SCJ* 29 (1998), 575–7.

Faculty in the following decade. It is in fact by examining and seeking to explain his activities surrounding the translation of Scripture that we begin to understand the motivations that lay behind his work and can identify the currents of thought that had influenced him. As we shall see by the end of this essay, if we do seek to categorize Benoist, we should turn to the vocabulary of a period much earlier in the sixteenth century, for his work recalls that of those working in pre-Reformation movements.[3]

Although Benoist was an influential figure for much of the latter half of the sixteenth century, few studies focus in any detail on the theologian or his activities, with the exception of interest in some aspects of the Bible controversy.[4] Benoist was born into humble surroundings not far from Angers.[5] After running away from the parental home and eventually beginning his theological studies and career in and around Angers, he moved to Paris, where he became a member of the Faculty of Theology in 1556; he was a student and then *docteur régent* at the Collège de Navarre. By 1559, he had gained a doctorate in theology in Paris; this in fact followed his first doctorate which had been awarded by the University of Angers. Benoist's public career began in earnest in the early 1560s. He travelled in 1561 to Scotland where he remained for a year as the confessor to Mary, Queen of Scots.[6] In 1568, he was appointed *curé* of the important Parisian parish of St Eustache, a post he held for around 40 years. It is from activities related to this position that he later gained the nickname 'Pape des Halles',[7] which bears witness to his popularity and power.

---

[3] For an examination of how Wanegffelen's terminology is helpful in this area, yet perhaps benefits from some modification, see Alison Ruth Carter, 'René Benoist and the Instruction of the Catholic Laity' (unpublished PhD thesis, Durham, 2003), esp. ch. 1.

[4] The main point of reference remains Émile Pasquier, *Un curé de Paris pendant les guerres de Religion: René Benoist, le Pape des Halles (1521–1608). Étude historique et bibliographique* (Paris, 1913). My doctoral thesis appears to be the only other sustained attempt to review his career.

[5] Here I follow Pasquier, *Un curé de Paris*, pp. 19–313. Pasquier's account of Benoist's life before he moved to Paris is sketchy, no doubt due to Pasquier's difficulty in obtaining and assessing sources covering this period. Pasquier's biography has drawbacks, but cannot be dismissed as unreliable; it is thorough and amply documented. The weakest chapters in terms of primary sources are those covering Benoist's early life and his year in Scotland as the confessor of Mary, Queen of Scots.

[6] An appointment usually attributed to the Cardinal of Lorraine. Alain Tallon, *La France et le Concile de Trente (1518–1563)* (Rome, 1997), p. 568.

[7] This name, which refers to '*les Halles*', part of the area surrounding St Eustache in which the market was held, was recorded by the diarist Pierre de L'Estoile in 1590. Pierre de L'Estoile, *Mémoires-Journaux 1574–1611*, ed. G. Brunet et al. (12 vols, Paris, 1875–96, 1982), vol. 5, p. 45.

Although a prominent Parisian *curé*, Benoist never joined the League, retaining his independence whenever possible.[8] Indeed, his relationship with those with Leaguer sympathies was sometimes tense; for instance, in 1592, when verbal attacks targeted those, including Benoist, who called for peace, he was singled out as 'le Diable des Halles'.[9] On the other hand, he enjoyed good relations with the monarchy; in 1572, he was appointed as the first *lecteur Royal* in Theology, a post established by Charles IX. But it was with Henri IV, two decades later, that Benoist appears to have had his closest ties. After playing an important role in the conversion of Henry to Catholicism, he was rewarded with appointment as royal confessor in 1593. He then accumulated the titles of *conseiller du Roi* and *conseiller d'État*. The King also nominated Benoist as Bishop of Troyes in 1593, although he was never granted the necessary papal bulls to confirm this appointment, nor those to another bishopric for which he tried to gain the Pope's support, that of Angers. After a decade of political manoeuvrings by Henri IV and his diplomats, Benoist resigned his claim. He could, however, comfort himself with the position of *gouverneur de Navarre*, which he gained in conjunction with his duties as the King's confessor; from this position, he was able to control the proceedings of the Collège de Navarre. His standing within the University of Paris increased further in 1598 when he became Dean of the Faculty of Theology, a position which he held for ten years until his death in 1608.

In addition to carrying out his various ecclesiastical offices with commitment and dedication, Benoist had a reputation for being a talented preacher. He was certainly a prolific writer, publishing over two hundred works, of which more than 90 per cent were in the vernacular;[10] he was by far the most prolific of the French Counter-Reformation theologians.[11] He followed in the tracks of the few in the first half of the sixteenth century, such as Jérôme de Hangest, who wrote in French and took on the Protestants on their own terms. His publications were a mixture of the polemical – attacking Protestantism and defending Catholic doctrine – and the

---

[8]   On the involvement of Parisian *curés* in the activities of the *Ligue*, see Michel Pernot, *Les Guerres de Religion en France 1559–1598* (Paris, 1987), pp. 269–70, 291, n. 48.

[9]   L'Estoile, *Mémoires-Journaux*, vol. 5, p. 162.

[10]   Pasquier, *Un curé de Paris*, pp. 319–76. It is hard to determine the precise number of works involved. Pasquier sometimes separates multiple works originally published as one volume, leading to overestimation, but the ephemeral nature of certain of Benoist's works means that other titles have probably been lost.

[11]   My thanks to Alexander Wilkinson, director of the Sixteenth-Century French Vernacular Book Project, Reformation Studies Institute, University of St Andrews, who confirms that Benoist's publishing output was unrivalled.

didactic and devotional. The unusually high proportion of works written in French for a Catholic theologian of this time shows a concern for disseminating the Catholic message to the literate laity, as opposed to the ecclesiastical elite. Although he was concerned with combatting heresy by responding directly to Protestants such as Jean Calvin, most importantly, his works were intended to aid the Catholic masses, whether as weapons in their armoury, in the case of polemic, or as devotional shields in the form of instructional material.

Generalizations about Benoist's work have frequently been uncomplimentary regarding the tone and content of his writing. For many, he has appeared to slot neatly into the category of so-called 'typical' Counter-Reformation polemicist, with little to distinguish him from the rest.[12] On closer inspection, the nature and style of his polemic, when taken as a whole, is perhaps surprising. He remained relatively irenic, unless circumstances demanded otherwise and his position was particularly precarious.[13] Whilst the themes he uses when discussing Protestants and his representation of heresy are undoubtedly traditional in nature,[14] in general, the tone of his invective is less violent and his polemic is less unpleasant and more moderate than that of many other Catholic authors.[15] His biographer, for example, talks of his 'conseils si mesurés'.[16] Moreover, Benoist does not confine

---

[12] For a summary of the long line of contemptuous dismissals of Catholic polemic, see G. Wylie Sypher, '"Faisant ce qu'il leur vient à plaisir": The Image of Protestantism in French Catholic Polemic on the Eve of the Religious Wars', *SCJ* 11 (1980), pp. 61–2. For a more comprehensive and sympathetic evaluation of the invective generated by Catholic polemicists, see Luc Racaut, *Hatred in Print: Catholic Propaganda and Protestant Identity during the French Wars of Religion* (Aldershot, 2002). For criticisms levelled specifically at Benoist, see Barbara B. Diefendorf, *Beneath the Cross: Catholics and Huguenots in Sixteenth-Century Paris* (Oxford, 1991), pp. 149–52; Robert M. Kingdon, *Myths about the St Bartholomew's Day Massacres 1572–1576* (Cambridge, MA, 1988), pp. 40, 117. See also Carter, 'René Benoist', ch. 2.

[13] Carter, 'René Benoist', ch. 2. Benoist's position was precarious at times under the *Ligue*: for example, at the beginning of 1595, his property was seized, the repercussion of a long-running dispute with the Chapter of St Germain, who claimed part of St Eustache's income: Pasquier, *Un curé de Paris*, pp. 139–40. The Duke of Mayenne is said to have frequently plotted to kill Benoist: M. de Bongars, *Lettres* (Paris, 1668), p. 263, cited in Pasquier, *Un curé de Paris*, pp. 226–7.

[14] Racaut's work demonstrates the extent to which certain arguments employed against heresy in the work of Benoist and his colleagues were traditional. For instance, he identifies Benoist's implicit association of heresy with lechery and his condemnation of Protestantism for its perceived 'feminization of society': Racaut, *Hatred in Print*, pp. 33, 89, 94. In this, Benoist is clearly conservative and far from innovative.

[15] For polemicists such as Robert Ceneau and Antoine de Mouchy, see Racaut, *Hatred in Print*.

[16] This refers particularly to his output from the time of the *Ligue* onwards. Pasquier, *Un curé de Paris*, p. 312.

criticisms to heretics in his polemic and frequently attacks the behaviour of those in his own camp, especially abuses within the clergy. But most importantly, Benoist's uppermost preoccupation was to minister to the needs of the Catholic masses and much of his time and energy were channelled into providing devotional and instructional material. This is not what we would expect of a typical Catholic polemicist – or indeed of Benoist, if we were to follow without modification the ideas of, for instance, Barbara Diefendorf in this area.[17]

It is clear that Benoist was deeply committed to defending the Catholic cause and that he was an enemy of Protestantism; the nature of his published works alone underlines these facts. Yet despite this, several of his activities enraged his own Church authorities. He puzzled his contemporaries and has continued to bewilder historians to the present day. He has been thought of as 'suspect';[18] one contemporary called him a 'dangerous fox';[19] later historians, noting his divergence from the norm, have used words such as 'wayward' and even 'mad'.[20] But if we turn to Benoist's attitude to the dissemination of Scripture in the vernacular and several texts associated with this project, we can explain these alleged inconsistencies and eccentricities.

In practical terms, Benoist recognized that the Protestants had the upper hand when it came to Scripture.[21] By the 1560s, the Protestants in Geneva had produced an accurate and well-written French Bible that was also being printed regularly within France's borders in Lyons. The Catholic Church in Europe as a whole took an ambiguous position regarding Scriptural translations, as is demonstrated by the different opinions expressed at the Council of Trent in the 1540s. Certain factions pushed for a sanctioning of translations into the vernacular, whilst others attacked this stance.[22] The matter of vernacular translations was to

---

[17] Diefendorf, *Beneath the Cross*, pp. 149–52.

[18] When Benoist was pursuing papal confirmation to the bishopric of Troyes, the nuncio, Silingardi, damningly reported that he was 'most suspect of heresy' ('sospettissimo di heresie'). Vatican Archives, *Nunziatura di Francia*, vol. 47, fol. 38, cited in Pasquier, *Un curé de Paris*, p. 244, n. 2.

[19] [Yves Magistri], *Le réveil-matin et mot du guet des bons catholiques, par Jean de la Mothe Escuyer* (Douai, 1591), cited in Pasquier, *Un curé de Paris*, p. 217.

[20] Joseph Bergin, *The Making of the French Episcopate 1589–1661* (New Haven, 1996), p. 216; Amédée Boinet, *Les Églises parisiennes* (Paris, 1958–64), p. 468.

[21] See Pierre-Maurice Bogaert (ed.), *Les Bibles en français: Histoire illustrée du Moyen Âge à nos jours* (Turnhout, 1991), pp. 48–91; Bettye Thomas Chambers, *Bibliography of French Bibles: Fifteenth- and Sixteenth-Century French-Language Editions of the Scriptures* (Geneva, 1983), pp. xi–xv.

[22] Bogaert, *Les Bibles en français*, p. 87; Hubert Jedin, *A History of the Council of Trent*, tr. Dom Ernest Graf (London, 1957–61), pp. 67–9, 71–3, 75–6, 83–5, 92.

remain unresolved. In France, the position taken was often openly hostile, particularly amongst the Faculty of Theology's senior rank. The Faculty had banned French translations of the Bible in 1523, following the publication of vernacular translations of parts of the New Testament by the evangelical Jacques Lefèvre d'Étaples.[23] This decision had not been rescinded. For less progressive members in particular, a complete French Bible was unthinkable; it was considered dangerous. In their eyes, the 'illiterate' and 'ignorant' could not hope to understand all that was contained in the Bible and the Church's guiding hand must always accompany the text to act as interpreter. Furthermore, their view was that the Catholic laity should obey Church tradition as well as following God's word in the form of Scripture.

Benoist acted in direct contradiction to several of these principles. If a member of the Catholic laity wanted access to a French Bible, he had no choice but to turn to an existing Protestant Bible, due to the Faculty of Theology's censorship of French Bibles.[24] The French Bible that Benoist published in the 1560s was intended as a practical move to counter the Protestant Bible.[25] He took the best Bible translation available at the time, the Genevan Bible, and replaced the 'heretical' words with the appropriate Catholic expressions. He removed annotations with Protestant interpretations and provided others espousing the Catholic point of view. His method of translation is not unusual; in fact, almost all sixteenth-century French Bibles were to some extent revisions of earlier versions.[26]

Benoist published the edition under his own name in folio format in 1566 in Paris, under the noses of the censors.[27] That year, he also published a small Latin–French New Testament, and in 1568 a bilingual

---

[23] Chambers, *Bibliography*, no. 31; James K. Farge, *Orthodoxy and Reform in Early Reformation France: The Faculty of Theology of Paris, 1500–1543* (Leiden, 1985), pp. 177–80; Francis M. Higman, *Censorship and the Sorbonne: A Bibliographical Study of Books in French Censured by the Faculty of Theology of the University of Paris, 1520–1551* (Geneva, 1979), pp. 24–5.

[24] A previous Catholic version translated by Nicolas de Leuze (the Louvain Bible) had been published once in 1550 (Chambers, *Bibliography*, no.145), but copies were not easy to procure. Bogaert, *Les Bibles en français*, p. 91.

[25] On the Benoist Bible controversy, see Bogaert, *Les Bibles en français*, pp. 91–102; Carlo de Clercq, 'La Bible française de René Benoist', *Gutenberg-Jahrbuch* (1957), 168–74; Francis Higman, 'Les *Advertissemens* des Bibles de René Benoist (1566, 1568)', in Higman, *Lire et découvrir: La Circulation des idées au temps de la Réforme* (Geneva, 1998), 563–71; Pasquier, *Un curé de Paris*, pp. 85–116.

[26] The notable exception is Sébastien Châteillon's Bible (Chambers, *Bibliography*, no. 202).

[27] Chambers, *Bibliography*, nos 371–4.

Latin–French Bible in a quarto edition.[28] These publications caused great controversy amongst his colleagues at the Faculty for whom French Bibles were not to be tolerated. Furthermore, the Protestant scholarship remained all too evident in places, in both text and marginal notes. Benoist refused to retract his work, but it was censored by the Faculty, from whose ranks he was expelled in 1572, and it was eventually condemned by the Pope in 1575.[29] But it was Benoist who prevailed. In spite of the disapproval in Paris, Christopher Plantin in Antwerp had taken the Benoist translation, gained approval from the Louvain theologians and a privilege from Philip II of Spain and published Benoist's New Testament from 1567 onwards.[30] Plantin published the entire Bible in 1578.[31] This version was the one on which subsequent French Catholic translations were based into the next century in Lyons, Rouen and eventually Paris.[32] Benoist's victory became even more emphatic when he was accepted back into the ranks of the Faculty in 1598, supported by Henri IV.[33] This followed a speech renouncing his Bible – by now meaningless words, as the Bible was in common use.[34] Significantly, Benoist did not reject all Scriptural translations, only the French Bible published under his name. Immediately after delivering these words, as the eldest member, he became the Dean of the Faculty of Theology.

Benoist's attitude towards the Faculty during the long-running controversy has been called 'stiff-necked'.[35] Contemporaries and modern historians have seen him as stubborn and perverse when recounting the twists and turns of the prolonged Bible controversy.[36] His intransigence in the 1560s and 1570s and refusal to kowtow to the

[28] Ibid., nos 378–9, 399–402. In 1568, at least two of the publishers involved in the 1566 and 1568 Bibles (Chesneau and Guillard) shared a Latin–French New Testament edition of Benoist's text (Chambers, *Bibliography*, nos 405–6); one year later, three of the publishers (Chesneau, Nivelle and Buon; Guillard had died) shared another Latin–French New Testament (Chambers, *Bibliography*, nos 413–15). Chesneau also published a French-only Benoist New Testament (Chambers, *Bibliography*, no. 416).
[29] *Collectio Judiciorum de novis erroribus*, ed. Charles Duplessis d'Argentré (3 vols, Paris, 1724–36, repr. Brussels, 1963), vol. 2, pp. 417, 442.
[30] Chambers, *Bibliography*, no. 385.
[31] Ibid., no. 439.
[32] Benoist's text was still being used at the beginning of the eighteenth century. Bogaert, *Les Bibles en français*, pp. 98–101.
[33] Bogaert, *Les Bibles en français*, p. 102; De Clercq, 'La Bible française de René Benoist', 174; Pasquier, *Un curé de Paris*, pp. 260–61.
[34] *Collectio Judiciorum de novis erroribus*, ed. Duplessis d'Argentré, vol. 2, p. 534.
[35] M.H. Black, 'The Transition to the Seventeenth Century', under 'The Printed Bible', in *The Cambridge History of the Bible*, ed. P.R. Ackroyd et al. (3 vols, Cambridge, 1963–70), vol. 3, p. 448.
[36] Pasquier, whose book received the Bishop of Angers's *imprimatur*, saw Benoist as stubborn, lacking humility and having a persecution complex: *Un curé de Paris*, pp. 168, 259, 303.

Faculty's decisions were only matched by the Faculty's single-minded approach on the matter. However, Benoist's motives have perhaps been misinterpreted. It is in fact clear that in addition to coping pragmatically with opposition as it arose, Benoist had a very specific agenda regarding Scripture. Making the Bible accessible to the masses in their own tongue formed an essential part of a broad programme for the vernacular religious instruction of the laity which linked back to the late medieval period and early sixteenth century before the spread of Lutheranism, when various movements within the Church – reforming or humanist – had advocated the dissemination of Scripture in the vernacular.[37]

The reasons underpinning the tenacious pursuit of his project are frequently expressed by Benoist: indeed, he engaged in argument in defence of Bible translation both outside and within the editions of the Bible translations themselves, often juxtaposing the polemical and the devotional. His central contention is that Scripture is the keystone; the most important weapon for the Catholic laity is the spiritual sword of God's word, expressed most purely in Scripture.[38] Benoist certainly did not undervalue sermons and was himself a popular preacher, although he often lamented the inadequacy of much of the clergy's preaching.[39] In prefatory material in all three of his Bible and New Testament editions, he underlined the importance of the Christian having God's word. In perhaps the most memorable, in the dedication of his 1566 French Bible, reprinted in his 1568 Latin–French Bible, Benoist introduced the idea of the four stratagems of Satan for attacking the Church; one of these, he claims, is Satan's suppression of Scripture.[40] In addition to these texts, he defended his actions elsewhere. For instance, one anonymous pamphlet in manuscript form, later attributed to Benoist (or at least to his secretary), was circulated in 1574 whilst the prolonged wrangling with the Faculty

---

[37] Carter, 'René Benoist', ch. 3.

[38] See Benoist's 1568 Bible (Chambers, *Bibliography*, no. 399), fols †2ᵛ–†3ʳ. This material can also be found in his 1566 Bible.

[39] For example, René Benoist, *Brieve et facile response aux objections d'une damoyselle, par lesquelles elle rejecte la Saincte Messe* (Paris, 1565: Pasquier, no. 23), fol. 10ʳ.

[40] Chambers, *Bibliography*, no. 399: fol. †2ʳ. 'Firstly, he [Satan] has removed good and effective pastors from the Church. Secondly, he has virtually hidden Holy Scripture and God's word. Thirdly, he has eradicated the love and fear of God from the hearts of men. Finally, he has sent false prophets, ministers of his lie and irreligiousness.' ('Premierement il a osté les bons et operaires pasteurs de l'Eglise. Secondement il a comme caché et absconsé l'escriture saincte et parole de Dieu. Tiercement il a desraciné l'amour et crainte de Dieu des coeurs des hommes. Finablement il a envoyé des faulx prophetes, ministres de son mensonge et impieté.') This comment is representative of much of what Benoist says in these and other works.

of Theology continued.[41] This contained the arguments used by Benoist from the pulpit and in public to defend the work.[42] Throughout his career, he praised Scripture in his treatises and, even after the papal condemnation of 1575, he advocated the availability of at least parts of the Bible in the vernacular.[43] Furthermore, he included French translations of parts of the Bible in more than one work. For example, a 1579 treatise on sorcery and infertility published in Paris is in fact dominated by a French translation of Tobit.[44] He was thus simultaneously offering his reader instruction through biblical translation, and defending a book regarded by the Protestants as part of the Apocrypha. Substantial sections of the Bible can also be found in one of Benoist's last publications, which contains material used in his sermons.[45] This long work of over a thousand pages contains many passages from the Old and New Testament in French.[46] These two works and Benoist's Bible all contain a vast quantity of annotations pointing out parts of the text supporting Catholic doctrine; Benoist may have believed in making Scripture available to the laity, but the guiding hand of the Catholic Church remains essential.

Thus Benoist showed a great determination to provide the Catholic laity with Scripture in the vernacular. His inspiration in doing so was certainly not Protestant and could well have been born principally of pragmatism in the face of the Protestant challenge. Whether access to Scripture was desirable or not, Catholics who were going to read the Bible in French – however much the authorities disapproved – might as well be provided with a Catholic text and marginal notes. However, his frequent expression of the idea that access to Scripture is indeed desirable seems to look back to a time before the Reformation schism and to the enthusiasm for making Scripture available to the laity expressed by Erasmus and evangelical humanists like Jacques Lefèvre d'Étaples early in the sixteenth century. Furthermore, it suggests a spirit of Gallican

---

[41] *Juste et necessaire complainte pour M. René Benoist*, in *Collectio Judiciorum de novis erroribus*, ed. Duplessis d'Argentré, vol. 2, pp. 435–41. See Bogaert, *Les Bibles en français*, p. 96; De Clercq, 'La Bible française de René Benoist', p. 173; Pasquier, *Un curé de Paris*, pp. 97–8.

[42] Pasquier, *Un curé de Paris*, p. 98.

[43] See, for example, René Benoist, *Traicté enseignant en bref les causes des malefices, sortileges et enchanteries* (Paris, 1579: Pasquier, no. 69), 'Advertissement au Lecteur', sig. Ii3ʳ (fol. 249ʳ).

[44] Ibid.

[45] René Benoist, *Notables resolutions des presens differens de la religion: Prononcees par diverses predications, en plus de cinquante caresmes, preschez tant en ce royaume, que hors iceluy* (Paris, 1608: Pasquier, no. 129).

[46] On these two publications, see Carter, 'René Benoist', ch. 3.

independence also lively earlier in the century. For Bernard Chédozeau, who interprets the hostilities of the controversy with regard to Benoist's translation as arising at least in part from tension between Gallican and ultramontane factions, Benoist's behaviour clearly conforms to a Gallican model.[47] And, of course, his frequent complaints concerning clerical abuses conform closely to longstanding Gallican preoccupations.

Benoist's commitment to his French Bible demonstrates that he was prepared to go against the wishes of the Faculty of Theology and, in spirit at the very least, against Rome, in order to promote the instruction of the Catholic laity by means of books in the vernacular.[48] Central as Scripture was to this programme, it was not the only strand; several other projects supported it. One year after the publication of his Latin–French Bible in 1568, Benoist proceeded to publish a French translation of the Book of Hours. This was a significant move in several respects; a vernacular Book of Hours had run into problems with the Faculty of Theology in the 1520s, in a debate which related to the controversy between Erasmus and the Faculty concerning prayers in the vernacular and whether people should be able to understand the contents of their prayers,[49] as well as to the Faculty's censorship of Scriptural translations. Not only were entire Bible translations censored, so too were works containing parts of Scripture in translation and therefore the inclusion of parts of the Psalter and sequences of the Gospel had resulted in the condemnation of Pierre Gringore's French verse translation of the Book of Hours in 1525.[50] One of the most popular religious books of the late medieval period, particularly amongst women, was thus rendered suspect if translated. We should remember that, as Virginia Reinburg underlines, use of the Hours did not necessarily imply literacy:

> As a devotional object the book of hours is located at the
> intersection of literate and not necessarily literate religious
> experience – particularly the visual, aural and tactile dimensions of

---

[47] Bernard Chédozeau, *La Bible et la liturgie en français: L'Église tridentine et les traductions bibliques et liturgiques (1600–1789)* (Paris, 1990), pp. 110–14 and notes. For instance, in 1569, Benoist took the matter to the *Conseil du roi*; Chédozeau underlines Benoist's Gallican tendencies in doing so (p. 112). For a different view, see Tallon, *Conscience nationale et sentiment religieux*, and Tallon's essay in this volume.

[48] Benoist was not, of course, the only Catholic theologian to write in French at this time: see Francis Higman, 'Theology in French: Religious Pamphlets from the Counter-Reformation', in Higman, *Lire et découvrir*, 353–70. Benoist was, however, unparalleled in the scale and volume of his literary enterprise and alone in providing a vernacular translation of the Bible.

[49] *Collectio Judiciorum de novis erroribus*, ed. Duplessis d'Argentré, vol. 2, pp. 45, 61.

[50] Higman, *Censorship and the Sorbonne*, pp. 77–9.

devotional practice. Owners of books of hours sometimes pasted or sewed amulets, pilgrim badges and medallions inside their books. Both manuscript and printed prayer books usually included devotional images.[51]

Nevertheless, during the middle of the sixteenth century, a few vernacular editions started to appear. In 1569, Benoist published a Book of Hours in French, as well as a Latin–French version; it was subsequently printed in well over 30 editions from 1569 to 1646, indicating its mass appeal.[52] As with his Bible, Benoist put his name on the title page – an unusual move – demonstrating that he wanted to be associated with the project. Indeed, such was his enthusiasm that he added prefatory material, something largely unheard of in Books of Hours, in which he defended vernacular Hours and prayers in the vernacular. This could be seen as a pre-emptive move, for in 1571, the authorities in Rome attempted, but failed, to suppress editions organized in the manner of the Benoist Hours and in the vernacular.[53] In fact, Chédozeau suggests that Benoist's translation of the Hours was a contributory factor in his not receiving papal bulls for his bishopric.[54]

Several conclusions can be drawn from Benoist's Hours. First, Benoist was concerned that the Catholic laity should be provided with devotional texts in French and his Hours were clearly very popular, genuinely responding to the laity's needs. Second, although Benoist did not have Protestant leanings (Protestants would most certainly not have been interested in a prayer book offering prayers principally to the Virgin),[55] he was unafraid to challenge the ecclesiastical authorities in Paris and Rome by the publication of a translation of this particular text and his support for vernacular prayers. Third, his position on prayers recalls once again that of those working in certain pre-Reformation movements. Finally, in presentational terms, Benoist's Hours formed a sharp contrast to many of the Latin Hours in circulation at the time, which retained gothic characters and whose Latin texts of the Hours of

---

[51] Virginia Reinburg, 'Books of Hours', in Andrew Pettegree et al. (eds), *The Sixteenth-Century French Religious Book* (Aldershot, 2001), 68–82, p. 71.

[52] *Heures de Nostre-Dame à l'usage de Rome* (1569 onwards: Pasquier, nos 145–6). Pasquier identifies 19 editions; my own searches to date have taken the total to around 40 and include a 1569 Latin–French version not listed by Pasquier.

[53] Carter, 'René Benoist', ch. 4. For the text of the papal bull, see BL C.65.k.9: *Officium b. Mariae Virginis, nuper reformatum, et Pii. V. pont. max. iussu editum. Cum privilegio, et indulgentiis* (Rome: in Aedibus Populi Romani, 1571), prefatory material.

[54] Chédozeau, *La Bible et la liturgie en français*, p. 111.

[55] This did not prevent Benoist from using the 1546 Genevan Bible (Calvin's own revision: Chambers, *Bibliography*, no. 128) as the source for the translations of at least some parts of the Psalter in his own edition of the Book of Hours. Carter, 'René Benoist', ch. 4.

the Virgin tended to lack visible forms of division. In Benoist's Hours, large roman type was used and the text was far easier to navigate; they were also distinctive in their lack of ornamentation and images. They were not intended to appeal to 'the visual, aural and tactile dimensions of devotional practice', but to be read and understood.

Finally, let us review briefly several other titles amongst Benoist's output that indicate his plan to publish devotional and didactic works for the laity and which have close associations to texts published earlier in the century. Benoist clearly linked these to his work surrounding the Bible. Émile Pasquier notes 'Benoist's plan to provide the faithful with "the Bible, which teaches us what we should believe, know and do; saints's lives, with examples which can help us; and works of Christian meditation, above all the *Vita Christi*, by which we are spiritually nourished and fortified".'[56] French translations of Jacobus de Voragine's *Golden Legend* and Ludolphus of Saxony's *Vita Christi* were exactly the kinds of texts that had been emerging from the presses around the early 1500s. Belgian and Lyonese editions of Jean de Vignay's fourteenth-century French translation of the *Golden Legend* had been published from around 1475. Slightly later in Paris, the demand for the work was so great that the well-known publisher Anthoine Vérard published five editions within seven years.[57] If we shift to a later period, Francis Higman records six editions of translations of the *Golden Legend* and four French editions of Ludolphus' work in the period 1511–51.[58] In the latter half of the sixteenth century, Benoist participated in preparing for publication versions of the saints' lives in French and contributed treatises to a new translation of the *Vita Christi*.[59] Both were expensive, folio editions. In spite of the cost, the hagiographical material was particularly popular and went through more than a dozen editions. Although this popularity indicates that

---

[56] Pasquier, *Un curé de Paris*, p. 166, n. 1, citing Benoist's *Catéchèses ou instructions touchant les poincts à présent controversés en la religion* (Paris, 1573: Pasquier, no. 43).

[57] Brenda Dunn-Lardeau and Dominique Coq, 'Fifteenth and Sixteenth-Century Editions of the *Légende Dorée*', *Bibliothèque d'Humanisme et Renaissance* 47 (1985), 87–101; Mary Beth Winn, *Anthoine Vérard, Parisian Publisher, 1485–1512* (Geneva, 1997), p. 238.

[58] Francis M. Higman, *Piety and the People: Religious Printing in French 1511–1551* (Aldershot, 1996), nos V71–6 (*The Golden Legend*, 1513–40), L74–7 (*Vita Christi*, 1521–44). Higman's bibliography begins in 1511 and it should be remembered that these and other texts and those which follow had often been printed before 1511 in some quantity (see previous note).

[59] *Histoire de la vie, mort, passion et miracles des saincts* (over a dozen editions, 1577– : Pasquier, nos 54–5); *La Vie de Jésus-Christ* (Paris, 1582: Pasquier, no. 78). Two further editions of the latter have been located by the St Andrews French Vernacular Book Project (both dated 1599). The hagiographical material was not related to the *Golden Legend*: it was a new venture.

Benoist's publications filled a gap in the market, it would seem that in this case a wealthier, possibly more educated audience was envisaged.

But Benoist's project extended beyond the texts mentioned above. He also provided religious texts in French for those with more restricted budgets and indeed for those whose level of literacy was not so advanced. He re-edited the *Grand Ordinaire*, one of the fuller manuals of instruction from the pre-Reformation period, and this appeared in the smaller, cheaper octavo format.[60] Editions had been published in 1490, 1492, 1502, 1506, 1514, 1530 and 1532; Benoist's 1580 publication came after a gap of nearly 50 years.[61] He published works of different levels of complexity – often both devotional and didactic in nature – for the diverse groupings within the laity. For example, Pasquier classes Benoist's new version of the *Manuel de dévotion* to which Benoist adds prayers and catechistic material as being 'pour les personnes plus instruites'.[62] Published in a small, inexpensive format (16°), it was no doubt cheap to purchase. In fact, some of the contents of this work are similar in several ways to those of the Book of Hours, Benoist's most popular publication, as indicated above. He thus ensured that vernacular religious works were available for the various types of lay-folk whom he recognized had different needs. Benoist was also evidently interested in the work of Jean Gerson, the fifteenth-century Chancellor of the University of Paris who had himself been much concerned with lay instruction. Benoist translated at least three treatises by Gerson[63] and quoted Gerson in his own work.[64]

Many of the works alluded to above – frequently works of popular piety – quite obviously look back to texts from the pre-Reformation era, as has been demonstrated by looking at the quantity in which some of

---

[60] *Le Grand Ordinaire ou instruction commune des chrestiens* (Paris, 1580: Pasquier, no. 159).

[61] Francis Higman, 'Theology for the Layman in the French Reformation 1520–1550', in Higman, *Lire et découvrir*, 88; Higman, *Piety and the People*, nos O9–11.

[62] *Le Manuel de dévotion: Extraict des escrits des saints Pères et Docteurs illustres, tant anciens que modernes* (Paris, 1574: Pasquier, no. 158). Pasquier, *Un curé de Paris*, p. 161. Pasquier knew of four editions (1568–80); a further, 1575 edition is preserved in Durham's Chapter Library (HIII.B.27).

[63] *La Manière et forme de vivre d'un chascun en son état* (Paris, 1579: Pasquier, no. 183); *Response à ceux qui preschent publiquement et au peuple qui croit que si chacun ouït la messe dévotement, il ne deviendra point aveugle ce jour-là et ne mourra pas de mort subite* (Paris, 1579: Pasquier, no. 184); *Traité de Gerson ou règle adressée à un ermite* (Paris, 1580: Pasquier, no. 147). Higman, *Piety and the People*, records seven editions of works by Gerson published between 1511 and 1551 (nos G14–20, 1519–47).

[64] See, for example, his *Petit fragment catechistic d'une plus ample catechese de la magie reprehensible et des magiciens* (Paris, 1579: Pasquier, no. 70), pp. 22–3; *Sermon de la disposition requise pour le lavement des pieds* (Paris, 1601: Pasquier, no. 122), p. 21.

these texts appeared earlier in the century. A significant comparison can be made with Mary Beth Winn's bibliography of Vérard, one of the major Parisian publishers at the turn of the sixteenth century. Vérard had published many of the titles which Benoist later produced, acting as reviser or editor: for example, Vérard had published the *Grant Vita Christi*, the *Golden Legend*, the *Ordinaire des crestiens* and a French verse Book of Hours. He was also the first to publish the *Bible historiale*, which brings us back to the most important text in Benoist's programme.[65]

But how typical in general were the kinds of texts we have been discussing in the earlier period? In fact, religious works dominated the presses in the pre-Reformation era; it has been estimated that at least 75 per cent of printed texts between 1445 and 1520 were religious in nature.[66] Commenting on the output of texts in French from the turn of the century to the 1520s, Jennifer Britnell notes that in France, the publication of religious works in the vernacular for the laity went relatively unchecked and was indeed increasing before the threat of Lutheranism.[67] The quality of the publications varied to suit all purses and works were intended to reach both the literate and illiterate, with prefaces often addressing those who will 'lire ou ouyr lire' ('read or be read to'). A variety of texts was available – works of popular piety evolving out of late medieval tradition and devotional practice and, in addition, more ambitious projects. They include the texts described above and also works concerning Mass, manuals of instruction containing the Ten Commandments and Articles of Faith, and more adventurous works such as Church Fathers and even Scripture. The work of Jean Gerson was particularly popular. Like Gerson, authors aimed to provide works that would teach the laity directly and also to effect renewal within the Church by ensuring that members of the clergy were well instructed and able to deliver effective sermons. As Britnell comments:

> Everything suggests that the trend towards providing the laity with books in French on religion was one which was gaining in strength during the first twenty years of the sixteenth century. It accompanies the efforts towards Reformation of the monastic orders which were going on at the same time. Indeed, the parallel is worth pointing out, for the two things often went together. Authors of religious books in French written at the time often came from Reformed houses or were themselves reformers.[68]

---

[65] Winn, *Anthoine Vérard*, pp. 547–51. On the French verse Hours, see ibid., pp. 153–60; on the *Bible historiale*, see Chambers, *Bibliography*, no. 13.

[66] Jean Delumeau, *Naissance et affirmation de la Réforme* (Paris, 1988), p. 70. The percentage appears to relate to texts in Latin and the vernacular.

[67] Jennifer Britnell, *Jean Bouchet* (Edinburgh, 1986), pp. 190–94.

[68] Ibid., p. 193.

This underlines the point that those seeking to provide the laity with such works were not necessarily evangelicals or those whom we would consider today as early Reformers. Indeed, Reformers often criticized these works, which, in terms of theology, provided only a basic explanation of faith and doctrine, although an attempt was also made to help the laity to understand prayers. Nevertheless, these works had prepared the way for the success of the different style of vernacular religious work emanating from Reformers, which included Scriptural translations and more comprehensive explanations of faith. In fact, Reformers sometimes borrowed established titles for more radical texts.

It was this, combined with the Reformers' use of Scripture and liturgy, which brought opposition from Catholic theologians to the more traditional works. The threat of Lutheranism and later Protestant movements stopped Catholic efforts to reform the Church from within in their tracks. Few Catholics seemed willing to put out editions of religious texts in French, wary of being labelled heretics. Not only did very few French Catholic theologians attempt to combat the Protestant threat in French, but the output in French of traditional works also fell off in the course of the century.[69] In the Counter-Reformation period, Benoist made strenuous efforts to reverse this trend.[70] Thus his work continued that of those within the Catholic Church before the Protestant Reformers posed a serious threat. Several of Benoist's works in the vernacular follow traditional devotional trends, whilst ensuring that the devotional experience of the laity when using these texts was grounded in understanding. This would no doubt have been the natural development of these texts at a much earlier stage in the century had it not been for the Reformation.

Benoist acknowledged the usefulness of traditional texts, whilst understanding the need for evolution; well-loved religious works in the vernacular were not to be forgotten and suppressed on the grounds that heretics worked in French. In fact, they were beneficial in the fight against Protestantism, replacing heretical versions of similar texts.

---

[69] See, for example, Francis Higman, 'Premières réponses catholiques aux écrits de la Réforme en France, 1525–c.1540', in Higman, Lire et découvrir, 497–514; Higman, Piety and the People.

[70] Although much research remains to be done in this area, it is certainly possible that others worked alongside Benoist with similar goals; the scope and success of Benoist's literary enterprise suggests that he, however, was the leading force who spearheaded such a movement if it existed. A wider reforming movement involving theologians and publishers is perhaps indicated by the formation of the publishing venture the Grand-Navire: Denis Pallier, 'Les Impressions de la Contre-Réforme en France et l'apparition des grandes compagnies de libraires parisiens', Revue Française d'Histoire du Livre 31 (1981), 245–7. See also Carter, 'René Benoist', ch. 4.

Benoist published these works after modernizing them, ridding them of archaisms, an old-fashioned appearance and (particularly in saints' lives) superstitious elements which had accumulated in late medieval times. He was quite clearly responding to the needs of the laity as the various texts he provided were very popular.

Combined with his interest in works such as the Book of Hours and his criticism of clerical abuses, Benoist's work to make the Bible accessible to the masses shows an agenda for reform and renewal of the Catholic Church comparable to the aspirations found at the beginning of the century amongst humanist, evangelical and, in some cases, Gallican groups. Benoist recognized the need to help his own Church to evolve, as had other groups earlier in the century. Renewal within the Catholic Church would revitalize it and strengthen its position so that it could oppose Protestantism and serve Christians well. These objectives were in line with the Counter-Reformation spirit and his aims to bring about a renewal of piety bear some similarities to those of the Jesuits. His criticism of clerical abuses and superstitions said to come from the medieval Catholic Church is reminiscent of certain post-Tridentine movements. But if the objectives were orthodox, the means proved controversial at the time. If we return to the question posed by Wanegffelen's work, it is evident that Benoist was most certainly Rome and not Geneva. It is wrong to think of him outside the Catholic camp, yet it is also clear that he did not always follow Rome's reasoning or dictates. There can be no doubt that, above all, Benoist's particular sympathies appear to be closest to those of pre-Reformation thinkers operating in France at the beginning of the century and that, against opposition from his own colleagues in the Parisian Faculty of Theology, who failed to appreciate the necessity of change and adopted more extreme positions,[71] he was attempting to steer the French Catholic Church in a direction marked out by those more moderate currents working within the Church early in the sixteenth century.

---

[71] See, for example, the anonymous *Observationes bibliorum lingua gallica editorum sub nomine M. Renati Benedicti* (undated). Pasquier ascribed this extensive attack on Benoist's Bible to Jacques Lefebvre, Syndic of the Faculty of Theology: *Un curé de Paris*, pp. 90–91.

CHAPTER TEN

Moderation under Duress? Calvinist Irenicism in Early Seventeenth-century Royal Hungary

Graeme Murdock

The Reformed Church in Royal Hungary was granted institutional autonomy and legal sanction to hold church services by its Habsburg rulers in 1608. However, the Reformed Church operated during the early seventeenth century within a context of political weakness, as a minority faith facing Lutheran and Catholic competitors and a hostile royal court. The response of some Reformed clergy in western Hungarian counties to this position was to make irenic appeals to Lutherans to unite with them to defend common Protestant freedoms against the Habsburg Court and Catholic hierarchy. In particular, Superintendent János Samarjai of the Upper Danubian Reformed Church province invited Lutheran clergy to recognize that they agreed with Calvinists on fundamental points of doctrine.[1] Leading Reformed clergy also set out forms of worship for their communities during this period which included some Lutheran practices and also retained some traditional forms of religious ritual. This Reformed agenda of irenic theology and a mixed pattern of ceremonies was in part driven by the political realities of Habsburg Hungary during the early seventeenth century. However, Reformed irenicism and moderation was much more than a short-term strategy or merely a hypocritical rhetoric which disguised a hidden dogmatism. Rather it reflected the personal commitment of some Reformed clergy to work for unity with Lutherans, and was also inspired by concern to meet the spiritual needs of local congregations. This essay will outline the context for the efforts made by some Hungarian Reformed clergy to reach theological agreement with Lutherans, and will then analyse their distinctive approach to forms of church services, sacramental ritual and exorcisms.

---

[1] The Upper Danubian Reformed Church province of north-western Hungary encompassed the counties of Moson, Pozsony, Komárom, Nyitra, Bars, Hont and Nógrád.

The religious liberties of Lutherans and Calvinists in Hungary were secured after the 1604 revolt of nobles led by the Calvinist István Bocskai against the Habsburg King Rudolf. By the terms of the Peace of Vienna of 1606, Bocskai relinquished his claim to the Hungarian Crown, while Rudolf accepted Bocskai's rule as prince of Transylvania. The peace agreed between Bocskai and Rudolf in June 1606 also offered the nobles, Royal towns and military garrisons of royal Hungary the free exercise of religion, and both the Lutheran and Reformed churches were given the right to direct their own affairs. These legal advances secured by Hungarian Protestants through the Peace of Vienna were only ratified by the Hungarian Diet in 1608. Protestant nobles took advantage of the struggle that year between the Habsburg brothers Rudolf and Matthias for control over Hungary and Bohemia. In return for noble support, Matthias endorsed the terms of the Vienna peace. After 1608, the religious allegiance of magnates and nobles was therefore decisive in determining the confessional colour of parishes across Royal Hungary.[2]

The rights granted to Reformed and Evangelical churches by the 1608 Diet were almost immediately threatened and undermined by the Court's backing for a campaign of re-Catholicization across the region. However, legal protection for the Lutheran and Reformed churches in Hungary remained intact at least in theory during the first half of the seventeenth century. This was because of continuing support for Protestantism from many nobles in the Diet. The Crown was also constrained by fear of further rebellion and by the need for noble cooperation to defend Royal Hungary against Ottoman forces. In addition, a series of Reformed princes in Transylvania acted to defend the religious freedoms of Protestants in Royal Hungary. Nevertheless, the position of both the Lutheran and Reformed churches steadily weakened during this period, as some leading Protestant nobles were won over to the Catholic Church by the Court with offers of titles and patronage, while others were persuaded to convert by clergy or by teachers in new Catholic academies and schools.

The increasing proportion of Catholic landowners, especially in western and north-western counties of Hungary, led to church buildings

---

2   K. Benda, 'Habsburg Absolutism and the Resistance of the Hungarian Estates in the Sixteenth and Seventeenth Centuries', in R.J.W. Evans and T.V. Thomas (eds), *Crown, Church and Estates: Central European Politics in the Sixteenth and Seventeenth Centuries* (London, 1991), 123–8; D. Daniel, 'The Fifteen Years' War and the Protestant Response to Habsburg Absolutism in Hungary', *East Central Europe* 8 (1981), 38–51; L. Makkai, 'István Bocskai's Insurrectionary Army', in J.M. Bak and B.K. Király (eds), *From Hunyadi to Rákóczi: War and Society in Late Medieval and Early Modern Hungary* (New York, 1982), 275–97; K. Péter, 'Az 1608 évi vallásügyi törvény és a jobbágyok vallásszabadsága', *Századok* 111 (1977), 93–113.

being returned to the control of Catholic priests and to the expulsion of Protestant ministers from newly-converted Catholic nobles' estates. In 1619 Protestant nobles argued at the Diet that the rights granted in 1608 were meaningless unless Protestants were able to gain access to a place of worship. Although Protestants continued to form a majority in the Upper Chamber of the Diet as late as 1613, by the time of the 1619 Diet held at the Hungarian capital at Pozsony (Bratislava) Catholics were in a majority. This Diet failed to resolve the extent of Protestant rights, and only offered an acknowledgement that there was disagreement on whether freedom of religion included access to a place of worship. The Diet's statement also recognized that there were differences of opinion as to whether the rights of landowners as church patrons, or the rights of a majority within local communities, took precedence in determining parishes' confessional allegiance.

The Protestant cause in Royal Hungary was then bolstered by the intervention of the Transylvanian prince, Gábor Bethlen. Bethlen took up arms against Ferdinand in October 1619, claiming to act in defence of Protestant freedoms. However, after the collapse of the estates' opposition movement across the Habsburg monarchy, Bethlen agreed a peace with Ferdinand in 1621. Thereafter, noble support for Protestantism in Royal Hungary, particularly in western counties, continued to decline. Royal grants of new titles to Catholic nobles as well as the effect of noble conversions meant that Catholics were established in a clear majority in the Upper Chamber of the Diet by the 1630s.[3] The Protestant churches' ability to exercise their legal rights had by then become severely restricted and the need for Lutherans and Calvinists to cooperate in order to win concessions from the Crown and the Diet was increasingly apparent.

Protestants in Royal Hungary had coexisted within a single church structure during the latter half of the sixteenth century. However, tensions between clergy who supported the Reformed and Evangelical camps came to the surface during the 1590s, both in north-western counties where Evangelicals were in the majority, and in counties further to the south where those of Reformed sympathies were more numerous. Synods of Protestant ministers held at Csepreg in 1591 and at Galánta (Galanta) in 1592 led to disputes over how to celebrate and understand the sacrament of Holy Communion. One leading Protestant noble patron, Ferenc Nádasdy, insisted that all the ministers on his estates sign up to the 1577 German Evangelical *Formula of Concord*. This province's Protestant Superintendent, István Beythe, was inclined towards the Reformed camp

---

[3]   P.G. Schimert, 'Péter Pázmány and the Reconstitution of the Catholic Aristocracy in Habsburg Hungary, 1600–1650' (unpublished PhD thesis, North Carolina, 1990).

and subsequently resigned his post in 1595. Clergy in this province then began to divide between two groups recognizing the leadership of rival seniors. When István Beythe died in 1612, separate Lutheran and Reformed superintendents were appointed which formalized the division of Protestants in the Western Danubian Church province.[4]

The divergence between the two Protestant groups was also reflected in doctrinal statements which were agreed by rival synods. In 1598 a synod of clergy in Sopron county agreed on canons which highlighted their Evangelical sympathies. These canons, for example, supported the practice of auricular confession and forbade ministers from administering Holy Communion using ordinary leavened bread.[5] In 1612 the new Reformed Superintendent of the Western Danubian province, István Pathai, led a synod at Köveskút which agreed new canons for churches 'of the Helvetic confession'. On the crucial issue of Holy Communion, these canons described how believers were spiritually united with Christ in the sacrament. The canons supported the use of leavened bread and ordinary wine rather than wafers to symbolize that the elements of Communion only represented Christ's body. However, the Köveskút canons encouraged clergy to be patient with simple parishioners, especially in the countryside, who wanted to continue to receive wafers in Communion services. The canons advised that clergy should only move slowly to the better practice of using leavened bread at a pace which was appropriate for their community as they received instruction on the true meaning of the sacrament. The canons followed a similar line in arguing against the practice of auricular confession, but allowing parishioners who had troubled consciences to ask their minister to hear their confession of sins.[6] The Köveskút canons also forbade ministers from taking Communion to sick members of their congregation for private consumption. However, in 1617 the Reformed congregation at Pápa decided to provide the sacrament to sick church members. Members of the Pápa congregation were encouraged to gather on Sunday afternoons at the house of a sick person, so that the minister could distribute Communion to the small gathered group of his parishioners.[7]

---

[4] The Western Danubian Reformed Church province included Sopron, Vas, Zala and Veszprém counties.

[5] *A dunántúli ág. hitv. evang. egyház 1598-iki törvénykönyve*, ed. Gy. Mokos (Budapest, 1892), pp. 74–107.

[6] 'Köveskút canons (1612)', in E. Thury, *A dunántúli református egyházkerület története* (Pápa, 1908), 145–67.

[7] Thury, *A dunántúli református egyházkerület története*, pp. 175–7, 182–3.

Separate Lutheran and Reformed Church structures, statements of faith and forms of worship also emerged only slowly in the Upper Danubian Church province. Some towns and villages including Nagyszombat (Trnava) continued to have united Protestant congregations worshipping together into the seventeenth century. There was also a concerted attempt to revive the cause of Protestant unity during the 1610s. At a synod held at Komját (Komjatice) in September 1615, Evangelical and Reformed clergy from the Upper Danubian and Western Danubian provinces agreed four key points of doctrine which they held in common and acknowledged remaining points of doctrinal division. On the issue of the nature of Christ's presence in the bread and wine of Communion, Lutheran and Reformed representatives at the synod were able to agree that Christ's body and blood were truly present in a 'sacramental manner' in the bread and wine.[8] While a doctrinal union between the two churches failed to materialize after the Komját synod, the manner of celebrating Communion adopted by Lutheran and Reformed parishes continued to have much in common. For example, Reformed congregations in towns such as Kiskomárom, Körmend and Németújvár (Güssing) only slowly changed to use leavened bread in Communion services during the 1610s and 1620s.

The founding synods of the Reformed Church in Hungary held during the mid-sixteenth century had offered clear guidance on how to conduct simple Communion services which were distinctive from the rituals of the Church's confessional rivals. A synod of clergy from eastern Hungary and Transylvania held at Debrecen in 1567 had adopted Heinrich Bullinger's *Second Helvetic Confession* and the 1562 *Confessio Catholica* of Péter Méliusz Juhász and Gergely Szegedi. The synod demanded that ministers abandon wearing traditional vestments, and that altars, statues and images be removed from church buildings. All these physical signs of Catholic worship were described as remnants of popery, and instruments of superstition and idolatry which prevented the pure worship of God.[9] The Debrecen synod had also agreed that Communion services could only take place when a congregation was gathered together. The conduct of the sacrament was simplified and the traditional liturgical practice of clergy asking congregations a series of questions, to ensure that parishioners understood the sacrament, was condemned as lacking any precedent in Scripture. Instead, clergy were to explain the meaning of the service and to read out the words of institution for the sacrament from the Bible

---

[8] 'Komját canons (1615)', ed. E. Thury, *Magyar Protestáns Egyháztörténeti Adattár* 7 (1908), pp. 155–6.
[9] *Confessio Catholica* (1562), in *A xvi. században tartott magyar református zsinatok végzései*, ed. Á. Kiss (Budapest, 1881), pp. 152, 189, 196–7, 200, 516.

before distributing the elements of bread and wine to the people.[10] The canons agreed by the Herczegszőllős synod in central Hungary in 1576, recognized by ministers from Hungarian counties west of the Danube, also provided clear statements on the appropriate way to conduct Communion in Reformed churches, for example insisting that it was not permitted to use 'the Pope's wafer' in the sacrament.[11]

When Superintendent István Pathai produced a service order-book for his Western Danubian province in 1617, he drew from some of these existing canons to produce a distinctively Reformed pattern of services, but he also allowed ministers to continue to use some traditional liturgical practices. Pathai's instructions to clergy on how to administer the sacrament of Holy Communion explained that such services were held to commemorate the events of the Last Supper when Christ had used bread and wine to symbolize his body and blood. To establish that the congregation had a clear understanding of Communion, Pathai maintained the traditional practice of providing a series of questions which were put to the congregation by the minister. Believers had to reply clearly that they accepted that they were sinners in need of God's mercy, that they accepted that Christ's sacrifice alone offered grace and forgiveness of sins, that they looked to Christ as their saviour, and that they turned away from their sins. Then the minister could distribute the wine and bread, which, according to Pathai, should not be any special sort of bread. Pathai acknowledged that in different congregations people knelt, stood or sat to receive Communion. For Pathai, this was a matter of indifference, and he encouraged ministers not to cause scandals or offend congregations by demanding changes to local practices. This liturgy which Pathai introduced for use in Reformed communities therefore offered some degree of continuity with past ritual practices. Pathai's instructions reflected the late and incomplete separation of distinct Evangelical and Reformed churches in western Hungary, as well as continued efforts to find doctrinal unity among Protestants through the discussions held at Komját. Pathai was also concerned not to introduce changes to the conduct of sacraments which went beyond what he believed congregations in the region were ready to accept.[12]

---

[10] Gáspár Heltai, *Az Urnak vaczoraiarol való közenséges keresztyéni tanitóc mind egész magyar országból, s' mind erdelböl a vásárhellyi szent sinatba töttéc es kiattác* (Kolozsvár, 1559).

[11] *A xvi. században tartott magyar református zsinatok végzései*, ed. Kiss, p. 685; *A Herczegszőllősi kánonok más egyházi kánonokkal egybeveté*, ed. Gy. Mokos (Budapest, 1901).

[12] István Pathai, *Az Helvetiai Confession való köröztyén praedikátoroknak Dunán innen, az egyházi szolgálatban való rend tartásokrol irattatot könijvechke* (Németújvár, 1617), sigs b5r–d4r.

This outlook was shared by leading Reformed ministers in western Hungary during the 1620s, some of whom were able to present their position using a newly acquired language of irenicism. Hungarian students who travelled to study at the University of Heidelberg in the Palatinate during the 1610s encountered arguments in favour of Protestant unity put forward by the Silesian-born teacher David Pareus. During the 1610s, 91 Hungarian Reformed students registered for study at Heidelberg, including Péter Alvinczi, Imre Pécseli Király and János Samarjai, all of whom went on to make irenic appeals for Protestant unity. This is not to suggest that Hungarian students at Heidelberg simply had their spiritual and intellectual outlook determined by the influence of Pareus. Rather Samarjai, Pécseli, Alvinczi and other clergy found his arguments useful in articulating their own agenda for the future direction of the Church in Hungary.[13] For example, Imre Pécseli Király, the Reformed minister at Komárom (Komárno) and then at Érsekújvár (Nové Zámky), published a tract in 1621 which questioned whether the labels Calvinist and Lutheran should be adopted by Christians. Pécseli's work was clearly influenced by Pareus's ideas on Christian unity, but was also directly relevant to the position of the Church in western Hungary.[14]

Another Reformed minister who promoted irenicism in Hungary was János Samarjai, the son of a Protestant minister at Galgóc (Hlohovec) in Nyitra county. Samarjai was born in 1585, and went to school at Nagyszombat before teaching briefly in the village school at Szenc (Senec). He then studied at the University of Heidelberg from 1609 until 1611. On his return from Germany, Samarjai first worked as rector of the school at Nagyszombat, a town which from 1590 had been the site of a seminary to train Catholic clergy. Samarjai was then appointed as minister at Nagymegyer (Čalovo) in Komárom county in 1613. In 1615 he moved to a parish to the south of the Danube at Halászi in Moson county. In 1622 he was elected as Superintendent for the Upper Danubian Reformed Church province, and remained in this office until his death in 1652.[15]

In 1628 Samarjai published *Hungarian Concord*, which was dedicated to Gáspár Szegedi and his wife Orsolya Eczi, who were leading members

---

[13] G. Murdock, *Calvinism on the Frontier, 1600–1660: International Calvinism and the Reformed Church in Hungary and Transylvania* (Oxford, 2000).

[14] Imre Pécseli Király, *Consilium Ecclesiae Catholicae Doctorum super ista Quaestione: An homo Christianus possit et debeat se cognominare Lutheranum vel Calvinistam ad Religionem puram ab impura recte discernendam?* (Kassa, 1621); Imre Pécseli Király, *Catechismus, az az: A Keresztyeni tudomannak Fundamentomirol es agairol valo rövid Tanitas* (Lőcse, 1635).

[15] G. Kathona, *Samarjai János gyakorlati theologiája* (Debrecen, 1939), pp. 1–33.

of the Reformed congregation at Nagyszombat. In this text, Samarjai attempted to promote Protestant unity between Calvinists and Lutherans. This *Hungarian Concord* included a translation of one part of the *Irenicum* of David Pareus, and Samarjai also attempted to demonstrate that the Lutheran 1530 *Augsburg Confession* and Bullinger's 1566 *Second Helvetic Confession* were entirely compatible with one another.[16] In the section of the *Irenicum* which Samarjai translated, Pareus had argued that sacramental theology was the only point of significant difference between the Evangelical and Reformed traditions. Pareus reviewed the history of efforts to reach unity among Protestants from Luther and Zwingli's meeting in 1529 at Marburg to Lutheran negotiations with south German and Swiss reformers during the 1530s. Pareus suggested that a new council should be called so that Evangelical and Reformed theologians could agree on a single confession of faith for a united Protestant Church. Pareus was optimistic about the chances of a positive outcome to these negotiations, since he found no trouble in accepting the 1530 *Augsburg Confession*, except for the tenth article on Holy Communion. However, Pareus claimed that many Lutherans, including Melanchthon, also did not accept this 'obscure' article, which explained the real presence of Christ in the bread and wine of Communion. Pareus suggested that the article should be replaced by words which simply indicated that 'the bread and the wine are truly the body and blood of Christ, which was given for us and was shed for the forgiveness of our sins'.[17] In addition, Pareus rebutted the polemical attacks of some Evangelical writers against Reformed beliefs, including the suggestion that since Reformed theologians denied the ubiquity of Christ's body, they also denied that Christ was really God and were Arians. Pareus also rejected the accusation that Reformed salvation theology made God the author of sin, or that Reformed theologians thought that God did not desire the salvation of all people and had created most men and women for damnation.[18]

---

[16] *Augsburg Confession* (1530) in *The Book of Concord: The Confessions of the Evangelical Lutheran Church*, ed. T.G. Tappert (Philadelphia, 1959), pp. 23–96; *Second Helvetic Confession* (1566) in *Reformed Confessions of the 16th Century*, ed. A.C. Cochrane (London, 1966).

[17] János Samarjai, *Magyar Harmonia, az az Augustana és az Helvetica Confessio articulussinac eggyezö értelme, mellyet Samaraeus Janos superattendens illyen ockal rendölt öszve, hogy az articulusokban fundamentomos ellenközés nem lévén az két confessiot követö atyafiak is az szeretet által eggyessec legyenec. Ez mellé Paraeus David d. Irenicumjából XVIII ragalmas articulusokra valo feleletek és az eggyesegre kétféle indito okok adattanac* (Pápa, 1628), pp. 229–30: 'Az Augustana Confessionac minden articulusit nyilvén javallyuc, az tizediktöl meg válva ... inkáb, hogy az kenyér és az bor, valosagossan az Christusnac teste és vere, mely mi erettünc adattatot, es ki ontatot büneinknec boczanattyára.'

[18] Ibid., pp. 187–231; David Pareus, *Irenicum, sive de unione et synodo evangelicorum concilianda, votivus paci ecclesiae et desideriis pacificorum dicatus* (Heidelberg, 1614).

Samarjai then moved on to consider the texts of the Augsburg and Second Helvetic confessions. He claimed that since there were not many copies of either confession available in Hungarian, ignorance about their contents had led to the widely-held view that sharp differences existed between the beliefs of Lutherans and Calvinists. By presenting the details of the two confessions alongside one another in the vernacular, Samarjai hoped that those who called themselves Lutherans would better understand both their own beliefs and their similarity to Reformed ideas. Samarjai thought that since he could demonstrate the harmony between the Augsburg and Helvetic confessions, this ought to bring an end to the offensive language sometimes used by both Evangelical and Reformed polemicists towards each other in Hungary. He called on all Hungarian Christians to recognize that their salvation lay in Christ, and did not begin in either Augsburg or Switzerland. Samarjai encouraged his readers to show Christian love towards one another, and not to focus on minor points of ceremonial difference between the two churches, such as the use of clerical vestments, or the presence of candles, altars, organs and images in church buildings.[19]

Samarjai's *Hungarian Concord* compared the equivalent sections of the Augsburg and Helvetic confessions, by using letters in the margin to highlight similar ideas, phrases and sentences in the two texts. Some articles in the confessions did not present Samarjai with insuperable problems in arguing the case for Protestant theological unity, and he was often able to make reasonable claims about clear differences between shared Protestant and Catholic ideas. On the issue of sacramental theology, Samarjai also claimed to have discovered harmony between the ideas set out in the two confessions. He cited the *Augsburg Confession*'s insistence that Christ's body and blood were really present in the elements of the Eucharist. Meanwhile, according to the *Second Helvetic Confession*, the bread and wine of Communion were 'holy signs' which 'outwardly represented' the spiritual benefits which God inwardly performs in the sacrament. However, Samarjai followed the line of argument which Pareus had adopted in trying to reconcile these positions by emphasizing what was held in common. According to Samarjai, both churches accepted that Christ's body was truly, essentially and practically present for those believers who received the bread and wine. Samarjai thus used a formula of words which came very close to the tenth article of the *Augsburg Confession*, but without explicitly accepting either the ubiquity of Christ's body or Christ's local presence in and under the bread and wine of Communion.[20]

---

[19]   Samarjai, *Magyar Harmonia*, pp. iv–xi.
[20]   Ibid., pp. 48–55.

Lutherans in the Empire had long rejected such attempts to gloss over differences between the two churches, and bitterly condemned any perceived crypto-Calvinist infection of their Church. Lutheran writers mostly looked instead to the 1577 *Formula of Concord*, which explained the articles of the *Augsburg Confession* and rejected both Catholic and Reformed theology. The *Formula of Concord* insisted that in the 'Holy Supper the body and blood of Christ are truly and essentially present', and that believers received the body and blood of Christ 'not only spiritually, by faith, but also orally'.[21] A Lutheran minister from western Hungary followed these arguments in rejecting Samarjai's appeals for unity. István Lethenyei, the minister at Csepreg and senior of his church district, dedicated his 1633 work to Vas county's high-sheriff, Pál Nádasdy. Lethenyei drew on a wide range of German Evangelical writers to deny that Lutherans and Calvinists were united in the fundamentals of their faith. He decried Calvinists' 'horrible and evil errors', and rejected any suggestion of similarities between the Augsburg and Second Helvetic confessions.[22] Lethenyei scorned the technique adopted by Samarjai of using letters in the margin to show the compatibility of the two texts. He described this as 'playful', and designed only to fool the ignorant. Lethenyei picked through a range of Reformed writers to highlight any number of differences between the beliefs and practices of the two churches, and focused in particular on Reformed attitudes towards the sacraments. Seizing on Samarjai's failure to accept that Christ was really present within the elements of Communion, Lethenyei concluded that it was impossible to argue that the two churches held identical positions on this vital issue.[23]

Lethenyei concluded that he would not accept fellowship with Calvinists until they gave up their many doctrinal errors. He also followed his German co-religionists in denying the honest intent of Reformed irenic appeals for Protestant unity. Calling his readers' attention to the many attacks made by Reformed theologians on Lutheran beliefs, Lethenyei claimed that Calvinists only wanted to pass themselves off as Lutherans when it suited their interests. This was also the verdict on Reformed irenicism offered by the Catholic Archbishop of Esztergom, Péter Pázmány. In 1620 Pázmány had ridiculed attempts to present unity between the Protestant churches, claiming that 'preachers,

---

21 *The Formula of Concord* (1577) in *The Book of Concord*, pp. 481–7.
22 István Lethenyei, *Az Calvinistac Magyar Harmoniaianac, az az: Az Augustana es Helvetica Confessioc Articulussinac, Samarjai Janos, Calvinista Praedicator, es Superintendens által lett ösve-hasonlétásánac meg-hamisétása* (Csepreg, 1633), sig. c3ʳ: 'szörnyü és kárhozatos tévelgési'.
23 Ibid., pp. 10, 76–82.

who row in Calvin's boat, often lie about what they believe, for friendship's sake'.[24]

Some Hungarian Reformed clergy continued to denounce Lutheran beliefs in forthright terms, including István Milotai Nyilas, who was Superintendent of the Eastern Tisza Church province. The Reformed Church held a dominant position in the confessional landscape of the eastern Hungarian counties of Milotai's province, which came within the territory of the Transylvanian principality. The service order-book which Milotai, another former student of David Pareus at Heidelberg, completed for his province in 1621 was dedicated to the Reformed Prince of Transylvania, Gábor Bethlen. Milotai's text laid down instructions for his clergy on how to conduct church services and administer the sacraments. At every turn, Milotai delighted in pointing out how the practices of true Christians were different from the ceremonies of both Catholics and Lutherans.[25] Milotai's description of services of Communion directed ministers in his province to explain that Christ was present in the sacrament for believers by faith and by the action of the Holy Spirit. Milotai set out a form of Communion service which began with a general confession followed by a set of questions read out by the minister which required the congregation to declare that they repented of their sins and acknowledged the saving sacrifice of Christ. Milotai detailed how the minister should then approach a table in the church, read out the words of institution for the sacrament from the Bible, break the bread into pieces as a symbol of Christ's body broken for his people, and distribute the bread and wine to the congregation.[26]

Milotai laid a particular emphasis on key distinctions between Lutheran and Reformed ceremonies in the Communion service, which symbolized their different beliefs about Christ's presence in the elements of bread and wine. Milotai permitted the use of either leavened or unleavened bread, but recommended the use of leavened bread. However, he dismissed out of hand the 'impudent' suggestion that wafers, 'the bread of the Antichrist', could be used. He rejected the argument that wafers could be retained for use by simple-minded parishioners who were not accustomed to receiving bread, and insisted that using wafers would only sustain superstition and idolatry. Milotai

---

[24] Ibid., sig. a4[r–v]; Péter Pázmány, *Rövid felelet két kálvinista könyvecskére* (Pozsony, 1620), pp. 436, 451.

[25] István Milotai Nyilas, *Agenda, az az: Anya szent egyhazbeli szolgálat szerént valo czelekedet: melyben az Uy Testamentomnak ket Sacramentománeak, az Szent Keresztsegnek es az Ur Vaczorájának ki szolgáltatásának es az házasulandoknak egjbé adattatásoknak mogya meg iratik azokhoz illendö hasznos tanuságokkal egyetemben* (Kolozsvár, 1621). Milotai's text was reprinted in 1622, 1634 and 1653.

[26] Milotai Nyilas, *Agenda*, pp. 52–60.

also rejected wafers on the grounds that the bread should be broken into pieces, which he argued was essential to follow the example set by events at the Last Supper.[27] He refuted the idea that wafers were in effect broken bread, requiring that 'the priest breaks the bread at the Lord's table, not the sexton in the kitchen'.[28] He derided Lutherans as 'waferists', who refused to break the bread into pieces, and suggested that Catholics felt at home in 'waferist' churches, which retained altars, images, statues and candles, and where the clergy wore traditional vestments. Milotai also recounted a story which he had heard while a student in the Empire of a minister in a town near Heidelberg who tried to use wafers in Communion, but was unable to do so when the wafers miraculously flew out of the plate as he prepared for the service.[29]

By contrast with Milotai's instructions, the service order-book which János Samarjai produced for his Church province in 1636 reflected his irenicism and supported a varied pattern of ritual practices for Reformed congregations in western Hungary.[30] On some issues Samarjai issued firm guidance to his clergy which mirrored the practices followed in other Reformed provinces. For example, Samarjai instructed Reformed clergy not to wear any traditional vestments, including surplices, during church services and especially when distributing Communion. He rather advised ministers to wear 'appropriate clothes' to preach and conduct the sacraments. Samarjai also required that candles and relics be removed from churches, but only instructed ministers and church patrons to remove images from church buildings where there was a clearly perceived danger of idolatry.[31] When Samarjai offered guidance to clergy on how to conduct church services, he also highlighted the danger of weakening the faith of simple peasant parishioners by abandoning all the familiar elements of their religious practices. Samarjai's instructions therefore mixed some obviously Reformed forms of worship with other traditional elements of religious life. According to Samarjai, Psalms and other songs were to be sung in Hungarian by the

---

[27] This issue also proved to be a bitter point of division between Lutherans and Calvinists in the Empire: B. Nischan, 'Ritual and Protestant Identity in Late Reformation Germany', in B. Gordon (ed.), *Protestant History and Identity in Sixteenth-century Europe* (2 vols, Aldershot, 1996), vol. 2: *The Later Reformation*, 142–58. A Colloquy of Reformed and Lutheran theologians finally met at Leipzig in 1631 and set out points of agreement and remaining doctrinal differences: B. Nischan, 'Reformed Irenicism and the Leipzig Colloquy of 1631', *Central European History* 9 (1976), 3–26.

[28] Milotai Nyilas, *Agenda*, pp. 184–99, 234–78.

[29] Ibid., pp. 198–200.

[30] János Samarjai, *Az helvetiai vallason levö ecclesiaknak egyhazi ceremoniajokrol es rend tartasokrol valo könyvetske. Az eggügyüveknek rövid tanétásokra köz akaratbol irattatott Samorjai Janos Halászi predikator által* (Lőcse, 1636).

[31] Ibid., pp. 4, 8–9.

whole congregation, unaccompanied by an organ or any other musical instruments. Ministers were to teach children and adults from catechisms, so that all could be educated in the fundamentals of their faith. However, when the congregation prayed in church, Samarjai allowed parishioners to stand or kneel, and stated his preference that they should turn to face the east when they prayed. Samarjai also required that the congregation knelt or bowed their heads when Christ was named. Prayers could not be said for the dead, but Samarjai allowed relatives and friends to continue the practice of spending the evening before a funeral with the body of the deceased. Samarjai recommended that ministers call 40 days each year as fasts when congregations were to show repentance of their sins through their dress and behaviour, but not in a 'hypocritical manner'. Infant baptisms were only to be conducted by clergy using ordinary water and were normally to take place in church buildings. However, Samarjai allowed for ministers to conduct baptisms elsewhere if required to do so by parents. He forbade parents from giving children any pagan names, but allowed the use of saints' names if they offered examples to people on how to live a godly life.[32]

Thus, the familiar themes of Reformed religious life emerge from Samarjai's service order-book, but with acceptance of some variations which were rejected out of hand in the vast majority of Reformed churches across the Continent and in other Hungarian Reformed Church provinces. This was also the case with Samarjai's instructions on how to conduct Communion services. Samarjai's description of how to administer Communion included a series of questions which ministers were required to ask the congregation, including whether they accepted that the body and blood of Christ was offered to believers in the sacrament for the forgiveness of their sins. Those who expressed this belief were allowed to receive the elements either standing or kneeling, and either distributed into the hands or directly into the mouths of communicants. Samarjai suggested that men should come up to receive Communion first, but argued that most local variations over the administration of Communion were matters of indifference. According to Samarjai, it was a matter of indifference as to whether his province's Reformed clergy distributed the bread and wine from a wooden table or served the elements from altars, and he only required that images be removed from view around the altar for the duration of the Communion service. Samarjai advised using normal leavened bread, either white or black bread, but preferably using white flour. He also permitted ministers to use either white or red wine, dependent on local availability. However, Samarjai allowed unleavened bread or even wafers to be used

---

[32] Ibid., pp. 40–41, 44–5, 56–9, 63, 138, 187.

by 'weak' members of congregations who were not yet ready to accept leavened bread. He also allowed for Communion to be served privately to the sick. While Samarjai showed a high degree of flexibility in his instructions for how clergy in the province should conduct services of Communion, he maintained that the bread must be broken before it could be distributed, but offered no comment on how this could be achieved where wafers were still in use.[33]

Samarjai was not alone in supporting some elements of traditional ritual in Reformed services and in permitting a variety of local practices in Communion services, some of which had been rejected by early Hungarian Reformed synods. The orders for the administration of Communion written by István Milotai Nyilas and Albert Szenci Molnár had also presented a liturgy which required congregations to answer a series of questions before the elements were distributed.[34] Samarjai's Communion service also had much in common with the order of service composed by another former Heidelberg student, Péter Alvinczi. In 1622 Alvinczi wrote *A Short Notice about the Lord's Holy Supper from the teaching of the Holy Apostle Paul* as part of his irenicist project in the Lutheran-dominated royal free town of Kassa (Košice) in Upper Hungary. Alvinczi also allowed both for wafers to be used in Communion and for the elements to be distributed from altars as matters of indifference, but again insisted on the need to break the bread before it was distributed to the congregation.[35]

Another striking example of Samarjai's approach to worship and ritual in his Reformed community was his support for exorcisms, a practice roundly condemned by Reformed leaders across the Continent as an invented papist ritual which encouraged superstition. However, Samarjai provided his clergy with an outline of how to conduct exorcisms, quoting Scripture and early Church history for support of the practice. Samarjai described the role of an exorcist as able to assist those who doubted their faith or who had given in to the temptations of the devil. He rejected the use of incense, holy water and relics during exorcisms, and advised clergy to read out relevant verses from Scripture, to pray and to fast in order to force Satan to depart.[36] Approval for exorcisms was not given in any other service order-book in the

---

[33] Ibid., pp. 90–95, 110–11.

[34] *A xvi. században tartott magyar református zsinatok végzései*, ed. Kiss, p. 238; Albert Szenci Molnár, *Szent Biblia: az az Istennec O es Uy Testamentomaban foglaltatott egész szent irás* (Oppenheim, 1612).

[35] Péter Alvinczi, *Az Urnak Szent Wacsoraiarol valo reovid intes az Szent Pal Apostol tanitasa szerent egynéhany szükséges kerdésekel és feleletekel egyetemben* (Kassa, 1622), pp. 28–9, 67–9, 80–81.

[36] Samarjai, *Az helvetiai vallason levö ecclesiaknak egyhazi ceremoniajokrol*, pp. 216–24.

Hungarian Reformed Church, and it has been suggested that the inclusion of this service of exorcism betrayed a Catholic infection of Samarjai's religiosity. The influence of the Catholic *Rituale Strigoniense* is indeed apparent behind the form of liturgy which Samarjai suggested for services of exorcism. This Catholic order-book, composed by Archbishop Péter Pázmány, had been agreed for use in Hungary by a synod held at Nagyszombat in 1629. It detailed how to identify people who were possessed through their strange behaviour or unnatural powers, and instructed priests on how to combat demons with fasting, prayer and ritual, but warned against using superstitious incantations.[37]

However, rather than see Samarjai's support for exorcisms as a sign of Catholic influence, it should instead be seen in the context of his irenic appeal for unity with Lutherans, and even more as a reflection of his desire to meet the perceived spiritual needs of his community. Among Evangelical churches the rite of exorcism was retained as part of the service of baptism in some, but not all, church order-books in the Empire. The practice of exorcism came to prominence among Lutherans from the 1580s as a means of marking out that children were reborn in baptism through the Holy Spirit. Meanwhile, for Calvinists, the water of baptism only symbolized that a child was being received into the community of the Church. Thus, when German princes converted from Lutheranism to Calvinism the rite of exorcism was taken out of liturgy for baptisms. For example, the crypto-Calvinist Christian I of Saxony prohibited the conduct of exorcisms in 1591, and Johann Sigismund tried to eliminate exorcisms in Brandenburg in 1613 but came up against a violent popular reaction in favour of this and other forms of Lutheran ritual.[38]

While Samarjai was perhaps unwilling to support a ban on Reformed clergy performing exorcisms (which would have become another mark of confessional difference between Hungarian Protestants in the Upper Danubian province), he did not support exorcisms in the context of infant baptism, but rather as a ritual for adult believers who doubted their faith. This readiness to respond to the spiritual demands of ordinary parishioners was the reason which Samarjai gave for allowing clergy to distribute wafers in Communion, the reason why Samarjai accepted that the sick could ask for the elements of Communion to be brought to their homes, why he allowed some images to be retained

---

[37] *Rituale Strigoniense, seu formula agendorum in administratione sacramentorem, ac ceteris Ecclesiae publicis functionibus* (Pozsony, 1625), ch. 12: 'De exorcizandis obsessis a daemonio'.

[38] B. Nischan, 'The Exorcism Controversy and Baptism in the Late Reformation', *SCJ* 18 (1987), pp. 36–7, 47.

inside church buildings, and why parents were permitted to call their children after saints if they so wished. Calvinists who looked for help from clergy against attacks from the devil were not to be sent away without receiving any assistance, and it seems that Samarjai was willing to provide a Reformed exorcism service rather than see parishioners turn to Catholic priests for help.

Samarjai was not alone in identifying the popular appeal of exorcisms in Hungary. When four Reformed ministers were suspected of having conducted superstitious services of exorcism in the Western Danubian province they were, however, called before the 1622 Pápa synod to answer for their actions.[39] Exorcisms were also being used by the Hungarian Catholic Church during this period as a confessional weapon to demonstrate the spiritual powers of their priests in fighting demons. In 1642 a 20-year-old woman living in Pozsony was exorcised of a ghost which had been tormenting her. The Catholic authorities took evidence from witnesses about how priests had sent the ghost from purgatory to heaven, and an account of the incident was then published with the approval of György Lippay, the Archbishop of Esztergom. Protestants responded with anxious rebuttals of these Catholic claims. Two Reformed students from eastern Hungary, Péter Szatmári Baka and István Szilágyi Benjámin, gave disputations on the incident at the University of Utrecht and gained affirmation from Gisbert Voetius about the fraudulent nature of the claims made by the Pozsony priests. While mainstream Reformed opinion continued to deny the validity of any supposed exorcisms, local Calvinists in the Upper Danubian province could hardly come to the same judgement. They could instead only agree with a Lutheran minister from Trencsén (Trenčin), Zacharias Láni, who argued that the spirits which the priests at Pozsony had controlled were indeed real, but evil.[40]

Samarjai's moderate position on theology and liturgy has mostly received a negative reaction from later Reformed historians. His only biographer concluded in the 1930s that Samarjai had weakened the Calvinist community in western Hungary because of his lack of commitment to a Reformed pattern of religious life and worship. Géza Kathona argued that Samarjai's friendly personal relations with Catholic priests influenced him to promote ritual 'of a Catholic spirit' in his

---

[39] Kathona, *Samarjai János gyakorlati theologiája*, p. 158.
[40] *Narratio rei admirabilis ad Posonum gestae* (Pozsony, 1643), also in German and Czech translations; Gisbertus Voetius, *Theologiae in Acad. Ultrajectina Professoris, selectarum disputationum theologicarum, pars secunda* (Utrecht, 1655), pp. 1135–40, 1141–93; Zacharias Láni, *Pseudo spiritus Posoniensis* (Trencsén, 1643); R.J.W. Evans, *The Making of the Habsburg Monarchy, 1550–1700: An Interpretation* (Oxford, 1979), pp. 391–3.

province.[41] Samarjai's outlook on religious life was certainly moderate in the latitude which he allowed over some points of dogma and forms of ritual but the suggestion of Catholic influence seems overstated. Certainly Samarjai's brand of moderate Calvinism did not indicate any unwillingness to defend the Reformed Church's rights against Catholic attacks. The Reformed Church presented a catalogue of complaints of mistreatment to the 1634 Hungarian Diet at Sopron, alleging that Catholic landowners had occupied dozens of church buildings, had prevented church services from taking place and had expelled Reformed ministers from their estates. Calvinists also faced obstruction from Catholic urban councils such as at Nagyszombat, where the Reformed community's plans to replace their old wooden church with a stone building were blocked at every turn. The Church pursued this case to the royal court and then to the Diet in 1637, when permission was finally granted for the building work to proceed.

Protestants gained some respite from Catholic repression in 1644 when the Reformed Prince of Transylvania, György I Rákóczi, invaded Royal Hungary. Ferdinand was anxious to bring peace negotiations held at Linz with Rákóczi to a successful conclusion, and conceded a re-definition of the meaning of Protestant religious liberties to include rights of access to church buildings and graveyards and permitted the use of church bells. Protracted negotiations then followed at the 1646 Pozsony Diet on how to interpret this Linz treaty. Lutherans and Calvinists claimed that 300 churches had been illegally seized by Catholics and ought to be returned, but could only name some 146 confiscated churches. Many Catholic nobles were anxious to settle the matter in the Diet and to avoid a decision on religious rights being left to a royal decree. In 1647 the Diet agreed that 90 church buildings seized by Catholics must be returned to the control of the Lutheran and Reformed churches. These concessions, however, did not long survive the waning of Transylvanian influence in Royal Hungary, and Catholic nobles soon steadily re-imposed restrictions on the free practice of Protestantism. After 1648 Lutherans and Calvinists turned to the Hungarian Diet for redress of their grievances about the illegal actions of Catholic landowners entirely in vain. Ministers were expelled from their parishes, Protestant churches and schools were either closed or destroyed, Protestants were forced to recognize Catholic holidays and to make payments to Catholic priests, and were unable to get married or have relatives buried without declarations of support for the Catholic Church.[42]

---

[41] Kathona, *Samarjai János gyakorlati theologiája*, pp. 32, 123.

[42] M. Zsilinszky, *A linczi békekötés és az 1647-ki vallásügyi törvényczikkek története* (Budapest, 1890); K. Péter, 'The Struggle for Protestant Religious Liberty at the 1646–47 Diet in Hungary', in Evans and Thomas, *Crown, Church and Estates*, pp. 261–8.

János Samarjai remained a determined advocate of the religious freedoms of the Reformed Church in Royal Hungary. His willingness to make concessions towards potential Lutheran allies and to respond to the perceived spiritual needs of his community aimed to shore up popular support for Calvinism and to prevent the Reformed Church from being submerged beneath the waves of Counter-Reformation in Royal Hungary. Samarjai's appeals for unity with Lutherans and the instructions which he issued to his own clergy on how to conduct church services thus reflected the political and confessional environment of early seventeenth-century Royal Hungary. This led to charges of hypocrisy by contemporary opponents on the grounds that Reformed clergy only supported union with Lutherans when they needed allies in the battle against Rome. However, Samarjai's support for exorcisms, and the advice which he offered to clergy on the administration of Communion and appearance of church buildings was not merely a strategy to advance Reformed interests but also reflected his view about those beliefs and forms of worship which were essential to salvation and those which could be treated as matters of indifference. Samarjai's appeals for Lutherans to support his call for Protestant unity were also shaped by the view that points of theological difference between the two churches were minor and could be reconciled. The Reformed Church's inability either to secure any agreement with Lutheran ministers or to retain the support of noble families in the region were both crucial failures in the face of a rising tide of persecution from the monarchy and Catholic hierarchy.

Conclusion

Moderate Voices: Mixed Messages

Mark Greengrass

On the Sunday after Pentecost, 14 June 1609, there was an unfortunate roadside encounter not far from the south-west French town of Libourne between Daniel Moulans, the Protestant pastor of Duras and his congregation, on the way back from celebrating Sunday worship at the place allowed them by law at 'Villaux' (that is, 'les Billaux'), and the redoutable Archbishop of Bordeaux, François d'Escoubleau Cardinal of Sourdis. It was a sectarian incident, and not without precedent. One of the inevitable weaknesses of the Edict of Nantes (1598) had been the establishment of authorized places of worship for the Protestants in locations at a distance from major towns. Protestants tended to congregate and leave for Sunday worship at the same time, and by the same gates, and to return *en masse* too, making them the focus for sectarian taunts from the majority Catholic population. It was probably no accident that the paths of the Cardinal and the pastor crossed on 14 June 1609.

What exactly happened during their encounter has to be reconstructed from the various depositions laid before Geoffroi de Malvyn and Jean de Gaufreteau, the two experienced magistrates of the *Parlement* of Bordeaux who were appointed the investigating judges of the subsequent lawsuit.[1] The Cardinal and his substantial retinue ('accompagné de force gens' said a young chambermaid, one of the witnesses), all on horseback, met the pastor, who was also on horseback although the majority of his congregation were not. The pastor prudently stepped to one side, pointedly ignoring the large crucifix being carried in front of the Cardinal but saluting Monsieur de Sourdis, as decorum dictated. From among the lackeys around the Cardinal, however, one of them (he was not identified by any of the Protestant witnesses, though one of their number, an elderly advocate in the *parlement*, noticed his bright red trousers and white stockings – immoderate dress on a Sunday, as he may

---

[1] The depositions are to be found in *Mémoires et correspondance de Duplessis Mornay pour servir à l'histoire de la Réformation et des guerres civiles et religieuses en France sous les règnes de Charles IX, de Henri III, de Henri IV et de Louis XIII, depuis l'an 1571 jusqu'en 1623 [...]*, ed. A.D. de La Fontenelle de Vaudoré and P.-R. Anguis (12 vols, Paris, 1824–25), vol. 11, pp. 473–80.

well have thought) stepped forth to belabour the pastor with a white cane, whilst another set about him with the flat of his sword, cutting his face, saying: 'Go away, go away, you have your fill, you notorious rake [*gueusard*]. I will teach you to pay your respect to the cross.' A contingent of de Sourdis's entourage then hassled the pastor and his flock as they rushed to the safety of their houses within the town walls at Libourne.

So far, so depressingly familiar: a microcosm of sectarian France as it had existed for over two generations in the 'wars of religion'. But there was a sequel. Before the end of the day, the priest in charge at Libourne and an envoy despatched to the town by the Cardinal-Archbishop offered the pastor the Cardinal's personal apology ('raison et satisfaction') for what had happened. It was against the King's edict and should not have occurred. On the Protestant side, the husband of the pastor's niece, a merchant and inhabitant of Libourne, made it his business to act as a go-between, urging the pastor 'qu'il debvoit accepter la satisfaction que M. le Cardinal de Sourdis lui voulloit faire faire'. The pastor was also afforded the healing ministrations of a surgeon and apothecary in the town, who also added their voices of moderation. In due course, the pastor agreed to meet the vicar and envoy from the Cardinal over supper. Dinner tables were, as Catherine de' Medici (among others) had often cause to discern, good places to encourage moderate voices. Food and drink were the physical manifestations of the spiritual message of commensuality, even though the theological dimensions of such a message were fraught with Reformation argument.[2] Over the meal, the discussion lasted well into the night. The pastor was keen to demonstrate his moderation. He wanted to accept the Cardinal's apology and, if the affair were simply a matter of his own injuries, he would gladly do so. But a lackey had behaved illegally and should be punished; social discipline was not a point to be lost sight of in the eyes of this Protestant pastor. He eventually declared that the integrity of 'all of France's churches' was at stake in the incident – an honour card in any suit of cards involving the notability when a dispute was likely to go to law.

So the issue was left to be resolved before the two investigating magistrates who were well-known advocates of the deployment of the mediating hand of justice (the far from secure foundation of the edicts of pacification). Geoffroi de Malvyn had given a notable speech before the Parlement of Bordeaux in August 1599 when the judges had considered

---

[2]   See Michel Jeanneret, *A Feast of Words: Banquets and Table Talk in the Renaissance* (Cambridge, 1991).

the registration of the Edict of Nantes[3] He admitted all the arguments in favour of one religion in a state: the sacred 'marriage' between the Catholic Church and the French kingdom; the recent evidence of the potential for sedition from Protestantism; the ancient truths of the Catholic faith and the importance of discipline and police that were instilled through religious faith and practice. And yet, in the second part of his speech, he argued in favour of the Edict on prudential grounds:

> There is nothing more fortunate than peace, nor anything more terrible than war, worst if internecine ... The old quarrels are the most difficult to unravel and it is necessary to get out of them as best we can ... We are all *concitoyens*, we breathe the same air and enjoy the same liberty under the same prince and the same laws.[4]

The magistrates in charge of the case knew and had rehearsed the prudential case for tolerating the two faiths and they could be trusted to produce a prudent outcome. Although M. Moulans sought the support of the Protestant community at large (notably from the provincial synod of the Bordelais), it is unlikely that Philip du Plessis-Mornay (to whom the pre-trial depositions were sent in due course) would make much of something as slight as a pastor losing face in the vicinity of Libourne. There were larger issues at stake – not least, the question of the survival of the Protestant cause in Jülich-Clèves – but worse still the fragile working relationship with the French monarchy would soon be questioned by the King's assassination in May 1610.

The moral of this story encapsulates the larger message of this book: that moderate voices in the Reformation were conveyed in fundamentally ambiguous ways. Moderation, more than just a doctrine to be espoused, was a confused living experience: the hard-won result of local and patchy mediations and negotiations that were part and parcel of religiously divided Europe. Moderation emerged (or not) in much the same way that a local feud among village notables or a noble feud might be appeased (or avenged), settled amicably or, again, become the object of a duel depending on circumstances. Honour, integrity, the influence of local notables, decorum, employment patterns, mixed marriages, family relationship and kinship ties were fundamental to the ways in which moderate voices were expressed, and heard, in the age of the Reformation. Moderate voices were thus a fundamental component in the reality of sectarian conflict – as real in the conflict when they were set aside as when they were applied, as notable when they came short of

---

[3] See Paul Courteault, *Geoffroy de Malvyn. Magistrat et humanite bordelais (1545?–1617): Etude biographique et littéraire* (Paris, 1907), appendix V, pp. 131–54.
[4] Ibid., p. 142.

mediating the issues in question as when they were emphatically and rhetorically adduced to appease them.

I

The traditional narrative of this subject is encapsulated in the phrase 'the rise of toleration'. Many recent works, however, have tried to deconstruct the smooth, secular transition from the Reformation to the Enlightenment that it implies. On the contrary, recent scholarship has identified in the Reformation a strengthening of the 'persecuting society' that was established in the central Middle Ages.[5] Even in the later seventeenth century, we now understand that the 'moderate voices' of the English epitome 'Act of Toleration' of 1689 emerged as a result of a muddy political accommodation.[6] The secure equation between Enlightenment and toleration itself has recently been replaced by an awareness of the ambiguities and religious sensibilities of rationalist philosophers' thought, and an appreciation of the pragmatic political and social realities that created whatever religious pluralism existed in eighteenth-century Europe.[7] For the earlier Reformation period, the tendency has been similar in minimizing the impact of any ideology of 'toleration' and emphasizing in its place the pragmatic, realistic and contingent nature of the various 'accommodations' that were arrived at in the sixteenth and early seventeenth centuries in order to avert the potential chaos of religious conflict.[8] As Heiko Oberman has observed, we need a 'social history' of toleration in order to contextualize the moderate voices themselves.[9] The advent of religious pluralism in the French wars of religion was, as a recent collection suggests, an 'adventure' as perplexing in its realization as it was contingent: dependant upon political and social circumstances.[10] As Laursen and

---

[5]   Robert I. Moore, *The Formation of a Persecuting Society: Power and Deviance in Western Europe, 950–1250* (Oxford, 1987).
[6]   Ole Peter Grell, Jonathan Israel et al. (eds), *From Persecution to Toleration* (Oxford, 1991).
[7]   Ole Peter Grell and Roy Porter (eds), *Toleration in Enlightened Europe* (Cambridge, 2000); see the revisionism concerning John Locke's toleration, discussed in the introduction to *Political Writings of John Locke*, ed. David Wotton (Harmondsworth, 1993), pp. 32 ff.
[8]   See the various studies collected together in Ole Peter Grell and Robert W. Scribner (eds), *Tolerance and Intolerance in the European Reformation* (Cambridge, 1996).
[9]   Heiko Oberman, 'The Travail of Tolerance: Containing Chaos in Early-Modern Europe', in Grell and Porter, *Tolerance and Intolerance*, 13–31.
[10]   Keith Cameron, Mark Greengrass et al. (eds), *The Adventure of Religious Pluralism in Early Modern France* (Oxford, 2000).

Nederman have argued, theories and practices of toleration existed and were discussed to an extent that we have not hitherto appreciated both before and during the Reformation.[11] But the living and talking reality of moderation was more like heated wax in a lava lamp: the endless, revolving suspension of an 'uneasy combination of principle, prudence and practicality' that oscillated between a complete rejection of toleration and the espousal of its necessity.[12] Moderate voices in the age of the Reformation, in short, always carried mixed messages.

II

To examine that mixture in a more specific context, let us briefly examine the uses of the term 'charity' in the sixteenth century. 'Charity' was at the heart of the Christian understanding of friendship, good neighbourliness and social accord. It was the basis of the shared *Pax Christi*, the moment of expressed sociability that brought together the living and the dead in harmony; indistinct, we are told, from the social purpose of the Mass.[13] In the Pauline Epistles, charity is slow to chide, meek and long-suffering – the embodiment of the moderate voice of Erasmus in the earlier sixteenth century. Yet this moderate voice gained a second meaning with the Protestant Reformation. In sixteenth-century France, charity was often presented as 'ardente' or 'violente', all-consuming in its perfection.[14] In John Foxe's martyrology (but the same is doubtless true of sixteenth-century Protestant martyrologies in general) the term 'charity' is used in a variety of contexts, at once combative and conciliatory. 'Burning charity' was how Foxe described the English Lord Chancellor's justification of the bishops' search for heretics: 'euen like as a good shepheard doth see to his flocke, that none of his sheepe hath the scabbe or other disease for infecting other cleane sheepe, but wyll saue & cure the said scabbed sheep'.[15] 'Burning charity'

---

[11] John Christian Laursen and Cary J. Nederman (eds), *Beyond the Persecuting Society: Religious Toleration Before the Enlightenment* (Philadelphia, 1998), p. 1.

[12] Randolph Head, 'Introduction: The Transformations of the Long Sixteenth Century' in Laursen and Nederman, *Beyond the Persecuting Society*, 104.

[13] John Bossy, 'The Mass as a Social Institution, 1200–1700', *P&P* 100 (1983), 29–61.

[14] As, for example, in the title and text of Thomas Gaillard, *Le Traicté des quatre degrez d'amour et charité violente* (Paris, 1507); see also the revealing text of Joseph Gauchier, *Sainct Augustin, de la Vie chrestienne, avec les traictez de Charité, de la Vanité de ce siècle et monde inférieur, d'Obedience et humilité, et l'Eschelle de Paradis [...]* (Paris, 1542).

[15] John Foxe, *Actes and Monuments of matters most special and memorable* (London, 1583), Bk 11, p. 1566.

and 'discreet severity' was how he depicted the chancellor of Oxford and London, Dr John Story's search for the ostensible heretic John Warne and his family.[16] If this can be seen as mere irony on Foxe's part, it is only part of the story. Elsewhere Foxe would refer to the Chancellor's 'antichristian charity' – the 'charity' that the fox shows the chickens whom he stalks, the 'charity' that Bradford claimed he found in Ottoman Turkey in his examination, but not in England.[17] In another vein Foxe accepted that charity was closely related to witnessing for the truth, citing 1 Corinthians 13 ('If I yield my body to the fire to be burnt, & haue not Charitie, I shall gayne nothyng thereby').[18] Charity was only as good, in short, as the righteousness of the cause in which it was expended: 'the goodnesse of the cause, and not the order of the death: maketh the holynes of the person'.[19] Charity was not simply a matter of keeping one's head down and getting on with the neighbours. It came from God. 'Charity keepeth Gods commaundements, a pure hart loueth and feareth God aboue all.'[20] Those that preach God's truth, providing that they do not aim to stir up sedition, are part of the 'chayne' of Christian charity. God's witnesses on earth, especially those who suffer for his truth, are at one with another in the 'knotte' of charity, separated, imprisoned, beleaguered in body, but 'present in the spirite, coupled together with the vnity of fayth in the bonde of peace, whyche is loue'.[21] Among the martyrs and their sustainers, there was, in short, a sense of charity, of belonging in Christian community to one another under God. So, for Foxe, the notion of charity was a sectarian weapon capable of rhetorical deployment against an enemy whose lack of charity demonstrated their depravity, and could be evoked in the name of a godly cause and in defence of the brotherhood of the elect.

Foxe was registering that sublimate of Augustinianism, traces of which were so widespread in sixteenth-century Europe. In the early fifth century AD, Augustine had responded to the threat posed by the Donatists by elaborating in a set of letters the principles that justified the use of physical coercion to punish those who deviated from the true faith. One of his central sources, of course, was the gospel passage from Luke 14:16-24 where Jesus told of a rich man who, when his guests declined his invitation to his feast, commanded his servants to go out into the streets and 'compel them to come in, that my house may be

[16] Ibid., Bk 11, pp. 1689, 1910.
[17] Ibid., pp. 1487, 1612.
[18] Ibid., p. 1769.
[19] Ibid., p. 1647.
[20] Ibid., p. 1833.
[21] Ibid., p. 1855.

filled'. *Compelle intrare* – to rescue those who had strayed from righteousness – was the message to the Christian Church and magistrates. Augustine presented it as a necessary wake-up call to those who were 'asleep' in their false belief, a 'sharp medicine' to reclaim sinners before it was too late. Here was 'charity' at work; saving souls who would afterwards thank their saviour for the action taken on their behalf, even if it had been a 'bitter pill' at the time. The Church of England's 'Homily on Charity' emphasized the responsibility placed upon the Christian magistrate to bring their subjects to embrace the true faith as a 'loving father correcteth his natural son'. Alexandra Walsham will have more to say about this in an important forthcoming book on the subject of toleration in England.[22] For the present, we should simply record the mixed message contained in the oxymoron 'charitable emnity'. 'Clemency', too, could be given the same ambiguous voice. It was the Dominican friar, Jacques Clément who killed Henri III in August 1589 on the grounds that he was a tyrant. League pamphlets proclaimed the assassination as an act of godly 'clemency', that quality of hearing and responding in mercy to petitions that Seneca had most applauded in a virtuous prince. The last Valois prince's murder of the Guise princes (on the festival of St Clement, as the League pamphlets did not fail to point out) was a treason against 'clemency', just as God's wrathful clemency thereafter was a sign that he had listened and responded in mercy to the pleas of his faithful people.[23]

The messages of 'charitable enmity' and 'wrathful clemency' could be turned on their head. What was wrong with tolerating those who opposed God's truth was that it was a form of auto-deception; a dangerous folly. In 1572, Elizabeth I was told by her bishops in an open letter to put away her 'foolish pitie' and order the execution of her Catholic cousin, Mary, Queen of Scots. This was not a matter of *adiaphora* in their eyes. She represented a real and present danger, and one from which the fledgling Protestant Church in England required active political protection. 'Foolish pitie' – another oxymoron – was repeated in a letter to Walsingham from Sir Amias Paulet, Mary's gaoler at Fotheringhay in the last months of her life. Writing in 1586 and reflecting on the decade and more of dithering in high places about the fate of the captive Queen, that 'bosom serpent' and 'root and well-spring of all our calamities', he reflected: 'Others shall excuse their foolish pitie

---

[22] Alexandra Walsham, *Charitable Hatred: Tolerance and Intolerance in England 1500–1700* (Manchester University Press, forthcoming 2005). I am grateful to Alex Walsham for letting me see a portion of this typescript in advance of publication.

[23] Anon., *Le martyre de Frere Jacques Clement de l'ordre S. Dominique* (Troyes, 1589), p. 2 ; 'Sonet'; pp. 4–5.

as they may.'[24] Patrick Collinson has located the phrase precisely in the margins of the English Geneva Bible, a treasure-house of Protestant instances of the finger-post. Against the passage in the second book of Chronicles about godly King Asa, who dethroned his idolatrous mother but then failed to kill her, the Geneva Bible has the marginal gloss: 'Herein he showed that he lacked zeal. For she ought to have died both by the covenant and by the law of God, but he gave place to foolish pity.'[25] And Paulet would have recognized instantly the 'law of God' in question described in Deuteronomy 13:

> If thy brother, the son of thy mother, or thy son, or thy daughter, or the wife of thy bosom, or thy friend, which is thine own soul, entice thee secretly, saying, Let us go and serve other gods, which though hast not known ... thou shalt surely kill him; thine hand shall be first upon him to put him to death ... Neither shall thy eye pity him.

The voice of the Old Testament was heard all too often in the sixteenth century alongside the voice of moderation. In the age of the Reformation, one cannot, in fact, dissassociate the two.

III

Let us stay in 1586 and cross the Channel to the little Court of Henri of Navarre, mostly resident that year in Nérac. The councils of the King were dominated by Philip du Plessis-Mornay – the embodiment of 'aulic Protestantism' in the smaller princely courts of the day. Can we count him as a moderate voice? He was certainly not a *moyenneur*, caught 'between Rome and Geneva', confessionally undecided.[26] He knew what side he was on. At that time, he was largely responsible for the articulation and publication of Navarre's propaganda against the emerging Catholic League. One of the major themes of the campaign was that confessional coexistence was possible, and even that an eventual reconciliation of Protestantism and Catholicism by means of a council was feasible – at least under certain circumstances.[27] It was a bold message of calculated political moderation in a rapidly worsening

---

[24] John Morris, *The Letter-Books of Sir Amias Paulet, Keeper of Mary Queen of Scots* (London, 1874), pp. 321, 291.

[25] Patrick Collinson, *The English Captivity of Mary Queen of Scots* (Sheffield, 1987), p. 5.

[26] Thierry Wanegffelen, *Ni Rome ni Genève: Des fidèles entre deux chaires en France au XVIe siècle* (Paris, 1997).

[27] Hugues Daussy, *Les Huguenots et le roi: Le combat politique de Philippe Duplessis Mornay, Travaux d'Humanisme et de Renaissance* 344 (Geneva, 2002), pp. 364–8.

political climate. Was du Plessis-Mornay simply playing to the gallery on behalf of his master? We must certainly admit the political efficacity of the strategy, designed to 'unmask' the League and reveal its radical religious exclusivism for what it really was. Despite the liberal mind's urge to find a consistent irenic strand in Europe's history, the moderate voices of the age of the Reformation were more often than not adopted for polemic purposes. But it was not a new stance for the Court of the Bourbon in waiting – indeed it had been heard on numerous occasions before.[28] And du Plessis-Mornay himself had already demonstrated his interest in 'intra-confessional' concord among the Protestants themselves – always the first step to a wider 'reunion' of the faiths in his book. Responding to the Lutheran *Formula of Concord* of 1577, he used his influence in the diplomatic corridors afforded him by his position at Navarre's Court to knock on the doors of similar smaller Protestant courts in northern Europe and float the notion of a 'universal synod' among Protestants.[29] In 1583, it became something of a personal crusade, with letters to William, Prince of Orange, Philip de Marnix von Sainte Aldegonde, Francis Walsingham and Beza, urging them to put their weight behind the cause.[30] The result was a formal proposal in black and white that he put before the national synod of the French Reformed Church at Vitré in May 1583.[31] With the synod's approval, Jacques de Segur, seigneur de Pardaillan, the *surintendant* of the King of Navarre's household, was despatched round the Protestant capitals of northern Europe in the following two years. Even if Segur was not perhaps the most convincing advocate of moderation, it was not his fault if he returned two years later with responses that varied from the faintly lukewarm to the outwardly hostile. The German princes sent him back with a copy of the Formula and the pointed suggestion that a detailed study of it would reveal the 'truth' to a prince in error.

So it may be right to imagine that du Plessis-Mornay's public stance in 1586 reveals something of his deeper convictions. He was from one of those families united in kinship but divided by religion. His uncle, with whom he remained in private and intimate correspondence despite the difference in faith, was Philip du Bec, Bishop of Nantes. In his treatise *De la vérité de la Religion Chrestienne*, first published in London in 1578

---

[28] W. Brown Patterson, 'The Huguenot Appeal for a Return to Poissy', in D. Baker (ed.) *Schism, Heresy and Religious Protest* (Cambridge, 1972), 247–57.

[29] See Robert D. Linder, 'The French Calvinist Response to the Formula of Concord', *Journal of Ecumenical Studies* 19 (1982), 22–5.

[30] *Mémoires et correspondance de Duplessis Mornay*, vol. 2, pp. 225–7, 235–41.

[31] John Quick, *Synodicon in Gallia Reformata: or, the Acts, Decisions, Decrees, and Canons of those famous National Councils of the Reformed Churches in France* (2 vols, London, 1692), vol. 1, pp. 143–53.

(thanks to the active assistance of du Plessis-Mornay's friend and pastor of the French Church at Threadneedle St., Robert le Maçon, sieur de La Fontaine), du Plessis-Mornay wrote a remarkable apology for the Christian religion in general. In this work he insisted on the commonality of Christian beliefs and practices and on their shared baptismal vows. The work contained no trace elements of anti-papal vitriol and even aimed at confessional neutrality. The real enemies of Christianity were the 'Atheist, Epicurians, Pagans, Jews, Mahomedans and other infidels'. This work would find its way into the marginal glosses of the moderate defenders of the Anglican Church in the early seventeenth century, looking for a way to sustain the case for its 'catholicity' against its puritan and Catholic detractors.[32] It would be one of the 'irenic' Protestant works cited in Jean Hotman's notable Syllabus or 'bibliography' of irenic works from the Reformation period, which was eventually published by the Strasburg historian and philosopher Matthias Bernegger in 1628. With the opening line 'The road of peace is from God; & violence is from the Devil', and proclaiming that it contained 'the proofs of the facility of an accord [between the different religions]', it was as good a reading list of moderate voices from the Reformation as one could hope to find.[33]

But in 1586, confessional coexistence, a national council of the Church and the eventual reunion of divergent Christendom within the French kingdom was 'the stuff that dreams are made of' in the context of France's domestic politics. Even du Plessis-Mornay was prepared to concede that the season was not perhaps the right one for voicing the sentiments he had expressed in De la vérité. In a letter to Du Bartas of January 1584, he referred to the recently published Latin edition of the work, adding that it had perhaps been premature to publish it at all: 'I have ideas, and this almost displeases me, because I do not have the leisure and this is not the season to elaborate them.'[34] But only two years later, he boldly advocated moderation once more. In a letter to King Henri III of October 1585, published a few months later, he argued that consciences could only be persuaded, never constrained. The earliest Christians had learnt the painful lesson that heresy was a matter of

---

[32] Anthony Milton, Catholic and Reformed: The Roman and Protestant Churches in English Protestant Thought, 1600–1640 (Cambridge, 1995), pp. 146 ff.

[33] [Jean Hotman], Syllabus aliquot synodorum et colloquiorum, quae auctoritate et mandato caesarum et regum [...] ('Aureliae: i.e. Orléans' [actually Strasburg], 1628), sig. D.3ᵛ. 'this discourse ought not to be omitted from this list, having always been read and approved by all men of judgment and piety, Frenchmen and foreigners, and translated into many languages.'

[34] Mémoires et correspondance de Duplessis Mornay, vol. 2, pp. 471–2 [du Plessis–Mornay to Du Bartas, Mont-de-Marsan, 13 January 1584].

personal opinion, which could only be removed by reason and argument. They had resorted to assemblies of wise heads from all parts and the result had been a reconciliation of discord: 'Each peacefully put forward what they knew. Opinion at last gave way to science, shadow to light, verisimilitude to truth, and sophistry to reason.'[35] Of course, the conditions for such a council had to be right: it had to be genuinely 'free' from interference by Rome. But such councils had taken place before. For instance the council of Basel (he helpfully reminded the French King) had ordered that they should be held once every ten years in order to purge the Church on a regular basis of its errors and corruptions. Not for the last time, du Plessis-Mornay would, in an apparently ecumenical spirit, cite a Catholic source in support of his position, whilst knowing full well that it would be a manifest embarrassment to his opponents – in this instance, the assembly at Basel had, in fact, never been accepted at Rome as a canonical council of the Church. The tactic was one that he would deploy many times in order to 'unmask' what he would later term the 'mystery of iniquity' in the Roman Church, a kind of progressive self-deception which was the hallmark of the Antichrist.

So even if du Plessis-Mornay had a moderate voice, it does not necessarily follow that he was a moderate. He emphatically did not find religious controversy to be a perverse or useless exercise. On the contrary, the majority of his publications were front-line contributions to the major religious issues of the day – ecclesiastical, Eucharistic and theological. And in due course, the battle scars of the conference at Fontainebleau in 1600 would vouch for his willingness to enter into the fray for his faith. Nor did he find it difficult to justify military conflict in defence of the truth. On the contrary, in his eyes, it was a necessary part of God's providence. In 1586, taking some time off from the busy schedule of council meetings, military preparations and diplomatic correspondence, he found time to compose a sonnet for Henri of Navarre which encapsulated the stoic paradox that human struggle was morally uplifting and spiritually life-giving. Using the familiar image of the 'ship of state' he pictured Henri of Navarre adrift on a perilous sea of political and religious turmoil:

> Boat: that floats among the hazards of the World;
> That sees the Air troubled, and the winds conspiring;
> The chasm is yawning, the waters looming;
> Without anchor, without refuge, without cable or fathom-line.

---

[35] Ibid., vol. 3, p. 200; Hotman also included this letter on his reading list of moderate voices [sig. D], noting its closing remarks: 'I dare to promise, Sire, to make you aware in due course of a means whereby the two parties will be brought to an accord and by which all mankind, using reason and not wanting to fool himself, will be able to discern the truth from a lie.'

In the final stanza of the sonnet, however, he justifies the voyage, and thus the King's decision to engage militarily with his League enemies, in terms of a paradox:

> Your harbour, is the Eternal, from which you shirk away:
> You want Calm or good wind? You ask for your Death:
> Because to come to Port, you need a contrary wind.

It was a paradox that du Plessis-Mornay would live and experience. And paradoxes were the stuff of sixteenth-century intellectual life – not just because, like the ancients, they could be used as a way of showing off rhetorically, but also because they were a way of expressing views that were contrary to the common multitude, different from the opinions of the people at large, so easily led astray by their base passions.[36] The moderate voices of the period of the Reformation were often humanist voices, expressing a paradox, and using it not as a literary conceit but as a way of understanding their world and defining themselves in relation to commonly held, but inadequately substantiated, opinions.

IV

Moderate voices can be found in unlikely places and improbable individuals. Staying in France but moving back a decade, we find ourselves at the opening sessions of the Estates General of Blois on 30 November 1576. The Estates General had been summoned by the King to undertake the Reformation of the kingdom in response to the Peace of Monsieur, the latest of the attempts to pacify the religious divisions of the kingdom. But the Estates would be remembered for the decision, taken successively in each of the 'orders' in attendance, to abrogate the pacification and return France, by force if necessary, to being a uniquely Catholic kingdom. Yet there were siren-voiced moderates there as well, those who doubted the wisdom, legality or religious legitimacy of such a move.[37] One of them was Pierre de Blanchefort, the noble deputy from the Donziois.[38] If the latter had been an English county, Blanchefort would have been termed a

---

[36] See R.L. Colie, *Paradoxia Epidemica: The Renaissance Tradition of Paradox* (Princeton, 1966), esp. introduction ('Problems of Paradoxes').

[37] For the background to the first estates of Blois, see Mark Greengrass, 'A Day in the Life of the Third Estate: Blois, 26th December 1576', in Adrianna Bakos (ed.), *Politics, Ideology and the Law in Early Modern Europe: Essays in Honour of J.H.M. Salmon* (Rochester, 1994), 73–90.

[38] See Mack P. Holt, 'Attitudes of the French Nobility at the Estates-General of 1576', *SCJ* 18 (1987), 489–504.

'backwoodsman' by historians. Arriving at Blois, he let his views be known to anyone who would listen. 'He who takes pleasure in Civil Wars is not of God, and needs to be prayed for', he wrote.[39] When challenged with the biblical injunction *Compelle intrare*, he had his response ready: Christ had not instructed us to pull out the tares from the field, but to leave them to God to winnow out at the final harvest.[40] Blanchefort was well read in the extensive literature dating back to the early civil wars in defence of religious pluralism.[41] The examples of Germany and Switzerland proved that it was not necessary to impose one religion by force. The attempts to exterminate Protestantism in France had gone on for over a generation and, since they had not achieved their objective, they did not carry God's approval. The word of God had not been spread by the sword but by the 'sword of the Holy Spirit', by the gentle persuasion of preaching and teaching, not to mention the exemplary lives of its earliest Apostles. What was needed was 'Une Reformation en nostre Esglize Catholique Appostolicque et Romaine ... par laquelle les hereticques peuuent estre vaillamment Combatus et ne fault douter que nous humilians deuant Dieu il ne fasse par la assouppir et esteindre touttes heresies schismes diuisions et differents.'[42] Such a Reformation might occur through a national council of the Gallican Church – here he was at one with the Protestant du Plessis-Mornay. He had no time for the canonists who claimed that such a body, summoned by the King, was against the constitution of the Church. But it might also come about by a collective Reformation of public morality: 'Car nos pechez attirent sur nous ses esmotions seditions et Guerres et ne peult on esperer la paix que de Dieu qui seul la Donne.' It was a moderate, but minority voice, recorded in the privacy of his journal rather than the official registers of the estates.

Another moderate voice at the Estates General of Blois is better known, albeit more delicate to interpret: Jean Bodin. Bodin openly opposed the imposition of one faith by force in the estates and thereby made enemies for himself. In his famous *Six Books of the Republic*, published that same year, he expounded the 'political' and 'prudential'

---

[39] BNF, MS Fr. 16250, fol. 55.
[40] Ibid.
[41] It is interesting to see how extensively Blanchefort documented, and was able to deploy, the arguments that had been developed in the 1560s in favour of religious pluralism – see Olivier Christin, *La Paix de religion: L'Autonomisation de la raison politique au XVIe siècle* (Paris, 1997), pp. 49–69.
[42] BNF, MS Fr. 16250, fol. 58.

case for moderation. Religion was a matter of faith and belief. Disputed religion brings the beliefs themselves into doubt and causes the ruin and destruction of the state as well. There was a case, he argued, for banning public disputes about religion by law, such as had been enacted in some German states. Where a new religion had found firm support in society at large, then it was a matter of common-sense prudence to tolerate it. To do otherwise was to risk the integrity of the state: 'Wherefore, that religion or sect is to be suffered, which without the hazard and destruction of the state cannot be taken away; the health and the welfare of the Commonweale being the chiefe thing the law respecteth.'[43] But it was far better to have a multitude of religious opinions in a state than just two, which would be the natural and inevitable focus of faction and strike, perpetually unharmonious one with another.[44] Sometime over a decade later, however, he returned to the subject in that masterpiece of the humanist moderate voice, the *Colloquium Heptaplomeres (The Sevenfold Colloquium)*. The work was composed as a sequence of six dialogues among seven wise men, all but one of them with implausible-sounding foreign names and each representing a different point of view: Lutheran, Calvinist, Catholic, Jew, Arab, Sceptic and Natural Rationalist. Bodin pictures the meeting taking place in an academy in the purest and most tolerant air imaginable in France in the late 1580s: Venice.[45] Everywhere else was threatened by civil war, divisions or tax revolt whereas Venice was:

> the only city that offers immunity and freedom from all these kinds of servitude. This is the reason why people come here from everywhere, wishing to spend their lives in the greatest freedom and tranquillity of spirit, whether they are interested in commerce or craft, or leisure pursuits as befits a free man.[46]

The host of the academy is the exquisitely civil and learned Coronaeus, the epitome of the Venetian notable. The work is arranged like an elaborate fugue into which all kinds of subjects are interwoven: miracles, magicians, *arcana*, divine law, the notion of the best, God, truth and its contrary, and so on. At the beginning of book IV, literally

---

[43] Jean Bodin, *Les Six Livres de la Republique*, ed. Christiane Frémont, Marie-Dominique Couzinet et al. (6 vols, Paris, 1986), vol. 3, p. 206; cited from Jean Bodin, *The Six Bookes of a Commonweale*, trans. Richard Knolles, ed. Kenneth D. McRae (Cambridge, MA., 1952), vol. 3, p. 382.
[44] Ibid., Bk 4, p. 540.
[45] See Marion Leathers Kuntz, 'The Home of Coronaeus in Jean Bodin's *Colloquium Heptaplomeres*: An Example of a Venetian Academy', in Richard J. Schoeck (ed.), *Acta Conventus Neo-Latini Bononiensis* (Binghampton, 1985), 277–83.
[46] Marion Leathers Kuntz (ed.), *Colloquium of the Seven About Secrets of the Sublime* (Princeton, 1975), p. 3.

the middle of the book, Bodin reaches the pedal-point of the fugue. The members of the academy reassemble and give thanks to God, each in accordance with their own custom, and sing hymns of praise to their soul's delight, and Coronaeus is moved to introduce the theme of musical harmony.[47] How is it, one of them asks, that some sounds blend so well, and others so badly? Why is it that, in nature, the most dissimular songs of birds blended together, produce a most sublime sound in the ears? Why is it that extremes of noise, light or heat are hurtful but, put the opposites together, and the effect is benign? Why, in order to appreciate pleasure, must we have a pain that precedes it – just as dissonance in music is necessary to appreciate the resolution of the harmony thereafter? Bodin, no stranger to paradoxes, was exploring that most elaborate paradox of them all, that harmony (in nature and in art) was produced from contraries. In the resulting chorale, the most important verse stanzas in the book, Bodin evokes the providence of God as the creator of that harmony from contraries:[48]

> Who, moderating melody with different sounds and
>   voices yet most satisfying to sensitive ears,
>   heals sickness, has mingled cold with heat and moisture with dryness,
> The rough with the smooth, sweetness with pain,
>   shadows with light, quiet with motion,
>   tribulation with prosperity [...]
> Who joins hatred with agreement,
> A friend to hateful enemies.
> This greatest harmony of the universe
>   Though discordant contains our safety.

'Concord' was not, we are told, 'toleration' in sixteenth-century thought; in Bodin's text, however, they come to much the same thing.[49] The form of the literary work matches the paradox at its heart; from the opposites of opinion the academicians produce a harmony of contraries in their discourse. At the close of the academy, the participants agree to part and not to return to converse on such subjects again.[50] Some have claimed that this was Bodin's way of indicating that it had all been a failure; a

---

[47] Ibid., p. 146.

[48] Ibid., p. 147; on the significance of the verse stanzas in the work, see Georg Roellenbleck, 'Les Poèmes intercalés dans l'Heptaplomeres', in various (eds) *Jean Bodin: Actes du Colloque Interdisciplinaire d'Angers, 24 au 27 mai 1984* (Angers, 1985), esp. 442–51.

[49] Mario Turchetti, *Concordia o Tolleranza? François Baudouin (1520–1575) e i "moyenneurs"* (Geneva, 1984); see Mario Turchetti, 'Religious Concord and Political Tolerance in Sixteenth and Seventeenth-Century France', *SCJ* 22 (1991), 15–25.

[50] Kuntz, *Colloquium*, p. 471.

'dead-end discourse'.[51] The alternative is to accept that this was a rhetorical device to bring it to a close, Bodin's intention being to allow us to recognize that they have all gained wisdom on the way and that, had one of them persuaded all of the rest of the rightness of his view, it would have signalled the real death of harmonious discourse. 'Concordia discors': another oxymoron and Bodin's ultimate mixed message.

---

[51] Quentin Skinner, *The Foundations of Modern Political Thought* (2 vols, Cambridge, 1978), vol. 2, p. 249.

Index